Sailing Alone Across the Atlantic

A Pensioner's Tale

TREVOR WILSON

Published by

MELROSE BOOKS

An Imprint of Melrose Press Limited
St Thomas Place, Ely
Cambridgeshire
CB7 4GG, UK
www.melrosebooks.com

FIRST EDITION

Copyright ©Trevor Wilson 2008

The Author asserts his moral right to be identified as the author of this work

Cover designed by Trevor Wilson

ISBN 978-1-906050-97-9

Printed and bound in Great Britain by:
CPI Antony Rowe, Chippenham, Wiltshire

PART ONE

I dedicate this book to those and their descendants who sailed to freedom aboard *Erma*. Without them it would never have been written.

Chapter 1

Even with a double-reefed sail *Ozama* sped through the darkness as if celebrating having found the Trades. Sailing at six knots she slid gracefully down the side of each following sea, her tan Chinese sail silhouetted against the black starry sky. The wind was from the northeast, force five, and we were on a broad reach. After wallowing aimlessly in a windless sea for several days I was ecstatic with our new-found speed. However this mood of jubilation was to be short-lived, for without any warning the yacht's rudder fell off. The thought of being adrift and alone in the middle of the Atlantic on board a yacht without a rudder is not my idea of a good time.

The junk-rigged yacht (a Trident 24), which I had bought just over five months ago in Barcelona, was on passage to Norfolk, Virginia, via Rodney Bay in St Lucia. I'd sailed southwards from Porto Santo in the Madeira Islands on Christmas Day hoping to find the Trades at about 25 degrees north.

Before these winds were found however, several days of total calm had prevailed. With the sea about as flat as a proverbial mill pond, I decided to heave myself to the masthead in a bosun's chair and attempt to fix the tri-light that had failed. Just as I had reached the truck of the masthead after lots of arm-ache I heard a noise similar to someone blowing across the rim of a beer bottle. Looking down I saw a huge, glistening whale lying almost motionless along the portside.

A mixture of what looked and smelt like oil and water gushed like an intermittent fountain from the blowhole on top of the creature's head. Although it had taken over half an hour to haul myself up the mast, I lowered myself to the deck as quickly as the gantline would run through my hands. Somewhere (it might have been on a television programme) I'd heard about the "Song of the Whale". Whatever induced me to carry out my next action will puzzle me for the rest of my days. Leaning over the portside and cupping my hands around my mouth I dipped my head into the water and made a screeching, wallowing noise that as far as I could remember resembled the "Song of the Whale". To my utter amazement this huge creature (it was over fifteen metres long) sounded and momentarily disappeared from sight, only to reappear heading vertically skywards as it propelled itself out of the water like a Polaris missile! On re-entering the water, its fluke – which must have been four metres across – slapped hard down on the surface, causing the yacht to heel violently to starboard. My throat immediately became dry with fear. The calm water surrounding the hull became disturbed as the whale swam beneath the keel.

What had come over me to do such a stupid thing I asked myself as I suddenly remembered reading about a whale that sank a yacht somewhere off the Galapagos Islands? Looking at the life raft in the cockpit I devised a hurried plan of escape. My imagination ran riot, thinking that an irate whale might suddenly send the keel crashing through the bottom boards. To my utter relief this huge creature appeared on the surface about a hundred yards to port.

That was one of the moments that I remember best of a voyage that had its creation over forty years before.

Chapter 2

Now at sixty years old and after over forty years of sailing, I look back with a warm contentment that has graced the autumn of my life. To think I hadn't set eyes on the sea until I was fourteen.

I was born in 1940 in Leicester, England, which is about as far from the sea as you can get in this Island of ours. My mother took me on a bus trip to Skegness and I first saw, with wonder and amazement, how big and awesome the sea was. I can remember as if it were yesterday seeing a distant ship on the horizon and deciding that this would be the life for me.

Leaving school at the age of fifteen meant that I would have to wait another twelve months before attaining the minimum age to join the Merchant Navy. In those days (the 1950s) employment was plentiful as Britain was undergoing a recovery programme following the devastation caused by the Second World War.

It was one week after my fifteenth birthday that I found myself being lowered down the mineshaft of the Desford village colliery in Leicestershire. I had enrolled as a pit-boy. Along with two other lads, my job was to take the wooden pit props to the coalface, where in the beams of light from the head-torches of scores of kneeling, sweat-drenched men, coal was being shovelled onto a fast-moving floor-level conveyor belt.

The journey from the bottom of the pit shaft to the coalface was three miles, and it took us over an hour to reach there. The pit props were loaded into miniature steel rail trucks (called tubs) that were about three feet high and six feet in length. To pull these tubs along the rail-track we had a piebald pony called Turpin. By the end of the shift, though, Turpin didn't look piebald at all but black all over!

The journey to the coalface was hindered by the rail-track being distorted by the constant movement of the mine floor that was under a massive pressure from the ground weight above it. We carried with us large nails called dogs which we would hammer into any part of the rail track that had been disturbed, as it was also our job to keep the tubs running. Another delay to our trek was when we reached a part of the coal-carrying conveyor belt that crossed and ran overhead of the rail-track. Turpin's harness had to be removed or it became entangled in the steel mesh grid that had been rigged at the underside of the conveyor belt as a safety guard.

In whitewashed stables hewn out of solid rock, the ponies were kept permanently below ground, with the exception of two weeks in the month of August, when much to their joy they were brought to the surface and let loose in a grassy field. Stabled with Turpin were eleven other ponies – or horses as the miners called them. The miners seemed to have a language all of their own. We were never called boys but 'yolf' (youth) so it would not be unusual to hear "Have you got your horse ready, yolf?" Besides every other word in a miner's vocabulary seemingly to be a swear word, terms like 'tub amain!' would be cried out if any of the tubs started to run away downhill out of control.

The same pony would be collected every day by the same group of pit-boys, as a bond seemed to develop between each animal and their human carers. This bond resulted in the ponies working in a more cooperative manner: it was not unusual for the 'horse' to deliberately pull the tub off the track if he became upset for any reason. Turpin would sometimes derail a tub if we were working overtime. I was beginning to think that he had a hidden clock, for as soon as the normal shift time ended he would run off towards the stables and, in order to stop his gallop, we had to switch our head-torches off and grope after him in the dark.

It was a surprise to me at the time to discover that there were hills and dales underground. (The rock and coal seams followed the contours of the surface terrain.) On reaching a steep upward gradient we would have to uncouple the tubs (there were six of them) and take them individually to the top of the brow. The pony could only manage to pull one full tub at a time and that was only with the help of two of us lads pushing from behind and another lad leading. By the time all of the tubs were up the hill Turpin was dripping with sweat and so were we.

Going downhill was easier, of course, for man and beast, although to prevent the loaded tubs from running away too fast and out of control when making a steep descent, it was very important to stop the wheels from turning. This was done by jamming stout wooden pegs (called lockers) between the wheel spokes. With the wheels locked in this manner, the pony would then be able pull the heavy pit prop-loaded tubs safely downhill as they slid along the rail-tracks. The final part of the journey to the coalface involved negotiating a very steep and long downward incline. It was imperative that the lockers were jammed into the tubs' wheels at this part of the trek as the road's height was abruptly reduced from seven feet to four feet where it met at the coalface. A tub 'amain' would have disastrous consequences for the poor horse.

When we reached the 'face, the hard work began as we crawled along the four feet high coal-seam, dragging the wooden pit props to where each face-worker was stationed. Sometimes the men would pause from their work when we reached them with their quota of pit props and, as a way of saying thanks, they would offer us a round tin of snuff, saying, "Ta yolf, duh yah wanna pinch?"

Whilst we were on the coalface, Turpin was left alone in the darkness, but even so he would find and help himself to anyone's 'snap' (packed lunch) if it was not left under a rock. My 'snap' was usually thick doorsteps of bread and jam wrapped in newspaper. Drinking water was carried in a steel khaki-coloured ex-army canteen. There wasn't a fixed time for a tea break but we took one when it would not cause any hold-ups to the pit prop supply line. Whilst sitting on the rock floor having our break, we quite commonly saw fossilised seashells embedded in the rock, although we were over a quarter of a mile underground and about a hundred miles from the sea.

When we were sitting down, the air felt quite hot, even without any physical exertion. This ventilation air had its origin at a surface opening at another colliery called Merrylees, which was seven miles away. To draw this air through the mine workings, rotating fans of twenty feet in diameter were housed at our pithead. In the beams of our head-torches the direction of this ventilating air movement could be seen in the millions of coal-dust particles floating along. This visual direction of air movement could actually be of immense help should you become lost in the labyrinth of tunnels. When we became lost (usually after being sent to recover abandoned equipment from a disused working) we would follow the floating coal-dust particles, knowing that they would give us a good inkling as to the whereabouts of the pit-shaft.

On one particular shift, the first inkling that we lads had of something being amiss was Turpin's distressed neighing and stubborn refusal to continue to pull the tubs along the track. It was only after yanking him by his reins and lots of shouting that Turpin moved forward. The only other times he had behaved like this had been during the coalface shot-firing, when the coal was being blasted with dynamite. The deafening explosions would resound for quite a good distance, but on this occasion we were too far away for Turpin to be affected by any loud noise. We were soon to be enlightened about Turpin's strange behaviour, for we reached the coalface to find it silent and abandoned. A pall of thick smoke hung along the roof of the coalface.

"FIRE! Get out the pit!" The cries came from an overseer who was frantically running down the hill towards us. "FIRE! Get out the pit!" he yelled again with a desperate urgency, and then turned and disappeared into the darkness. Uncoupling Turpin from the tubs, we ran up the steep hill together and headed towards the pit-shaft. On reaching the conveyor belt that crossed our path we tried in our panic to push Turpin under it without removing his harness. This was a huge mistake, for the harness became caught in the steel mesh on the underside of the conveyor belt track. It took twenty minutes to free Turpin, who was now showing signs of distress as the smoke became thicker.

We finally reached the bottom of the pit-shaft to find hundreds of men waiting their turn to be taken out of the mine that was now threatening to suffocate all of us. The pit shaft resembled the inside of a giant chimney flue as the ventilation fans drew the smoke up to the surface. The steel lift cages were running at the coal-hauling speed, which was twice as fast as the man-lifting rate.

Along with the other distressed animals, Turpin's rein was pulled hand-by-hand to the front of the queue by lines of desperate men. When we eventually stepped out of the lift cage into the dazzling sunlight our task was to fill hessian bags with sand, from a mountain of it that had been dumped at the pithead. These bags of sand were used to block the tunnels and so smother the fire.

It was to take a week to finally smother the underground inferno that had had its origins at the Merrylees colliery. During that week Turpin, along with his other stable-mates, gambolled across the pithead meadow like newborn lambs.

It was such a joy when I was recognised by Turpin and he galloped across the field to see me.

With the 'All clear' being given, we began returning to our work underground. As I led a reluctant Turpin into the lift cage I did not realise that it was to be the last time he would ever see the light of day.

Turning sixteen on the 3rd of July, I had handed in my notice and by Wednesday 1st August 1956 I had just three days remaining to work at the colliery. On that day, the shift had been running quite normally and Turpin had resigned himself to hauling the pit prop-laden tubs without too much resentment after his impromptu holiday in the meadow.

On reaching the brow of the hill at a place where the rail-track followed the steep downward incline that ended abruptly at the coalface, we stopped the heavily laden tubs. In the beam of my head-torch I could see that Turpin's coat was covered in sweat and coal dust; he probably welcomed the brief rest. As we began to reach inside one of the tubs for the wooden lockers in order to jam the tubs' wheels, a mighty shot-firing explosion reverberated through the tunnel. Before we had time to grab hold of the terrified animal's rein; he had bolted, dragging the tubs with him into the darkness and to his death.

As I turned to walk away from the colliery for the very last time, I glanced at the now empty pithead meadow, and some small specks of coal dust must have settled into my eyes. That was of no consequence, though; for now I was a man and going away to sea.

So at sixteen I joined the Merchant Navy and for eight glorious years of my early adulthood explored our wonderful planet. The ships I sailed were classed as tramps that searched for cargoes in every corner of the globe. It was with these tramp ships that I was first introduced to sailing. Standing lug-sail were the rigs of the ship's lifeboats that we sailed. And looking back now I realise how clumsy they were. In our mind's eye then they were J class yachts. Having been torpedoed in the Second World War, only a decade or so before, the Captains were keen to teach their crews how to sail these lifeboats. At every chance the ship's boats would be lowered into some foreign harbour, the rope falls clattering through the davit blocks. When these clinker-built boats landed, the water would come pouring through the seams until they were swollen.

After eight years at sea I 'swallowed the anchor' (went to work ashore) and lived on the banks of the River Mersey opposite Liverpool. The famous ship *Great Eastern*, Isambard Kingdom Brunel's creation, was broken up there. And it was whilst I was rummaging through second-hand books at the local market, hoping to find one about this ship, that I came across a book called *Sailing to Freedom* by Veedam and Wall.

It was a true story of a group of Estonian people who, to escape their country at the end of the Second World War (it was taken over by Russia), bought a small wooden yacht called *Erma* and sailed to Norfolk, Virginia, U.S.A. This book, which cost the princely sum of sixpence, I started reading at eight o'clock in the evening and finished at three o'clock the next morning. I just could not put the book down. At the end of this epic tale I was so deeply moved by the voyage that they had endured, I vowed that I would one day sail single-handed across the Atlantic Ocean in memory and out of profound respect for these brave souls.

This day came when I retired from work in July 2000. The children had flown the nest. Though over the years I'd sailed coastwise and to Ireland and the Isle of Man many times, I had never sailed 'deep sea'. Having decided that the wooden twenty-one-foot clinker-built yacht I owned was not suitable for this voyage, I began looking for one bigger and more suitable.

Chapter 3

After many weeks of scouring through local papers and yachting magazines I came across a junk-rigged yacht for sale in Barcelona that had been made ready for an Atlantic crossing and the project abandoned owing to domestic troubles. Never having sailed a junk-rigged yacht, I enrolled in trail sail on a similar yacht from the haven of Warsash near Southampton. Afterwards I decided that this would be the ideal rig for a single-hander. Reefing couldn't have been simpler: ease away the main halyard, and that was it; except for taking up the slack in the luff-hauling parrel.

Having set eyes on her (she was called *Blue Moon*) I knew that this junk-rigged yacht had been prepared for an Atlantic crossing. The scuttles were boarded up, the cockpit reduced in size and the chain pipe had a wooden bung ready for sea. So there and then I decided to buy her, and allowed myself to be talked out of having a survey carried out. Then I gave my hand on the sale, adding to the seller: "Tell me now if there is anything that needs attention so I can sort it out before I sail across the Atlantic." He shook his head and uttered, "Nutting at all." So it was that this Belgian sold to me a potential death trap.

Blue Moon? I didn't like this name. So I decided to change it. Now, my wife and I had recently been on holiday to the Dominican Republic and travelled along a river called Ozama.

In the language of the indigenous people (according to our guide), *ozama* means 'deep water'. So *Blue Moon* became *Ozama*. And no sooner had I painted out the old name and painted in the new than the war in Afghanistan had broken out. *Ozama* was the least popular name in the world. People would point and ask me if the yacht was named after Ozama bin Laden. Too late; the paint was dry and *Ozama* she stayed.

The day came in that September to sail for Gibraltar, with the first port of call in Ibiza. So with my pal Dave, with whom I'd sailed for over thirty years, we waved farewell to Barcelona and headed out to sea.

It was after the first twenty hours that the first sign of trouble began. The barometer started to fall and the seas were dotted with white horses. A deafening clanging filled the cabin as the heavy steel drop keel swung from side to side with such violence that it was as if we were inside a church bell. Sleeping was impossible and we both cursed the keel, the sea, the weather and myself for not having a survey carried out in Barcelona. Running before a quartering sea and strong wind, and with two panels reefed, we sailed after two days into the lee of the mole of Santa Eularia. Peace at last. The clanging had stopped. Just the sound of music and laughter from a quayside bar filled the night air. The next day Dave flew back to England. Who could blame him?

When *Ozama* was cradled out of the water with the giant mobile lift, the problem with the lift-keel was evident. The bearings were worn away. The local marine engineer, after much thought and moving the keel from side to side, decided it would be too big a job to replace the obsolete bearing. Bolting two heavy pieces of angle-iron either side of the keel and to the stub keel solved the problem. And *Ozama* became a fixed-keel yacht.

After tying up alongside the marina pontoon I went ashore for a cold beer and to phone my wife Janet to see if she would like a fortnight's holiday in Ibiza.

Sailing is not high on Janet's list of pastimes, though I do try to show her the good side. It was with good intent that whilst she was making a cup of tea in the cabin, I slipped the mooring, gently raised the main and silently sailed out to sea. Her hand, holding a cup of tea, poked out of the hatchway and as she looked around she cried, "Where's the jetty gone?" With laughter filling the air I came about and headed to the harbour. She was having none of it. We spent time exploring the island by bus, calling into the tapas bars and always ordering the local dishes. It was a chance also to practise the Spanish I'd started to learn, so when a totally different dish arrived at the table from that I had ordered, I kept quiet and pretended that it was just the very thing!

Looking through the airport lounge window, I watched the plane turn to a northeasterly course, and Janet was on her way home.

Chapter 4

Cartagena was to be the next port of call on our journey to Gibraltar, so after clearing the newly allotted berth of the marina, I doused the little six-horse diesel engine. I fully set the mainsail and with a force four easterly wind we steered (the yacht and I) south by east to clear El Pila de la Mola at the southern tip of Formentera. Sitting in the cockpit supping a cup of hot tea, watching the vane of the Narvik self-steering gear gently dip to bring her back on course, and with the absence of a clanging keel, I was at peace with the world.

The next day the wind died away, but we were clear of the land and halfway there. Whilst we were bobbing about, a tiny yellow and green bird perched itself on the coaming, then, quite unafraid, it flew into the cabin. As quietly and gently as I could, I peeped below to see it hopping on and examining everything that was shiny: the brass dividers, the tell-tale compass, the kettle. After ten minutes the inspection must have seemed satisfactory and in order, so it flew off. It is seemingly small, unexpected events like this that, to me, make sailing all worthwhile. They are treasures that cannot be stolen.

Only three miles from Cartagena and I still could not make out the entrance to the harbour. Everything seemed to blend together against a backdrop of brown mountains. How the Romans managed to sail there, rape and pillage, baffled me. I couldn't find it with a G.P.S. As the sun sank below the horizon, the illumination of the harbour lights guided us in, which tallied with the G.P.S.-derived line of longitude that we were sailing along. Jumping ashore with the two back springs made *Ozama* fast, and when I was satisfied that she was secure in her new berth I went ashore, paid the berthing fees (which seemed to be less the further south we sailed) and ambled into town to find virtually everywhere closed. It was one of the many festival days that the Spaniards celebrate. Still, it was a change to be able to walk so far without falling into the water.

One of the sights that really interested me there was mounted in a cradle on the promenade. It was a submarine from the First World War, pock-marked with age though well maintained. The legend read that she carried one torpedo and a crew of five. Brave souls. Passing a pile of watermelons heaped up on the roadside, I bought the biggest one in the heap from a jovial lady sitting under a giant parasol. This was a mistake, for as I traipsed around the town, this thing seemed to become heavier, and rolled around the bar-top of the dockside tavern.

The next morning we sailed away, the melon safely stowed in the rope locker, and steered for Almería. The wind was east four to five, and under shortened sail we docked the next evening. There I met a fellow lone yachtsman, Wilhelm, and we swapped yarns aboard his yacht. He had sailed these waters for years and I was glad of any advice he could give. When I mentioned the easterly gale that was forecast he told me that they are very good if you are sailing west: do not be afraid of them, as the seas are not big, but westerly gales are very bad. So with this in mind we said *auf wiedersehen* to our new-found friend the next day and set course for Gibraltar.

The wind did pipe up and the self-steering was having trouble coping with this following easterly. During the night she gybed the boom, clouting my head and knocking my head-torch over the side. Helm down, I brought her smartly through the wind. The head-torch, still shining brightly in the water, was tantalisingly just out of the reach of the boathook. Three times we came about but just could not manage to fish it out of the sea. Donning a spare head-torch I set a new course north of west and brought the wind onto the starboard quarter. The self-steering could cope with this, so I went to put the kettle on, having one last glance astern at the fast-receding light dancing in the water.

After just over two days the wind had backed to the north-west and eased to five, and we stood south of the Europa light at the entrance to Gibraltar. Hard on the port tack we sailed at four knots through the water but did not make any progress over the ground, even with the help of the engine. After eight hours of this frustration of sailing over the same piece of seabed, it was two o'clock in the morning. With the light of the Europa Point mockingly shining on our portside, I bore off and headed for Estepona, about twenty miles to the north-northeast. So it was as the sun began to peep over the horizon that we docked. This was not our intended destination, but it was near enough. Having one last look around at our new surroundings, I got my head down and slept for twelve hours.

The bus didn't take long to reach Gibraltar. Strolling down towards the docks and passing an ex-R.A.F. aircraft hangar on the way, I made my way to the marina office. The information I needed to work the tides to make the passage were all in a neat little 'pilot' sold in their shop. Little wonder that I had struggled to make headway. There are three currents running parallel to each other and setting in different directions and speeds at various states of the tides. These sailing directions needed to be studied carefully before I could make another attempt. So after dropping the hook half a mile east of 'The Rock' I lit the oil-filled anchor light and settled down to await the early morning fair tide to take us in.

Whilst sitting in the cockpit looking at the shore lights and headlights of cars appearing and disappearing like a swarm of fireflies, out of the darkness the unlit silhouette of a patrol vessel came into view. Suddenly a huge searchlight was switched on, and I put my hand over my eyes, trying to make out who was shouting at me in Spanish. It was the maritime police, checking for illegal trafficking, which goes on in the Strait. After a quick once-over of *Ozama*'s cabin and asking a few questions, they disappeared into the night. At the Queensway Quay marina reporting berth the next morning I hopped ashore to register. Whilst I was filling out the obligatory papers, a uniformed man who was looking across the harbour turned his head and said, "Hope we didn't startle you last night."

Chapter 5

The time in Gibraltar was spent mainly loading stores and water for the next leg of the voyage to Porto Santo in the Madeira archipelago.

The water was carried in five-litre rigid plastic bottles. I'd been using three and a half litres a day, so the twenty-five bottles seemed ample for my needs and *Ozama* could carry the weight without losing too much more of her already low freeboard. Yarning with my waterborne neighbours, many of whom had sailed the Oceans alone and with crews for years, I learnt valuable information from their experiences and local knowledge of ports they had called at. *Keep a good lookout for tunny fishermen in the Straits* was one piece of advice I was given one evening whilst sitting at a cabin table as the cheer flowed freely. And sound advice this would turn out to be.

The sun was dipping below the horizon in a blaze of orange and red as we slipped our mooring and gently glided into the Straits. With a fair wind and working the currents from the new 'pilot', we headed south of west for Porto Santo, the beacon on Tarifa shining its friendly light to starboard. Ships of all shapes and sizes overhauled us as they converged at the narrows of the Straits, their powerful engines thundering away into the darkness, with an urgency to meet a rigid commercial timetable. A powerful torch was always at hand to beam at the bridge when one of these ships came too close.

The tri-light at our masthead could not be relied upon to be seen, as I'd learnt over the years of coastal sailing.

Clearing the Narrows I sighed with relief, as with more sea room and the sea traffic dispersing, I could think about making a hot cup of tea. Engaging the self-steering and having a quick look about the horizon, I went below to put the kettle on. We were sailing full and bye. The tea was brewing and I was rummaging in one of the ex-army kitbags to select a couple of tins of something to heat up for my dinner. Usually it was pot luck that came out and some interesting concoctions were created. Whilst smiling at the tins of pilchards and Irish stew that came forth, and at my decision to mix them in the one stew-pot, the yacht came to a violent halt and I was thrown forward.

Moving smartly into the cockpit I could see the huge tan mainsail still full of wind, but we were not moving through the water. Turning on my head-torch I looked over the side to see, just under the surface, a half-inch-diameter wire holding a fishing net: small buoys spaced at intervals suspended it vertically like a tennis net. Dousing the sail, I grabbed the boathook and tried to free the keel from this tunny fisherman's net. All to no avail, until turning on the engine and going full astern forced the net to let go its hold.

We weren't out of the woods, for as I shone a powerful hand torch about the surface there appeared yet another net. This to me was a nightmare: how could we find our way out of this, what seemed like a labyrinth? The answer came as an Arab fisherman turned on his lights and began shouting and yelling at me in what seemed a torrent of abuse. Then to my alarm he headed for me. My thoughts raced to Joshua Slocum's encounter with pirates off this coast. Even if I knew the way out of those nets I could not show him a clean pair of heels as *Spray* had done. Just when I thought this fisherman was going to invite himself aboard over the transom, he went about and headed the other way. This performance happened three times. Then the penny dropped when I could make out

18

through the darkness a crewman beckoning me to follow. They were trying to show me the way out of the nets. So at the fourth time that he went about I followed him. Lines of nets running parallel to each other rushed past and seemed to run for ever. To my relief he carried on steaming ahead, slowing down at times lest I lose sight of him. After what seemed ages a ship's whistle blasted U.W. through the night air and he was gone. We were clear of the nets.

With a happy heart I set a course again for the open sea and the last of the coastal obstructions, I hoped. Going below, I lit the stove, made a fresh pot of tea and carried on at where I had left off hours before, cooking my dinner. Pilchards and Irish stew could not have tasted better.

With the wind still on the quarter we sped onwards into the Atlantic, the windvane now having to work harder as the following seas started to pick up. Standing astride the side-benches of the cockpit I kept a futile lookout for unlit fishing nets for the remainder of the night. Looking astern as the sun peeped up, and against all logic, I felt safer now that the daylight was nearly here. So it was with a happy heart I could get my head down. Having one last look around, I went below. Just one last thing to do or I would not rest easy. Flipping through the seaman's bible, the 'Reeds Almanac', and turning to the pages of two-letter signals, I found U.W. It means, 'I wish you a pleasant voyage'.

The wind had backed to the north about force three, and for several days under full sail we ploughed gently to the southwest. High above us, on a more southerly course, the vapour trails of holiday jets bound for the Canary Islands made white chalk-marks upon the sky.

At the time I thought of how the distances they travel in one hour would in favourable winds take us a week, although to me sailing is not about getting somewhere fast, it's about the experience of being at sea and at one with it. In days of calm, to see in the water minute creatures being chased by other fish the size of sticklebacks, a turtle floating by, Portuguese men-of-war looking like pink transparent Cornish pasties bobbing about the surface ... these are some of the sights I had not seen from the decks of the tramp ships I sailed. To miss all of this when I had the chance would be like an unopened gift ... thrown away.

It was on one of those days of flat calm that we were halfway between Gibraltar and Porto Santo and I was leaning over the side scrubbing off some of the 'grass' on the water-line. Singing to myself and absorbed in the task at hand, I involuntary lifted my head for the usual lookout. There, to my shock, was a huge Merchantman less than a quarter of a mile off our starboard beam, her propellers not turning. The name *Rosalind* was clearly painted on her bow. Grabbing my hand-held V.H.F. radio from the cabin, I stood in the cockpit and called her. The ship was on passage to a port in the Gulf of Mexico to load liquid gas. After spotting the tan sail and yellow hull of *Ozama*, they had wondered if I needed assistance. This is the true brotherhood of the sea: this huge giant had been stopped by her Captain to render assistance to us, a humble yacht. I was grateful and moved beyond words. For over half an hour we chatted, asking each other questions about our different vessels. I discovered that there were nineteen crew on board, made up of eighteen men and one of the engineers being a woman. A detailed weather report for the area was relayed to me, which I hastily scribbled down so as to compare later with the barometer readings in my log. They would be at sea for Christmas and we agreed to raise a glass to each other on Christmas Day. As I waved goodbye to half of the crew lining the port rail, her giant propellers started to turn. And she was gone. I had not felt at all lonely at sea before this encounter, but as I stowed the now-silent hand-held V.H.F. radio in its rack, an unfamiliar sense of being alone engulfed me. Luckily this feeling did not last for long, as I told myself that I was here of my own choosing and fortunate, as there were lots of folk going about a humdrum existence, never having this golden chance.

A voyage made by one person is often called single-handed or lone – well neither of these words gives proper credit to the most important factor of any sea journey, the yacht. Sailing alone is like being one part of a seaborne duet, where the performances of the yacht and its skipper are both important. But yachts have been known to cross oceans crewless, having broken away from their moorings. Though I have never heard of anyone doing this yachtless.

The flat calm lasted for two days until the high pressure system started to shift and once more we were underway. It must have been midway to our destination that I sighted dead ahead a floating buoy. Immediately I thought it was a marker for a fishing net that had broken adrift. Unlatching the self-steering gear I swiftly gave this unwelcome stranger a wide berth. Looking through binoculars I noticed that the buoy supported an aluminium radar reflector mounted on top of trelliswork. The surface of the sea surrounding it was broken and disturbed. This did cause me to feel alarmed as I knew the water must be at least two miles deep. *Ozama* was not fitted with an echo sounder so I had bought a hand-held one. Leaning over the side I plunged it into the water. One hundred and eight feet was the read-out. This could not be right? After taking three readings with the results roughly the same, I knew it was. Looking astern until the buoy was just a dot on the horizon, I dipped the echo sounder again. No bottom! Feeling more relaxed now, I reset the self-steering, still puzzling about our strange encounter. I entered it into the log.

Who can forget their first deep-sea landfall? After two weeks at sea, there in all its glory and profoundly clear, the shape of the island of Porto Santo popped up over the horizon. The sun's dying rays outlined it clearly. Feeling like Christopher Columbus discovering the New World I let out a cry of joy and patted *Ozama*, adding, "Good girl."

So it was, with the red and green beacon lights marking the entrance to the harbour, I dropped the hook to await daybreak. It was whilst reporting with my passport and ship's papers to the official in the marina office that I mentioned the radar reflector that we had nearly run into. On one of the walls, and partly hidden by a large Christmas tree, hung a relief chart of the seabed. The official explained that the buoy was anchored on the top of an underwater mountain and was being studied by a Portuguese scientific research group.

The yachts in the marina were mostly local craft. The last of the Atlantic crossing fleet that had been waiting for the hurricane season to end had sailed a week ago. The only other foreign yachts were two French ones which had beautiful sea-kindly-shaped hulls and were sailed single-handed. One was owned by Mike, whom I considered the French version of Scrooge: to avoid paying the docking fee he anchored outside the harbour until the marina staff had gone home for the Christmas holiday. His fellow countryman, Olivier, was a trainee monk and totally opposite in nature. He was taking his ketch-rigged yacht to give as a gift to an orphanage in Uruguay. Olivier's parents had bought the yacht for him and having never sailed before in his life, he had enrolled in a crash course in seamanship. Sitting in his teak-panelled saloon during the evening I would teach Olivier simple bends and hitches. Religious icons and pictures hung from the bulkheads, and against the backdrop of the richly coloured timbers a feeling of quiet warmth and peace prevailed.

Olivier's parents were flying out to stay with him over Christmas. Afterwards they would organise having the stem of the bow repaired, that had been stove in after colliding with the breakwater during the entry. A new anchor and chain would also have to be purchased. He explained that whilst anchoring outside the harbour, and not realising that the bitter end of the chain was not made fast, he saw the last link disappear. And to add to this injury, he had started the engine and at full speed rammed the harbour wall whilst trying to release the jammed auto-pilot. Unfortunately the yacht's dinghy had been swept away from the davits in bad weather during the crossing from Gibraltar. Explaining how he had had to helplessly watch it disappear between the troughs, Olivier was quite philosophical, saying, "I did not expect this voyage to be easy," and pointing to a wooden figure that was screwed to the chart table. "With His help I will make it." Then, producing a bottle of wine made by his Brothers at the monastery, given as a going-away present, he poured two large glasses, and we wished each other fair winds.

Over the following days he practised different bends and hitches: he would proudly demonstrate a bowline made with a turn of his wrist. A round turn and two half hitches with which he had replaced the 'snowball' hitches on the yacht's fenders followed. In my stores I came across a new Irish linen tea towel depicting knots and splices. After wrapping it in a piece of disused Admiralty chart that I had decorated with coloured pens, I gave this to Olivier for Christmas, adding 'not to be opened' until then.

Every Saturday I had a strict routine of three things that I would carry out:

1) run the diesel engine for twenty minutes;
2) practise a lifeboat drill; and
3) cut my hair.

Cutting my hair could not have been simpler, as not having very much I cut it to the 'wood' with an electric cutter. My wife Janet had given me a haircutting kit before I left home, and a very professional outfit it was too, with three sets of scissors, two combs, brushes and electric cutters and an assortment of other items, all displayed in an open-out soft leather folder. The only item I ever had to use was the cutter, which was just as well as I haven't a clue how to cut hair.

It must have been a Saturday when, as I was leaving the marina shower block with a newly scalped head, I met Mike.

"Who cut your hair?" he asked in a strong French accent.

"I did it myself," I replied, and proudly laid open the haircutting outfit for him to see.

"Can you do the same for me?" he enquired, rubbing his hands together in glee at the thought of saving a few Euros.

"Of course I can," I answered, beckoning him to come with me to the shower block. Mike was a good-looking fellow with a full head of jet-black hair. I thought he wanted all his hair off like mine: well, it would take ages for it to grow again and it would be more comfortable for him when he sailed south for his next port, Bakau in Gambia, West Africa. This was my reasoning, anyway. Reasoning that turned out to be a mistake.

No sooner had a path been cut across his head from the back to the front, than he let out in French what I took to be swear words. Then, clasping both his hands on top of his head he stood up and yelled, "I do not want a haircut like this!"

"Too late now," I said. "You'll have to have it all off."

"No, no, my wife is flying from Le Havre to stay with me – do something with scissor!" he pleaded. When I explained that I did not know how to use the scissors, a look of disbelief crossed his face and he uttered, "You are not a barbear?"

"No," I said, "I used to work in the boiler house at Vauxhall Motors."

He insisted that I try to make the best of a bad job with the scissors. With tears streaming down my face I could hardly do anything for laughter as I hacked away at the remainder of his locks. To make matters worse, on the way along the pontoon we met Olivier, who, after I explained why Mike's hair looked the way it did, fell about in fits. Laughter is the best medicine, I've heard it said, but too much makes your stomach ache, as I found out the next day.

The next day was spent restocking the ship's stores and water and painting the name 'Ozama' and the legend 'Caernarfon Dec. 2000' on the harbour wall. The local supermarket was a mile or so along the coast road. So, trundling my set of shopping trolley wheels, I made several trips to ensure that there would be enough food for the Atlantic crossing. A leg of smoked pork was included in the stores after remembering how Wilhelm, the lone yachtsman I had met in Cartagena, told me how he had lived on smoked pork for weeks at sea after running out of tinned food. So the time came to say farewell to Mike and Olivier and their respective families. Whilst I was clearing the mooring lines Olivier thrust a present into my hand. I stowed it away, saving it until later.

Ozama, with her engine chugging away, headed through the gap between the harbour walls to meet the heaving ground swell. (*Ozama* and me) were on our way to St Lucia. It was Christmas day.

Chapter 6

Night was falling and so was the barometer. With the main halyard eased away, two panels were soon reefed. The wind from the northeast, force four, was gradually increasing. Could this be the start of the Trades? At thirty-two degrees north, it was too far north. Probably wishful thinking on my part. The old sailor men that I have had the privilege to listen to in my lifetime used to say: "There are two things that a seafarer cannot predict – one being the start of the Trades and the other the heart of a woman." By midnight a near gale was blowing, but now under only one panel of the tan-coloured Chinese sail we ploughed southward at about four knots. *Ozama* did not have the luxury of a built-in or trailing speed log, so I used to throw a Dutchman's log over the stern and count the seconds it took to run out. It was a twenty-foot log I'd made, so for example if it took three seconds to run out, the ship's speed through the water would be four knots. This was an extremely accurate way of finding the ship's speed through the water and it didn't need batteries. When compared to the speed over the ground on the G.P.S. read-out, a good indication of the current's speed and direction was found.

Four points off the port bow a light sprang up: a green and two whites showing clearly through the binoculars. Taking a hand compass-bearing on the ship, I was hoping the angle would alter, as I did not fancy having to alter course in that strong wind. After half an hour the angle stayed the same, so I put the helm down and hove to. The compass bearing on her was altering now, and I breathed a sigh of relief as she crossed our bows, seemingly oblivious to our presence.[1]

It was time to put the kettle on and open the Christmas present Olivier had given to me. It was an audio tape of (according to the picture on the box) a choir of monks singing in a monastery.

So, with the melodious sounds of a choir in the background and a hot toddy in my hand, I gave a belated toast of "Merry Christmas" to everyone and wished for peace on Earth. The northeasterly wind was still howling, though beginning to moderate in strength. Climbing into the cockpit to have a lookout for any lights upon the horizon, I noticed that our own navigation tri-light at the masthead had failed. The powerful hand-torch was stowed in readiness in the cockpit to beam at any passing ship, so I was not unduly concerned.

New Year's Eve was celebrated with the island of La Palma in the Canaries twenty miles on the port quarter. We had made good headway south, averaging eighty nautical miles a day. The gradually dying wind had finally disappeared and left us on a sea that was like a millpond. I was pleased with our progress. This would be the chance to haul myself up to the masthead and sort out the faulty tri-light. Sitting in a bosun's chair and with a gantline and single block hauled aloft, I began this laborious task, which took over half an hour. Having reached the truck, I heard a noise like someone blowing across the rim of a beer bottle. And the rest is history.

The following day, January 2nd, the wind was as elusive as ever, but the sky was cloudless and the sea calm. According to the Admiralty chart we were in the Canary Current that runs at a rate of one to one and a half knots in a southerly direction, turning southwesterly as it joins the North Equatorial Current. So I felt happy that, although not moving through

---

1   See collision course in the glossary for an explanation of this incident

the water, at least we were being swept along in roughly the right direction.

The tri-light still needed attention, and I did not relish the idea of another long haul to the masthead. But this was not a task to be put off. I told myself, quoting the old adage, "Make hay while the sun shines" (or "Climb aloft while the wind does not blow" in this case). I am not an expert by any means on 'electrics' but have an elementary knowledge of the simple basics. So after linking an electric circuit tester to the tri-light wiring and fuse decided it probably was the bulb at fault. The 'tool-box' that I used aloft to hold the bits and bobs needed for the job at hand was a black rubber bucket. Attached to this bucket was a lanyard, more than long enough to reach the masthead. There is nothing worse than hauling yourself aloft to find that you have forgotten a tool or something. I would jot down in a small note pad that I kept for the very purpose everything that was required, and would double-check this before the ascent. Sailing alone does concentrate your way of thinking to that of self-reliance, a sound attitude on board maybe. Ashore I find that this independent spirit is hard to put aside and unwittingly causes offence to family and friends who want to help in some way, only to find that their offer of help is turned down.

Sitting in the bosun's chair, and after half an hour of arm-aching heaving my own weight inch by inch aloft, once more I was at the top of the mast. I was beginning to feel like that spider called 'Incy-Wincy' in the children's nursery rhyme, who was washed down the drainpipe and climbed up again. Unscrewing the tri-light lens and placing it in the rubber bucket that was now secured to the upper shroud, I removed the old bulb from its holder. Before I had left the cabin I had turned the switch on the tri-light to the 'on' position. When I twisted the new bulb into place, it immediately lit up – and so did I, with a shout of "Eureka!"

Being able to shout or sing or even talk to yourself without fear of upsetting someone or having them cart you off to some institution is another bonus to enjoy when sailing single-handed. In books by lone sailors that I have read, they seldom write of talking to themselves, in case, I suppose, people think that they must be mad. On talking with different single-handed yachtsmen that I've met on my travels, most of them have said (usually after I tell them that I do) that they talk aloud whilst on board. They also immediately understand that we' can mean 'the yacht and I'. Perhaps this talking to ourselves is nature's way to keep us sane, unless we are mad in the first place. But I don't think so.

The tri-light would only be used in an emergency so as to conserve the electric power. *Ozama* only carried one twelve-volt main battery, which I avoided using if at all possible. The only means of restoring any power to this battery was by means of a small solar panel bolted to the afterdeck, which produced twenty watts. After using the battery to start the small diesel engine, for example, it would take up to one week to replace the energy used, depending on how strong the sunlight was. The alternator mounted on the engine, that should have easily recharged the battery in minutes, had stopped working. Luckily I had bought, among the ship's stores taken on in Porto Santo, a ten-litre supply of lamp oil. This oil was not paraffin; when burning it gave off a fragrance not unlike lavender and burnt brightly without making the lamp glass black and sooty. Before darkness fell I would fill the hurricane lamp and, after setting the wick alight, would hang it on the backstay. Hurricane lamp? If ever a title contravened the Trades Descriptions Act it must be this. I have never known one not to have its flame quenched in winds above force five, and usually less. A solution I found was to cut the top off a clear plastic five-litre water bottle and place the lamp inside. This all-round white light hardly conformed to the maritime rules but it was better than nothing at all. Before going below I would have one last glance at the hurricane lamp and shout into the night sky: "Your lights are burning brightly, sir!"

These were the some of the lessons that had been taught to me as a boy at a sea training school on board an old nineteenth-century sailing ship called the *Vindicatrix* moored on a canal in Sharpness, Gloucestershire, England. This ship was constructed in steel and had carried three masts in her sailing days. Built in 1893 on the banks of the river Clyde, Glasgow, under her original name *Arranmore*, she had sailed all over the world with a variety of cargoes: grain, coal and sulphates, and hay feed for the war horses in South Africa being among them. In 1939 she became a sea school for merchant navy boys. Of course it wasn't the night sky but the officer on watch that the call "Your lights are burning brightly, sir" was supposed to be aimed at, by the man coming off the lookout. I was trying to maintain an old maritime tradition: that was the excuse I told myself for such a display of apparent lunacy.

During the hours of darkness, if I was awake, the cabin would be illuminated by an oil lamp that was hung in a gimballed holder above the small chart table. Unless I was plotting our position or writing in the ship's log etc. the wick of the cabin oil lamp was turned down low enough that I could move about without groping. I used fuel sparingly – in fact with all commodities I practised this, remembering that there weren't any shops in the middle of the Ocean.

Light from the alcohol-burning stove also lent its glow to the visibility. This stove, with the exception of making a cup of tea, was only lit after the sun had gone down, as I found it too hot to eat a cooked meal before then. I promised myself that at the first opportunity this stove would be changed for one that used bottled gas, as I found it difficult to obtain the methylated spirit that it used. In fact the fuel I was using in the stove after I had run out of meths was a Spanish-bought product made for domestic cleaning purposes. Evaporation also caused the fuel that remained in the firing chamber after the flame was snuffed out to be wasted, even though the caps were put on top of the extinguished burners. Even so, on that stove I rustled together meals that I thought were wonderful.

Wholemeal pasta and brown rice were in plentiful supply in the ship's stores, and a handful of these were usually added to the cooking pot along with the tinned meat or tinned 'lucky dip', sundried tomato pulp, fresh potatoes and onions and spices – always spices, they would add such a variety to the taste. The meals that emerged I enjoyed, but more importantly, they contained the nutrients that my body needed to carry on working properly. With this in mind, every day I would also take an 'over-fifty' multi-vitamin tablet.

Incidentally, the idea of the fresh onions that were included in the stores and would keep for months without going off, was a tip from the pages of *Sailing to Freedom*. The very book that had inspired this voyage. In this book, the onions – and there were four sacks of them bought in Maderia by Rommy, one of the crew members of *Erma* – would be eaten raw by him but caused an uproar among his crew mates owing to the odour they gave off. No such complaints from the crew of the *Ozama* though.

It was during the third night of being becalmed that I was awakened by the sound of water passing alongside the hull. We were underway again! On shining my head-torch onto the tell-tale compass that was mounted on the cabin sole, and making out that a westerly course was being steered, I wriggled out of my sleeping bag and climbed into the cockpit. The seas were starting to build up, and water began to sluice across the foredeck. Unlatching the self-steering, I brought *Ozama* to a heading south of southwest. The wind from the northeast blew steady at force four to five. At our position, twenty-five degrees north and eighteen degrees west, this was where it was written in the 'pilot' that the Trades could be found in January. The Chinese sail was made of seven panels and after I had reefed it down to four, the seas stopped inviting themselves aboard.

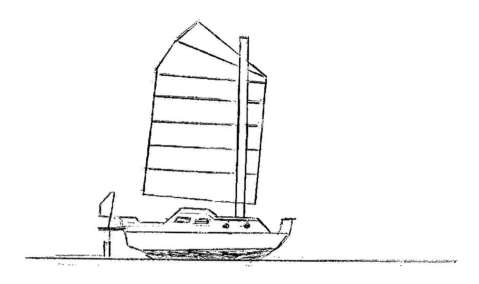

Ozama with her junk sail.

With the wind on the starboard quarter we were rushing headlong down the now ever-increasing following sea. The masthead was swinging across the black velvet sky like a giant stick trying to knock the stars across the heavens. I could not remember *Ozama* sailing as fast, and during the hours of darkness I have found that I tend to over-estimate the rate. The Dutchman's log has no such illusion, so laying out the twenty-foot log line and with stopwatch in one hand I dropped the triangular plywood 'log' into the water. This simple log and stopwatch told that in the two and a half seconds that it had taken for the triangle to reach the end of its log line the ship's speed through the water was nearly five knots. At this rate the Tropic of Cancer would be crossed in the next two days, as this invisible sea-mark lay two hundred miles to the south. A bottle of Rioja wine lay cradled in the bilge to be opened in celebration of this (to us) historic event. I found it satisfying to make an achievable target and then have an excuse to have a reward, be it a bottle of wine or a hot cup of tea and piece of the Christmas cake that my wife had brought out with her to Gibraltar.

The sudden whistling of the kettle jolted my thoughts back to our present position of not being in the tropics. No time for daydreaming, I told myself, feeling elated at our new-found speed. I opened the hatch and climbed back into the cabin, and filled the teapot that was hooked onto the stove by a piece of rubber shock-cord. To port, the sky was beginning to show the first rays of the sun. Daybreak was a sight that I never tired of. So, balancing my cup of tea in one hand, I crouched under the canvas spray hood to witness this spectacle. It was whilst perched there that a rogue wave came on board to join me and give my teacup a free refill.

The seas that came on board did not feel unpleasant, but it was like having a warm shower – unlike the bone-chilling water in the high latitudes that I was used to. Throwing the remains of the tea to leeward I went below to have a breakfast that would keep me going all day. This meal usually consisted of a porridge-like cereal that I had bought in Porto Santo. This finely milled grain was intended for infants, I discovered on interpreting the Portuguese label. I added to this cereal a quarter of a cup of sunflower seeds or dried apricots and honey, and milk powder mixed in a cup of water.

The drinking water was carefully monitored and was never used for personal washing: seawater was used for this and to wash the dishes. Only on a Saturday would I allow myself one cup of fresh water for shaving. During the voyage to date I had been consuming three and a half litres of drinking water per day. By 4th January there remained seventy-two litres of fresh water out of the one hundred I had sailed with from the last port. Time to reduce my daily fresh water usage to two litres per day. I supplemented this by using half seawater and half fresh to boil potatoes or rice. During the thunderstorms I would place a bucket in the cockpit and invert into it a giant umbrella that had its fabric perforated around the centre. This bucket would sometimes be filled with rainwater only to be spoiled by a breaking sea. It may have been psychological, but the pure

Ozama at Porto Santo December 2000
A month earlier, this harbour was full of yachts of every nationality
waiting for the hurricane season to end before crossing the Atlantic.
Photo: Trevor Wilson.

water that I did catch tasted absolutely wonderful. Should any drinking water be caught, the amount would be logged.

Inside the chart table that I grandly called the pilot desk were several notebooks, which included a fresh water book and a 'to-do' book in which I would jot down things that needed doing on board either at sea or in port. Although the list of things to do seemed to grow faster than I could mark them off as *done*, it gave to me a feeling of satisfaction and a sense of organisation when in red ink a tick appeared alongside each completed entry. After washing the breakfast dish and spoon in the sea I would open the to-do book and decide on the task to be carried out for that day. The state of the sea and weather, of course, played a major part in the selection of any job that I could carry out. The 'rule' was that I would only work until about local noon, as after that time it was too hot, belying the myth about mad dogs and Englishmen. On this particular day I had selected from the to-do book a rope-splicing job. Two mooring lines and two back springs, I had decided, needed permanent eyes instead of the bowlines. Being single-handed, every little helps when jumping onto the jetty to tie up. Gathering a wooden fid, deck knife and whipping twine – items that would be needed for splicing – I climbed into the cockpit. A big sea was running, the waves being about six metres in height, but the distance between the crests was, I estimated, a quarter of a mile. Down the slope of each of the following seas *Ozama* slid with a grace that befitted a ballerina. Rummaging inside the cockpit locker I fished out the mooring lines and, sitting on the side-benches, began splicing, feeling at one with the elements.

Chapter 7

On January 5th we crossed the Tropic of Cancer. We were in the tropics! This caused memories to come flooding back.

"When we are in the tropics, 'Pegs', put these wind scoops out of the portholes in the mess room."

Those were some of the words spoken to me by an old bosun after signing on my first ship after leaving the sea school at Sharpness. I was sixteen years old then. Now, at sixty years old, I can remember as if it were yesterday joining that ship: she was M.V. *Port Brisbane*, registered in London and owned by Port Line. I joined this ship in February 1957 while she was loading cargo in the K.G.V. docks in London. As a deck boy you had all the menial tasks to carry out, one of these being to wash the dishes and generally look after the more experienced crew members.

As the bosun continued to relate the duties on board ship that I was to carry out, my mind went blank after hearing him mention 'tropics'. Tropics! Where was the ship bound for? I dared not ask anyone this in case they thought that it was a stupid question and I was thrown off the ship. Every day I would cheerfully put my heart and soul into any task that I was set, often working from five o'clock in the morning until sometimes eight o'clock at night. And in those days there was no such thing as being paid for working overtime for us deck boys. You just got on with it. Nothing at all mattered then, only that I had the good fortune and honour to be allowed the greatest adventure in my life – to sail upon the sea and to a foreign country. Even being called 'Peggy' did not upset me, though I must admit that I thought it odd at the time.

'Peggy', I found out later, came about from the days of yore. When a seaman badly injured one of his legs, whether it be in battle upon the high seas or from falling to the deck in bad weather whilst handling the sails aloft, his leg would be amputated by the ship's surgeon or, as in many cases, the cook, who was skilled in butchery. The poor man's wound would then be dipped into boiling tar to seal it and to prevent infection and then fitted with a wooden leg. This wooden stump was called a peg leg. As if to add insult to injury, the owner became known as 'Peggy'. The duties of the man who was unfortunate enough to have undergone this treatment were naturally very restricted and usually he was allotted the task of attending to the needs of the able-bodied crew members. After learning of how this name came about, I was quite proud to be called Peggy, or Pegs for short.

The ship carried three deck boys and we would each take a turn every third week to work entirely away from peggying and be on deck under the supervision of one of the experienced crew. In those days we were taught not to answer back or give any cheek to our elders, as it was quite common to receive a clout around the ear for doing so, and this was accepted as normal. With this policy in mind the A.B. (able-bodied seaman) with whom you were working on deck would give you any part of the job that he didn't fancy doing. For example, in the ship's bows is the chain locker where the anchor cable is stowed. Our job one week was to chip the rust scale from the inside of this locker and finish the bare steel with a coat of anti-corrosive compound called red lead. After an electric lamp was lowered into the black abyss of this chain locker, a huge pile of giant links of the ship's anchor cable was revealed. A rope ladder was thrown over the side of the coaming and down we climbed.

"Now, Pegs, this is what we have got to do," said Stan the London docklands-born A.B. who was in charge of me that week; "you see all that rust scale on the ship's side? That's what we have got to chip off and paint with this red lead." Why he said 'we' I don't know, for after lowering down two buckets made from empty five-gallon paint drums, he stayed on deck hauling up these buckets with the rust chippings as fast as I could fill them, which was not very fast, as most of the time I was hanging on with one hand as the ship rolled from side to side. I did not mind in the slightest how hard I worked and was only too glad to be thought of as a useful member of the crew.

Being young and naive, us deck boys were open to all kinds of trickery, as I was to find out at the end of the trip. It was two days after sailing from the London docks when George, an A.B., approached me and mentioned that I would need a 'steering ticket' if I wanted to be promoted at a later date. This ticket was only obtainable at the mate's (officer of the watch) discretion after he had observed how many times and how well I had steered the ship, according to this A.B. "Listen, Pegs," he went on in a kind of whisper as if he was bestowing some good turn, "I will let you take my wheel tonight for two hours." (He was on steering watch duties.) "Come up to the wheelhouse at 20:00."

That evening, after I had washed all the dishes and my peggying duties were finished for the day, I went up to the bridge. It was 20:00. Peering into the unlit wheelhouse I could just make out the helmsman silhouetted in the green glow of the compass binnacle. "Over here, Pegs," George called through the gloom. With eyes squinting to adjust to the unfamiliar and dark surroundings I made my way to where George was standing. "Now," he began, "see that lubber line? Keep it on 243 degrees." And then he disappeared from the wheelhouse without waiting to hear my reply to his instruction, which would have been "How do I do that?" Too late now – the clanking noise he made hurriedly descending the steel ladders away from the bridge faded into silence. He had gone below to play cribbage and have a drink with his fellow off-watch A.B.s. There I was, alone at the wheel of a twelve-thousand-ton ship and feeling full of dread. The ship was steered by a gyro compass and I had not a clue how to respond to it in order to keep a steady course. At the sea school we had been taught steering on the old traditional magnetic compass. My eyes were fixed on the compass lubber line, and it was not long before the 243 degree mark moved to the right of this important line, which represented the ship's heading or direction. When a ship's wheel is turned it is not like being in a car, where the response is immediate – a ship will take several seconds before any movement is seen. Sweat was beginning to form across my brow and without knowing the reason behind my logic I turned the wheel to port. This turned out to be the wrong direction, as the ship herself had strayed off course to port. The figure against the lubber line soon read 200 degrees; the ship was 43 degrees off course. Frantically I turned the wheel even further to port, making matters worse. Wrong way, I realised, as we were heading south, and proceeded to swing the helm the opposite way in a blind panic.

Hurried footsteps came rushing out of the chart room as its door was flung open and the third mate yelled, "What do you think you are doing?" Throwing me aside he took over the wheel and after three or four minutes of skilful corrections the ship was steady once again on 243 degrees.

After the third mate had regained his composure he patiently showed to me the basic fundamentals of steering a true course. "Leave the wheel a minute, Pegs, and follow me." This is *it*, I thought, I am going to be reported to the *Old Man*.

Instead, and to my utter relief, the third mate pointed to a paper roll chart mounted on the bulkhead that recorded the straightness or otherwise of the course being steered. A fairly straight line was displayed in ink on this scroll where the four-to-eight watch (and George, who was on the eight-to-twelve watch and had been on the helm for five minutes from 19:55 to 20:00) had steered. The marks on the course recorder where I had been left on the wheel resembled the marks that a spider might have scrawled if its legs had been dipped in ink and allowed to crawl across the chart at random. Apologising to the third mate for the commotion that I had caused, I returned to the unmanned helm and, uttering a silent prayer of thankfulness under my breath, gently brought the ship back on course.

Almost six months later, at the end of the voyage, the total steering hours that I had amassed by taking the wheel tricks for the A.B.s was two hundred and seventy. These hours were written on the Board of Trade steering certificate that the third mate had signed and handed to me just before I had signed off the ship in the London docks. This was when I discovered that the number of steering hours required for obtaining one of those tickets was ten.

Although there had been low wages of £11.15s.0d per month (£11.75 in decimal money), and sometimes long hours of unpaid drudgery, the whole experience of that first voyage was worth everything to me. In fact one vivid recollection I still have of it was at the beginning of the trip, on the morning of the fifth day at sea. After gathering together a tin of Bluebell metal polish, sandstone and the remnants of a flag in preparation for going to polish the brass bell on the fo'c'sle, I stepped over the storm step into the working alleyway. There in all its glory was a sight to behold! A blue-coloured mountain top that looked as if had just broken the surface of the ocean was clearly visible less than five miles away. Rushing back to the mess room and feeling as if I had just made an important landfall, I blurted this news to the watch-keepers, who were eating their breakfast.

Casually looking up from his plate one of them said, "That's the Azores, Pegs." My eyes searched his face for signs of delight and wonder at the news that I had just announced. It was with disbelief that I watched him carry on eating his breakfast. I had half-expected them to fly out on deck to marvel at my discovery. The Azores, where were they on the map? The World Atlas that I had bought from Woolworth's for ten shillings revealed all. It was whilst looking at this atlas that one of the A.B.s enlightened me as to the itinerary of our ship and was quite amazed at my ignorance. He added that it was the first thing I must ask before signing on any ship.

Our first port of call was to be Port of Spain in Trinidad and on to Auckland in New Zealand to discharge the remainder of the outward-bound general cargo that included a variety of items from tons of cement to bales of cloth. Once this cargo had been discharged, the holds would be cleaned ready for the homeward-bound freight of frozen lamb and crates of apples to be stowed in the refrigerated holds. The Panama Canal had to be traversed first, of course, before reaching Auckland.

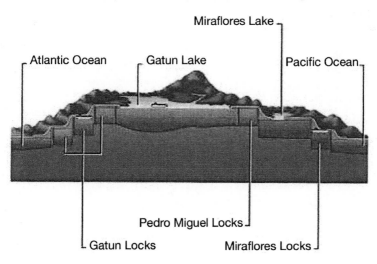

Panama Canal Lock System.
Sketch: Trevor Wilson collection.

We deck boys had been instructed by the crew to save all the stale bread for the mules that would pull the ship through the sets of locks that were needed to raise and lower the water level in the canal on our journey to the Pacific. It was amid howls of laughter on reaching the canal that a sack of stale bread was hauled on deck. We then discovered that the *mules* we had heard so much about were in fact giant diesel engines that ran on tracks either side of the locks. It was these motorised monsters, harnessed with their built-in towing cables, that would pull the ship along. As we emptied the sack of stale bread over the side, a flock of seagulls swooped down and, being totally unaware of their face-saving actions, ate the lot.

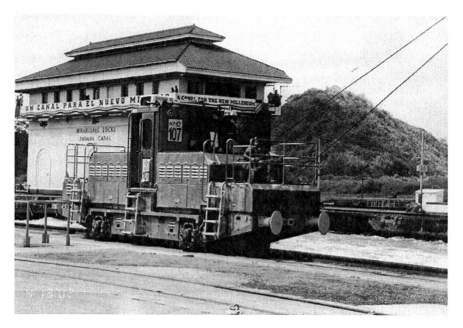

Panama Canal mule at Miraflores locks.
Photo: Trevor Wilson collection.

On the homeward-bound transit of the Panama Canal four months later, on entering the Pedro Miguel locks we deck boys felt slightly stupid on seeing the *mules* again. The A.B.s did however spare us any humiliation by not mentioning how we had been kidded on our first encounter with these steel workhorses. Perhaps our fellow shipmates were tired of playing tricks on us.

The American pilot guided our ship on its meandering forty-eight-mile journey past magnificent scenery of lush jungle foliage, and through natural lakes and artificial swathes cut into solid rock. One of these cuts is nearly eight miles long and called the Gaillard Cut or Culebra Cut. How the labour force managed to hack away at this rocky terrain day after day is a marvel in itself. A bronze plaque set onto the side wall of the rock face of this cut, bears testimony to the sacrifice that those men gave. It is said that every yard of excavation cost the life of one man.

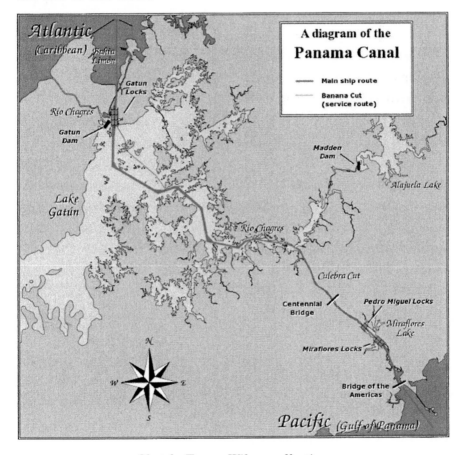

Sketch: Trevor Wilson collection.

Passing through the Gatun Locks that marked the Atlantic side of the Panama Canal, a pilot cutter raced alongside the ship to a rope ladder that had been thrown over and made fast.

Leaving the ship's telegraph set at 'slow ahead', the pilot was ready to leave the bridge and be taken ashore in the cutter that looked the size of a walnut shell. The skills of his pilotage were no longer required, as the expanse of water widened with every turn of the propeller.

A young cadet officer, whose surname happened to be Darling, stood on the 'monkey island' above the wheelhouse. He was waiting there in readiness for the order from the Old Man to lower the international code 'H' flag flying above his head that indicated 'we have a pilot on board'. Everyone seemed to be in readiness and preparing for going 'deep sea'. To prevent the mooring ropes from being washed over the side in bad weather, the bosun ordered all the deck boys and some of the A.B.s onto the foredeck and afterdeck to start to stow them into the rope lockers. These huge manila coils would not be needed until we docked in the London River in about three weeks' time. On coastwise passages they were left on deck, secured with cordage to eye-bolts.

Shaking hands with everyone on the bridge, the pilot wished us a safe voyage home. As he climbed down the pilot ladder, he heard our Captain bellowing up to the monkey island: "Take the H flag down, Darling!"

Chapter 8

Ten days out from Panama, we were about six hundred miles south-southwest of the Azores – in latitude 35 degrees 50 minutes north and longitude 40 degrees 20 minutes west. We had sailed into an area of the Atlantic where in two months' time, after I had signed off the M.V. *Port Brisbane*, a tragedy would unfold.

Having spent a few weeks on shore leave at my home in Leicester, I packed my kitbag and caught the train back to the London docklands. Feeling a lot more confident now that I had at least been on one trip away to sea, I went to the 'pool' as we seamen called the offices of the Shipping Federation (a kind of maritime labour exchange). There I was offered several ships that required deck boys. Remembering the advice the A.B. had given, I asked the clerk where each ship was bound. Deciding that I would like to see Australia, I joined my second ship: the general cargo carrier M.V. *Cretic* of the Shaw Saville Line that was loading in the busy, bustling King George V dock.

The outward-bound cargo-stowing was nearly completed except for a three-ton ship's kedge anchor and two thousand tons of plate glass that were to be loaded in Antwerp. After spending only twenty-four hours loading in Antwerp, the fragile glass sheets were safely stowed down in the holds in specially made racks, and the kedge anchor secured to eye-bolts as deck cargo. The third mate, whose duties included the overseeing of the loading and discharging of the ship's cargo, gave the order to the bosun: "Batten down the hatches and make her ready for sea."

Battening down the hatches involved quite a laborious task. Every hatch opening was first covered with three-inch-thick pitchpine boards and draped over the top of these were three sheets of heavy-duty tarpaulin, each measuring about sixty by forty feet. It would take four of us to lift each bundle of tarred canvas between our shoulders and carry it from the forecastle where they were stowed, trundling along the deck dropping them at each hatch. These tarpaulin sheets were then fastened into place by hammering thick wooden wedges along the side of the hatch coaming. Having a clip around my ear, courtesy of the bosun, reminded me to secure these wedges with the wider end facing forward, so any seas coming on board would drive them further in. During bad weather a ship risked foundering should she lose her hatch covers as a result of the securing wedges being washed away. Several strong, flexible metal bands bolted across the top of the hatch completed the process of battening down the hatches.

At the time, and being still green, I thought that all the care and attention given to the detail of this hatch security was a bit over the top. How naive could I have been? Soon I was to find out.

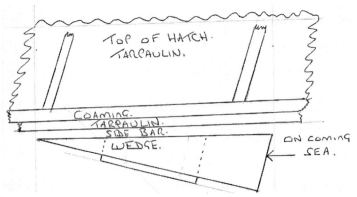

Now fully laden with the last of the cargo, and with her waterline just showing the Plimsoll mark of Winter North Atlantic, our ship was to be made ready for sea.

With all of the hatches battened down, the derricks (ship's cranes) had to be lowered into their holding crutches. As the head of each one of the twenty derricks slotted into its holding cradle, the deck would be festooned with wire ropes and guys and all the paraphernalia needed to operate them. To my inexperienced eyes this entanglement seemed impossible to sort out, so I just followed the A.B.s and heaved away and coiled ropes when they did, most of the time not having a clue what I was doing. I had studied in some depth the rigging and cordage that the old square-sail ships carried and how the seafarers of old had to know the function and place of every fathom of rope in the dark. The problem that I faced would have seemed laughable to them. These thoughts only increased my admiration further for those sailormen of yesteryear.

A sudden shout from the bridge quickly brought my thoughts back to the present day. "All hands on stations and stand by the tugs!" the Mate yelled down to the bosun, who was just about to have a rest and roll a cigarette after working non-stop for several hours.

"Okay you lazy bastards – you heard what he said," and with that the bosun threw a heaving line to one of the tugs. This was our leaving of Antwerp. Two tugs were made fast at the bow and stern of our ship, the tugs' steam whistles then filled the dockside air with the morse code signal Q D, 'I am going ahead', adding to all the other noise and confusion of sounds that came from the twenty miles of this busy Belgian waterfront.

The tugs' mighty engines turned their propellers, which began thrusting the water as two lone figures on our section of the quay threw the eyes of the mooring ropes from the shore bollards. Taking a couple of turns with each rope around the revolving drum of the electric docking winch, we soon had all the mooring lines (which had been holding our ship alongside the quay) on board. When these mooring lines were actually mooring the ship it was the duty of the deck boy to fit a rat guard to them. These guards were simply hinged pieces of sheet metal about two feet in diameter that fitted onto each mooring rope that led from ship to shore. This was a precaution, of course, to stop any rats from setting up home on board via a ropewalk. Whilst we were tending one of the tugs as they pulled our ship away from the quay towards the River Scheldt, an A.B. pointed to the towing cable of this tug and with straight face said, "Put a rat guard on that, Pegs." This brought back to mind the sackful of bread that on my last trip I had saved for the Panama *mules*. Feeling like an old salt I shook my head. I was having none of it.

Amid further blasts from their whistles the two tugs pulled and pushed our twelve-thousand-ton ship past the other ships that lay at anchor. Once clear of the busy harbour and into the river, we cast off the towing ropes, dropping them into the water. After making sure they were clear of our propeller the second mate called the bridge on the deck phone that was housed inside a cast iron box. This was followed by the ringing of the ship's telegraph to the engine room. The screw began to turn, and as our giant hull gathered momentum the shore lights on the river bank seemed to be flying past, although our speed was restricted to ten knots. It would be eighty miles of negotiating the twists and turns of the River Scheldt before we reached the open North Sea.

During that time the chippie (ship's carpenter), whose job it was to work the windlass that weighed and dropped the Admiralty-patent anchor, stood on the forecastle awaiting orders to 'let go the hook' should an emergency arise. A thankless job it was, too, as he crouched in the rain whilst trying to keep his hand-rolled cigarette alight and – as it was No Smoking on the forecastle –hidden from the eyes on the bridge. Every two hours the standby man of the watch would make a hot drink for the chippie and go and relieve him for thirty minutes from his lonely station. So it was with much joy for the carpenter that in the early hours of the next morning we had reached the delta of the river. Out of the darkness the lights of a vessel showing a white light above a red came towards us. It was to take our pilot ashore. The date was 14th September 1957.

Passing through the bottleneck of the Straits of Dover, ships of every nationality sped by: it was like the marine version of the road traffic in London's Piccadilly Circus. Although I had just acquired my steering ticket, the thought of being on the wheel in the confines of those busy waters made me glad that I was still a peggy. The Old Man stood on the wing of the bridge in a quiet confidence that came from many years at sea, instructing the helmsman when to alter course. During these long vigils on the bridge, the Captain's personal steward (who was referred to as the Captain's tiger) would bring to him a tray laden with a steaming pot of tea, complete with a china cup and saucer. "Why can't you bring us a brew, Pegs?" the wheelman, who had just come to the mess room from his stint at the helm, would ask me as he poured himself a hot drink from the chipped enamelled pot. These kinds of questions I regarded as a test by the A.B.s to ascertain how gullible I was.

Our ship carried another deck boy called Dave. It was his first trip to sea and, learning that I had sailed on my last ship to Auckland, he regarded me with much undeserved reverence. After I had told Dave about the numerous tricks that had been played on me on that last voyage, and that only ten hours was required to obtain a steering ticket, he thanked me for these revelations. To make him realise that I was still green I put him at his ease by saying, "In the land of the blind, the man with one eye is king."

With the Straits of Dover fading below the horizon, the Old Man left the bridge, as we had more sea room. The English Channel lay before us, and westward the ship was being steered. As the south coast slowly passed by, our progress would be reported to the hands in the mess room by the last wheelman who had had a peek at the Admiralty chart that lay spread across the table in the chartroom.

In coastal waters the ship's position was plotted every hour by the mate on watch who, with compass in hand, would be constantly taking bearings of anything that helped him to pencil in our whereabouts. This was in the days before the U.S.A. G.P.S. (global position system) came on the scene. A radio navigation system called Decca was available then, but usually it was used by fishermen and coasters, as its accuracy was affected by seasonal and night-time errors. It was during the night that the lookout man stood upon the fo'c'sle head keeping a vigil for any lights from the shore or sea. The sighting of these lights was brought to the attention of the watchkeepers on the bridge by the lookout man tugging at the rope on the ship's brass bell, which reverberated with deep clanging tones: one ring for a sighting of a light or object to starboard, two for port and three for dead ahead.

During the second night in the Channel a solitary clang of the bell indicated a sweeping loom that had popped up above the distant horizon. It was the Bishop's Rock Lighthouse, which stands on a rocky ledge four miles west of the Isles of Scilly. This magnificent piece of Victorian engineering is exposed to the full force of the Atlantic Ocean. It had been nearly one hundred years since the 1st September 1858, when the beam at the top of this granite beacon first swept through the darkness, marking these rocks where many ships had foundered. Probably the most famous loss on these rocks occurred in 1707, when four ships of the squadron of the British fleet led by Admiral Sir Cloudsley Shovel came to grief. It was the loss of these ships of the fleet and the death of two thousand seamen that prompted the decision by the Elder Brethren of Trinity House to build a lighthouse on the most westerly danger of the Isles of Scilly, the Bishop Rock.

The engineers of the day first designed a lighthouse that was supported on cast-iron legs sunk into solid granite. The idea was that the ocean waves would meet with less resistance as they swept between these supporting legs. This initial attempt to erect a lighthouse on this granite outcrop began in 1847, but on completion the whole structure was in service for only a few months before being washed away during a storm.

Back to the drawing board, and after years of labourers working in atrocious weather conditions, and 5700 tons of solid granite blocks later, we have standing today this strong maritime tower. The solitary clang of our ship's bell, rung by the lookout man who had spotted the silent warning loom of the Bishop Rock lighthouse, justified the sacrifice given by those builders of yesteryear. By morning the loom of the light had disappeared and a new course was set towards the Straits of Gibraltar.

Bishop Rock Lighthouse. Position 49.53 N 06.26W.
Photo: Trevor Wilson collection.

Chapter 9

September 21st 1957. It was at six o'clock that morning I was awoken by the cabin light being switched on and someone violently shaking my shoulder and shouting, "Look lively, Pegs, and get your gear on and listen to what I'm telling you!"

As I shot upright in the lower bunk bed, there stood Frank, the A.B. from the four-to-eight watch, who was now repeating the same instructions to my cabin mate Dave, who was in the top bunk. The first thing I noticed about Frank was the water glistening on the full suit of yellow oilskins and sou'wester that he was wearing. As he continued with his message there was urgency in his voice that I sensed he was trying to play down. "We are in for some bad weather – go and batten down all the dead-lights in the mess rooms and recreation room."

These hinged dead-lights were thick steel circular plates that covered the glass in the portholes and were bolted into place, so preventing damage from a heavy sea. As I gradually woke up and began to gather my wits I could hear water swilling about in the alleyway outside our cabin. Frank, hurrying out of our cabin doorway, turned to us and as an afterthought said, "You'll need your sea-boots."

A sense of fear coursed through my blood, and for the first time at sea I had a feeling of not being safe. Hoping Dave would not notice my anxiety, I put on a brave face. As I turned to tell him everything would be alright, he had his head in the wash basin, being sick. "Come on, Dave, get your sea-boots on – you'll feel alright when we are out of this cabin and into the fresh air," I told him, not believing a word I was saying. Our tiny cabin felt even more stuffy and claustrophobic now that Frank had battened down our single porthole, and I started not to feel too good myself.

At the sea school, it had been drummed into us that on a merchant ship there was no room for passengers among the crew, and to be ill was looked on as some kind of crime. In fact it was very rare for a general cargo merchant ship to carry a doctor in those days; the only medical treatment to be administered was by the mate, who would read the instructions from a medical book. The rest of the crew, should you happen to be ill, would treat you with contempt. I'm ashamed to say it now, but over the years I took on the same attitude towards any of the crew who had the misfortune to be laid up.

Stepping from the cabin, I was glad that I had put my sea-boots on. A wave of sea water about six inches high was running to and fro along the whole length of the alleyway with every roll and pitch of the ship. Before the storm-doors were battened down, a rogue sea had hurled itself into the crew's quarters.

When we had secured all of the dead-lights the next job was to get rid of the water in the alleyway. The bosun allotted this task to me. Armed with a bucket and a dustpan that served as a scoop, I began throwing this water out of the leeside door. Each time I peered through this door the seas seemed to be getting bigger and the motion of the ship was taking on an increased roll, each one lasting longer than the last. Suddenly I was overwhelmed by a feeling of nausea and prayed to God that I would not be seasick. The shame of it! I would not be able to face anyone again. Hanging on to the half-filled bucket and kneeling in the water that still filled the alleyway, I vomited violently, not caring now if I died.

Feeling slightly better afterwards, and with eyes filled with tears as a result of the retching, I carried on bailing. Grateful that no one had apparently witnessed my weakness, I dipped my hand in the water and swilled my face. "If you are not feeling too good, Pegs, eat some of this." There stood two A.B.s holding several rashers of raw bacon that they proceeded to slide down their throats. No hiding my seasickness now, and with a loud sound coming from my throat that could be heard above the noise of the increasing seas, I retched helplessly into the alleyway. With sounds of laughter receding into the messroom, they left me to carry on with the task at hand. Determination and resolve were the next feelings to spur me on. I will *not* be a passenger among the crew, I told myself, and as it was seven o'clock, went to the galley to collect the breakfast for the men on the eight-to-twelve watch.

The old cook, who was dressed in a light suit of checked cotton, looked refreshingly clean compared to me in the water-soaked and stained outfit that I wore. As he walked across the galley with the balance acquired from years at sea, he handed to me the breakfasts, saying, "We are in for a blow, Pegs."

The veracity of the cook's words began to become apparent as the ship's rolling and pitching was now being accompanied by a deafening mechanical scream from the stern. This was caused when the propeller thrashed wildly into the air as it was lifted clear of the water each time the bow dipped into the enormous head seas. Every time this happened, a violent shaking of the whole ship followed as the giant bronze rotating screw re-entered the sea on its downward see-saw-like stroke. I looked for signs of concern on the faces of the A.B.s who were eating their breakfasts. The crew, to my relief, seemed more interested in holding their plates down on the messroom table whilst shovelling food into their mouths with a free hand.

It was as if the mighty ball of a demolition crane had struck the ship's side when the panelling that covered the mess room bulkhead resounded from a blow by the heavy seas. These seas were now sweeping across the deck with every roll, striking anything that stood in their path with uncontrollable might.

Glancing at the dead-lights that now protected the glass in the portholes from this onslaught, I became thankful to the unknown person who had invented them. At the time that I was battening down these dead-lights I did not realise how vital they were to be. I had much to learn.

Frank the A.B. who had just come into the mess room after being on the wheel for the last two hours of his watch, grabbed his breakfast from the hot oven and at the same time informed us that the Old Man was on the bridge. It was from the bridge, by blowing through a mouth-whistle, that the Old Man would summon the standby watchman. On that day, however, it would have been futile to expect the sound of a whistle to be heard above the roaring noise of the bad weather that was all around us. It was no surprise, then, when the captain's 'tiger', who was being used as a substitute for the Old Man's mouth-whistle, came flying into the messroom and, with the urgency of someone who had just witnessed a major disaster, blurted out: "The Old Man wants the bosun on the bridge NOW!"

Coming back from the bridge, the bosun poked his head through the messroom doorway. "Call all hands and tell them to put their wet weather gear on and come to the messroom straight away." He turned to leave and, as if in afterthought, said, "You as well, Pegs."

Fourteen of us donned our oilskins and sou'westers and stood in line along the bulkhead and held on to the grab-rail. Each one of us probably looked like that picture of an old mariner you can see on a tin of sardines. Dave, my pal, was ordered to stay below and have ready a pot of hot coffee. To this day I can still see the look of admiration and bewilderment on his face as he saw me standing among the men waiting for the bosun to reveal what was happening. A churning feeling was filling my stomach as I listened to the A.B.s who were trying to guess what lay in store. These guesses ranged from the chain locker being full of tons of seawater to the cargo shifting.

"We could be in trouble." These were the first words the

bosun calmly uttered to us, and then carried on: "The three-ton kedge anchor has broken adrift on the foredeck." He went on to explain how two ventilation shafts that led to the number two cargo hold had been sheared off and water was pouring down into the bilge. This was as a result of the kedge anchor being thrown all over the foredeck like a toy, smashing into anything in its path in the frenzied pitching and rolling of the ship. The bosun had devised a plan to temporarily secure this maverick anchor to the deck eye-bolts with lengths of rope and chain. First we had to 'catch' it. His plan involved unwinding the thick wire cables (called runners) from around each drum of the four electric winches. These winches stood at each corner of the cargo hatch and by criss-crossing their cables and shackling the ends to the deck rings, then tightening, a 'cat's cradle' would be formed. The idea was to snag the fluke of the anchor as it flew about. That was the theory.

Following the bosun through the opened doorway that led out on deck, we were confronted by the full might of the storm. Tons of water were being scooped over the bulwarks as the ship laboured at the bottom of the mighty troughs. The ship was now being turned to face into the fury of the wind and sea (hoving to) to lessen the chances of us being swept over the side. From the shelter deck we could see the anchor that we had to secure being tossed across number two hatch. Never having witnessed such atrocious weather conditions before, I began to ask myself if it had been a good idea to go to sea. Once again I had the feeling of being unsafe.

Black clouds were racing across the sky, which seemed low enough to touch as we ran to the cargo winches. No time to be frightened now, I told myself as we started to unshackle one of the wire runners and begin roving its end through the deck ring-bolts to form the criss-cross pattern of the giant cat's cradle. Sheltering under the leeside of the hatch coaming as each sea swept across the deck, we pressed on with the job at hand, totally ignoring the mad anchor that was flying to either side of the ship. I suppose our thinking must have been like that of an ostrich that buries its head in the sand: if we took no notice of the danger, perhaps it would go away.

The Old Man was looking down on us from the wing of the bridge, and though we didn't hear him at the time, he was shouting for us to take cover. Just as we thought it safe to carry on dragging more wire ropes across the decks, *whoosh!* A screaming, hissing giant wave engulfed the foredeck. The sudden coldness felt like a thousand knives sticking into my body as this rogue sea swept four of us tumbling headlong into the lee scuppers. For one horrifying moment I thought that I had been washed over the side. As I fought for breath and with arms flaying like a windmill, the will to survive took over. I dragged my legs, that were sticking out of the side of the ship, and crawled to the lee of the hatch coaming where the bosun and the rest of the men were crouching. Pointing to the three A.B.s nearest to him to stay put, the bosun cupped his hands around his mouth and shouted above the screaming of the storm: "The rest of you stand by in the shelter deck whilst we tighten the cargo runners," ending with the determined words, "I'll hook that bastard yet!" that were swept away with the wind.

We held on to the steel handrails that ran the length of the shelter deck, and from its relatively safe position we could see the bosun and the three A.B.s dashing to the control handles of the four winches.

The water was still cascading across the deck and covering both men and winches as the cargo runner cables were slowly stretched bar-tight. The finished result of all our labours suddenly became apparent to me as I gazed at the appearance of an intricately woven spider's web made from giant steel rope. The 'fly' we hoped to catch had just collided with another ventilator pipe, causing it to bend in half. Waiting for the chance to run for shelter, the four men scrambled from the exposed winches to where we stood. Before we had started to go onto the fore deck, the bosun had prepared several lengths of heavy-duty manila rope, each piece being about twenty feet long and two inches in diameter, and various lengths of chain with shackles. As tons of water rapidly ran back into the sea through the scuppers, it revealed the flukes of the runaway anchor snarled among the 'web' we had made! "This is it, lads, let's go!" the bosun yelled, and we grabbed the ropes and chains and, ignoring the consequences, followed him into the raging turmoil that met us as we ran from the shelter deck. Swarming over this now immobile anchor with ropes and chains, we criss-crossed the binds in all directions, each man oblivious of the actions of the others. When all the ropes and chains had been used, the giant anchor looked as if the Lilliputian people out of Jonathan Swift's *Gulliver's Travels* had paid it a visit.

Correct position. Incorrect position.
Senhouse slip.
(Black lever is released when holding link is knocked away.)

It was with a great sense of relief that we all scrambled back to the refuge of the shelter deck, the bosun clutching in his hand the cause of the anchor coming adrift. These were the quick-release shackles called senhouse slips, usually used to secure the ship's lifeboats into their chocks etc. The senhouse slips that had been used to secure the kedge anchor had been fitted upside down, that is with the black lever pointing downwards, so that the releasing link that held this lever in place had been shaken away from its holding position. The most likely explanation for this mishap was the violent vibration through the ship as the propeller came out of the water during the storm.

Dripping wet and soaked to the skin, we headed in single file for the messroom, where we hoped Dave had a pot of hot coffee ready.

The sea had not finished with us yet, though, for as we hurried over the storm-step and before we had time to shut the watertight door that led to the accommodation, another wave followed us and threw itself along the inboard alleyway. We made our way into the crew's messroom still having to hold on to the grab-rails as the storm showed no sign of abating. To our surprise, waiting for us there, with Dave and the hot coffee, were the Old Man and the Mate (first officer) holding a bottle of whisky and a bottle of rum in their hands. "You've done well, lads," were the first words the Old Man uttered to us as the Mate unscrewed the bottles of spirits and added, "Now, what's your poison?"

Scale of three-ton Admiralty pattern kedge anchor on board M.V. *Cretic*, September 1957 (Anchor that broke adrift).

At the same time as our group assembled in the mess-room another drama was unfolding in mid-Atlantic. News of this came by means of a faint Morse code distress message picked up by our radio officer. A ship had been knocked on her beam ends (side) in hurricane-force winds. This ship was sinking as their radio officer tapped out a last frantic plea for help. The ship's name was *Pamir*, a four-masted sailing barque. At nearly one thousand miles we were too far away to render assistance. Our hearts could only go out to the poor souls who would be struggling to survive.

Pamir at Falmouth docks, England, 1956.
Photo: Courtesy of Philippe Bellamite.

Weeks later, after we had docked in Melbourne, we learnt that out of a total crew of eighty-six aboard the *Pamir*, including fifty-two cadets, only four crewmen and two cadets were rescued alive. The *Pamir* was a German sail-training ship, and having loaded nearly four thousand tons of barley grain at Buenos Aires, was on passage to Hamburg. Owing to a dockers' strike, this cargo, which should have been loaded in bags, was loaded loose instead. When grain is loaded in this manner, to prevent it moving during bad weather (which would make the ship unstable) a wall made from a series of heavy wooden boards is fitted along the entire centre length and height of each cargo hold. These boards, known as shifting boards, were omitted during the loading of her cargo. The tragic outcome could have been so different following *Pamir*'s encounter with Hurricane Carrie had these vital wooden planks been in place.

At that time, however, the sea that does not differentiate between anything or anybody that chooses to be upon her, carried on battering *our* ship. As each sea swept over the foredeck, water was still flooding into the hold through the damaged ventilators.

Pointing to two of the A.B.s who had just swallowed their noggin of rum that the Old Man had poured, the bosun said, "You two are volunteering to block off the vents that have been knocked down." Turning towards me as I was trying to stop myself from spluttering from the rapid intake of half a glass of neat whisky, the bosun carried on: "Never mind, Pegs, you'll have forgotten all about this when we are in the tropics."

Chapter 10

The tropics! Here I was, over forty years later, once again having just crossed the invisible line that circles the globe, the Tropic of Cancer. It was 5th January 2001. This time, however, I was alone aboard my twenty-four-foot junk-rigged yacht *Ozama*. The northeasterly winds were holding steady at force four to five. On working out the day's run at noon I was very pleased to find that we had covered one hundred and eight nautical miles over the seabed. (To those who are unfamiliar with sea measurements, thirteen nautical miles are equal to fifteen land miles.) If this progress could be maintained, we should be dropping the hook (anchoring) in Rodney Bay, St Lucia at the beginning of next month. Once there, the plan was to explore the islands in the Caribbean whilst making our way northwards, and to arrive in Norfolk, Virginia, at the beginning of May. That was the plan, and apart from a general outline of a sailing plan to work the sea currents and seasons etc, I concentrated on the day-to-day working of the yacht.

Three hundred miles to our southeast lay the Cape Verde Islands. Soon I would have to head on a more westerly course, as I didn't want to venture below latitude twelve degrees north in case the winds disappeared in the Doldrums. The Trade Wind route that I was sailing is usually devoid of any commercial traffic. During the hours of darkness in these areas I would get my head down and only venture to look out if I was woken up.

I *was* woken up with a start at three o'clock one morning. The yacht's head had come into the wind, and the junk sail was threatening to shake itself to pieces. Scrambling into the cockpit, I switched on my head-torch and examined the self-steering gear. Everything seemed in order so I unlatched it and took hold of the tiller to bring the yacht back on course. There was no feel or response to the helm – the rudder was missing!

Standing astride the after deck I pulled on the thick lanyard that held the drop spade rudder. As I desperately heaved away on this lanyard, the heavy steel pear-shaped plate of the rudder appeared on the surface. Balancing myself with legs akimbo on the wildly pitching deck I hauled the now useless rudder over the pushpit and lowered it onto the sole of the cockpit. It seemed beyond reason that I should have struggled to retrieve the rudder that weighed about a hundred and twenty pounds. It would have been impossible to relocate as the weld holding it in place had carried away under the yacht's counter stern. At that time, however, I was in shock so I may not have been thinking logically. Rummaging through the after locker I dragged out the sea anchor and its three-hundred-foot warp and paid it out through the bow roller. After dousing the sail I went below and lit the stove to make a pot of tea. I had to gather my thoughts and work out a plan.

The amount of drinking water I had remaining was my main concern. There was enough of it for twenty days, or forty on emergency rations. There was a wooden emergency rudder that came with the sale of the yacht, and though I did not pay much heed to it at the time, now it became a thing of major importance. This emergency rudder consisted of a wooden sleeve that was fitted with pintles (hinge parts – the sort designed for a dinghy) and was hung from the transom.

Through this sleeve slotted the rudder, made from a one foot by four foot length of marine ply. The problem was that the timber had swollen and the rudder would not fit into the sleeve. After two days of carefully chiselling away at the layers of ply, the rudder was drastically reduced in thickness but it fitted into the holding sleeve.

The seas had built up to about twenty feet and the wind was blowing at force six. After dismantling the self-steering gear and imitating a wobbly tightrope walker, I had got the emergency rudder in place. It would mean hand-steering, but the alternative was not an option. Setting the junk sail to three panels I hauled the warp and sea-anchor on board and brought *Ozama*'s head to a westerly course. The reduced thickness of this rudder worried me and as I looked over the side I noticed it was bending to and fro with every roll. Hoping against hope it would stay in one piece until we reached Barbados, the nearest island, about eighteen hundred miles to the west, I began hand-steering. The self-steering gear was now unusable of course, owing to the emergency rudder on the transom.

The sun was blazing down and the apparent wind's strength was reduced now that we were running with it on the quarter, making the cockpit feel like the inside of an oven. After four hours of hand-steering in that heat I realised that my thirst was becoming greater, tempting me to drink more than my daily water ration. Something had to be done to alter the situation.

Over the years of sailing I have always carried in my kitbag various lengths of rubber shock-cord and plastic snap-hooks. One of the many uses of these rubber ropes is a makeshift self-steering rig. It looks a Heath Robinson affair when set up, but provided the wind is steady and not too far abaft the beam, it will allow the tiller to be left alone for a while. It was with great joy that after fiddling about and experimenting with different strengths of the pulling power that these shock cords put on the tiller, the yacht was steering herself. The heading was now several degrees north of the westerly course that was required, as I had to bring the wind further towards the beam to make the new self-steering work. After having a quick glance at the bendy rudder, and glad to be relieved of hand-steering, I went below to plot our position. In the last four hours we had covered sixteen miles over the ground: if the wind held steady we could reach the islands in nineteen days. Having looked at the tell-tale compass on the cabin sole and seen that a reasonable course was being held, I decided to prematurely break open the bottle of Madeira wine that I was saving to celebrate the crossing of the halfway mark. This was a celebration in itself – to think that two days ago I'd lost the rudder and here we were sailing merrily on our way again, even if a little bit to the north of our required course.

A splintering, cracking sound coming from aft put a sudden end to any celebrations before they had begun. Flying out of the cabin, I was just in time to make out the remains of the emergency rudder floating up the side of the huge following sea. My heart sank as I watched helplessly as, again rudderless, the yacht began to turn into the wind. Streaming the sea anchor and dousing the sail once again, we lay with the oncoming seas about twenty degrees on the port bow.

Despair was the only feeling I now had as I sat in the cabin among the remains of the wood shavings that had weakened the emergency rudder. Looking at the bottle of wine that lay unopened on the bunk, I rummaged for the corkscrew, saying out loud: "Sod it, I'll have a drink anyway." Facing aft I watched the sun start to dip below the horizon. Darkness in the Tropics comes about quickly, as if with the flick of a light switch. Lighting the oil lamp I hung it on the push-pit rail, hoping against hope that someone would see its glow. I knew the chances of being seen were slim, as we were out of the shipping lanes. Sitting in the cockpit, legs outstretched and bottle of wine in hand, I watched the huge and now black velvet seas rolling past. And I realised how absolute its power was. As the night wore on I would stand upright on the side-benches and look out for any signs of another human being on our planet. Into my upward gaze the brilliant starry sky twinkled with a million diamonds, and suddenly I felt so very small and humbled by its enormity.

It was on 10th January 2001 that, aboard the now rud-derless yacht, I began drifting across the Atlantic. Gathering my wits, I decided that I must think positively and tell myself that I would survive. Thinking back to the World War Two experiences told to me by the British Merchant seamen who had been adrift in ships' lifeboats following being torpedoed thousands of miles from land, I took solace. Now was the time to take stock of the situation.

It was approximately eighteen hundred miles to the islands, and we were drifting over the ground at eighteen miles per day. Without any rainfall I had enough drinking water for forty days using one litre per day. Food was in abundance and the leg of smoked pork that I had bought in Porto Santo had been hardly touched. The V.H.F. radio was a hand-held type, the range being at the maximum fifteen miles in good conditions. The routine I had devised was at four-hourly intervals to send out a Mayday. The distress call went like this: "Mayday. Mayday. Mayday. Position: [*whatever my position was at the time*]. This is yacht *Ozama*. I require immediate assistance. Lost rudder." I would repeat this three times in a clear and calm voice – the reason for this calmness probably was that I really did not think anyone would hear it. In this distress call, the G.P.S. position would be given immediately *after* the words *Mayday*, and *not* after the name of the yacht, as the sequence is stated in the book of maritime rules. My reasoning is that the name of the yacht is of secondary importance, should the radio suddenly fail whilst transmitting a Mayday message.

An important part of the rescue plan that I was devising was to attract the attention of any passing ship. This of course sounds obvious now, but at the time I had to make an effort to think clearly. Without this concentration I found that my thoughts were carried into a dreamlike world. Perhaps this is nature's way of protecting us from shock.

During our slow drift westward the time was mostly occupied with tasks that I had set myself. Besides jotting down every idea that came into my head that would aid being rescued, I constantly spoke these instructions out loud. One of the tasks was to lay out on the bunk all the distress flares. I am ashamed to say this now but I did not fully understand how to set these flares off. After carefully reading the instructions on each type of distress signal I went through a practice routine, until I knew each one by heart. At the four-hourly intervals that the Mayday was sent out I would afterwards go through the distress flare operating routine. In further preparation for a rescue I had stowed in a haversack several of the most important items that I could safely carry on my back. These included: passport; wallet containing two credit cards and a twenty-euro and a twenty-dollar note; ship's log books; a last letter to my wife; ten rolls of film and camera; and a spare G.P.S. With these preparations ongoing I would wind up the tin alarm clock and set it to give me a four-hourly warning for sending out the Mayday. This routine was strictly carried out through every twenty-four-hour period. Sometimes I did resent being rudely awakened by the tinny rattle of this alarm clock, as I found sleep to be an escape from my true dilemma.

Whilst keeping a lookout from the cockpit at night, many times I would mistake a rising star for a ship. As *Ozama* climbed to the top of each wave more stars would appear, immediately raising my hopes of a rescue. To me they all seemed to look like the steaming lights of a vessel. After managing to focus the true identity of these lights through the wobbly lens of my binoculars, my hopes sank like a stone thrown into a pond. Some of the stars and planets as they popped up over the horizon ahead gave off a red glow that I also tried to will into being a port navigation light.

On the third night of being adrift, the northeasterly wind started to increase to force seven, making the seas build up to over twenty-five feet.

Tethered to a sea anchor with a warp of three hundred feet in those conditions, the yacht's head was sometimes dragged through the top of those oncoming waves. The time was 22:00 on that night and I suddenly felt a sense of despair and helplessness as I hooked my safety harness to the eye-bolt in the cockpit and ducked for shelter each time a sea smacked into us. Hope of a rescue was also receding as I reminded myself that we were out of the shipping lanes. This was when I prayed to God, the first time in my life that in earnest I had done so. "Please God, do not let me die, let someone rescue me, please answer my prayer." These words, that I said out loud, were swept away into the darkness by the roaring of the sea and wind that was turning uglier by the minute. Somehow I felt better after saying that prayer.

The tinny rattle of the alarm clock brought me back from a world of meadows, trees and streams to one of reality. Time to send out a Mayday call. It was 04:00 ship's time on 13th January 2001.Taking the V.H.F. hand-held radio from its solar charging rack I climbed into the cockpit to transmit a distress signal. The black night sky that greeted me was still studded with a jewel-like brilliance of which I never tired. Sending out the Mayday message became routine, as it was always the same call except for a few minutes' difference in our position. At the end of the third Mayday I switched off the transmitter and stood astride the side-benches for the usual lookout. As *Ozama* climbed out of the trough and glided to the top of the next wave she would pause a few seconds on the crest before descending down the next watery slope.

As the yacht was momentarily balanced at the top of one of these waves I could clearly make out the steaming lights of a ship! Lights that were bearing fine on our port bow: one red, one green and two white lights. The ship was heading for us! Down we plunged and the lights disappeared. With my heart racing and hands that suddenly started to tremble totally out of control I fumbled in my smock pocket for the radio transmitter and turned it on.

"Yacht in distress – send a flare to indicate your position."

These were the first words that came issuing forth and were repeated constantly in broken English. As soon as the receiving message paused I made radio contact and said in a voice that I hoped would be understood: "Rescue ship, rescue ship, I am sending parachute flare now." Snaking into the night sky, the yellow tail of the distress flare arched a course determined by the strong winds. Bursting into a bright red ball of fire at about six hundred feet high and checked by its now opened parachute, it was being swept rapidly downwind. From the inside of my smock pocket the radio came alive with the message: "We have visual contact ... We have visual contact. Stand by for rescue. Stand by for rescue."

The black silhouette of the ship could be clearly seen as she approached from the weather side, sheltering us in her lee. Arc lamps suddenly illuminated a cargo net hung over the side of this massive ship. Diving back into the cabin I donned a life jacket and grabbed the haversack. The bag had been prepared full of the essential items as I mentioned earlier. A ship's crew member threw down a heaving line only to see it blown over the top of *Ozama*'s mast. After three attempts I managed to grab the heaving line and, holding on for my life, made it fast to the mooring post forward.

Immediately the yacht swung along the ship's side and began to smash into her steel plates with such violence that I wondered if we would stay afloat. The wind was blowing from the northeast at force six, making the rollers that were sweeping past lift us halfway up the ship's side. Poised like a monkey ready to leap, I waited until the next wave lifted us to its top, then sprang onto the cargo net. A problem soon became apparent – I could not climb the net as it was hanging too close against the ship's side, preventing my feet from getting a grip. Ten heads were bent over the ship's bulwarks looking down at me clinging to the net like a crab. "Climb up!" they shouted. "Climb up!" The crewmen were quick to weigh up the situation and started to haul the net upwards hand over hand, with me clinging to it like grim death. Reaching the taffrail on top of the bulwark, my arms were aching as they were supporting all my body weight. A forest of arms leant over the ship's side and grabbed hold of my life jacket and safety harness and hauled me on deck.

Getting to my feet on the now relatively stable deck I crawled out of the net that was now heaped up in a pile and immediately started to stagger like someone who was drunk. The crew helped me to a hospital cabin that was equipped with a shower and fresh towels, soap and a razor. The ship's Master and first officer came and shook my hand and welcomed me aboard their ship, M.V. *Baynes* that was registered in Limassol. The Master was Icelandic and named Hakon Isaksson, and First Officer Eugeno Marasigan was from the Philippines, as were most of the remainder of the twenty-one crew members. After telling me he would try to save the yacht, they left the cabin and I had the luxury of a hot shower. Owing to the big seas that were running and the wind, it proved impossible to get a man on board to save *Ozama*. The yacht, after being constantly and violently thrown against the steel plates of the ship, was holed below the waterline. With her mooring line cast off, the mortally wounded *Ozama* disappeared forever into the darkness.

Chapter 11

M.V. *Baynes*, a bulk carrier, was on passage to Owendo, Gabon, West Africa. Fully laden with a cargo of coal from New Orleans, the twenty-two-thousand-ton ship, steaming at fourteen knots, would take another week to reach her destination. As an ex-Merchant seaman I was interested to compare the way the ship was run to the tramps that I had sailed. The second mate gave a guided tour of the *Baynes*, including a visit to the engine room. The advancement in the use of the latest electronic technology to navigate was astounding. The charts that constantly displayed the ship's exact position, electronic weather systems and facilities to send emails and voice messages all over the world, were some of the things that impressed me most of all. The crew could not have been friendlier and as I would take turns to dine one day in the officers' messroom and the next in the ratings' mess, I got to know everyone on board.

On being passed as okay health-wise, I was transferred from the hospital to the supercargo cabin. This cabin was fitted out with every facility and included a refrigerator that I would always find stocked with several cans of beer (the benefactors being a mystery). The young crew worked hard and played hard, and there was a genuinely cheerful atmosphere throughout the ship. Although my offer to work on deck was refused (something to do with insurance cover)

M.V. *Baynes.*
Photo: Collection Trevor Wilson.

I was never left out of any of the activities, like the safety
meetings that took place in the wheelhouse, or lifeboat drill.
At the end of each day's work there would be a party in one
of the crew's cabins. The beer would flow, yarns were told and
we would each take a turn at singing. None of us would win
any prizes for our efforts but it didn't matter, it was great to
hear the out-of-tune songs sung in different languages. On
one of the evenings the Captain organised a barbeque on the
boat deck and happily dished up sizzling sausages, chicken,
hamburgers and everything that makes a party go with a
swing. Unsurprisingly, at sixty years of age I was the eldest
on board. The young crew, who would have been about the
same age as my children, kitted me out for the do with shorts,
sandals and tee-shirts of vivid colours and emblazoned with
U.S. baseball team names and the like.

It took some time before I could take in the almost total
lack of division between officers and ratings, unlike that I had
experienced in the British Merchant Navy. Everyone worked
together for the common good of the ship and respected each

other for the part they played in it. As I talked to the first mate one day, he explained how it was during his watch that he had heard my distress call coming through on a small hand-held V.H.F. radio that hung on a peg in the wheelhouse. After the Captain had been alerted, all available hands were called to the bridge for lookout duties and the engine room put on standby. It was whilst the mate was relating to me the sequence of events that led to my being rescued that he casually mentioned something that left me with a feeling that made my blood run cold. "You know," he said, "you are very lucky because we do not sail on this route as a rule." He went on to explain how on the night before the rescue, at about 22:00 the Captain came on to the bridge with the order: "Alter course to the south to see if we can get out of this bad weather." If these orders had not been given and the ship had stayed on her usual heading, then our courses would not have converged, making it impossible to be in range of my Mayday call. As we gazed ahead out of the wheelhouse windows the mate continued chatting to me, totally unaware that I was in shock and his words were no longer registering in my brain. My mind had raced back to the night and the time (about 22:00) that I had prayed to God for someone to save me. It was the time during that night when the seas were building up and I was feeling really sorry for myself at the thought of drifting unnoticed and dying of thirst. Coincidence – the ship altering course after my prayer? I prefer not to think so. I have not turned into some religious fanatic, but vowed that I would never deny God again.

TO ATH/OFFICE
CC JHC
FM MV BAYNES
13.01.01
GDAY
APPROX 0500 THIS MORN I WAS CALLED TO BRIDGE, MAYDAY RELAY,
GIVEN POS 18-27.13N-028-35.2W.ALL CREW ON STBY,ENG INFORM.
0604 ONE PERSON OBSERVED IN THE DISTRESSED YACHT -LOST RUDDER.
0608 RESCUED PERSON ON DECK,ASSISTED TO HOSPITAL,TRIED TO SAVE THE
YACHT BUT IMPOSSIBLE DUE TO WC ENE-6 SWELL NE-5
INFM OFFICE AND MRCC DOVER.
RESCUED PERSON
NAME: WILSON, TREVOR AMOS
NATIONALITY: BRITISH
DATE OF BIRTH:03 JULY 1940
PASSPORT NO:010511272
NAME OF THE YACHT: OZAMO
RESCUED IN POS :18-22.5N - 02835.0W
MR WILSON TOOK A SHOWER AND CAME TO MESS ROOM,HE SAID I AM TIRED
BUT HAPPY TO BE ONBOARD A BIG VSL AFTER BEEN DRIFTING 3 DAYS.
MR WILSON TRANSFERRED TO SUPERCARGO CABIN AND IS OK.

SAILING ON SCHEDULE TO OWENDO

NICE WEEKEND

BRGDS/H.ISAKSSON

========== End of Message Print ==========

Radio message sent to ship's owners by Captain Isaksson.
Collection: Trevor Wilson.

Chapter 12

2 0th January 2001. After I had been a week on board, M.V. *Baynes* was tied up alongside the jetty at Owendo in the Gabonese Republic, West Africa, to discharge her cargo of coal.

Gabon, as it's usually called, was formerly a part of French Equatorial Africa. Since its independence from France in 1960, the Republic has been ruled by a total of only two autocratic presidents. A country that has an abundance of natural resources is also rife with corruption in many of the governmental institutions, resulting in the majority of people living in poverty. Armed robbery at the point of a knife or gun and killings by these impoverished people were a daily occurrence to anyone who ventured ashore without the protection of an armed guard. It was with mixed feelings, then, that after we had docked I found that the crew would not go ashore for recreation, even though they had been at sea for nearly three weeks since leaving New Orleans.

To leave Gabon I had to first obtain a visa, a routine procedure, I thought, with the immigration offices being close to the jetty. It was not going to be like that, for the official who was on board 'clearing' the ship told the Captain that I would have to pay a 'fee' of two hundred U.S. dollars before he would issue a visa that would be valid for only twenty-four hours. Thankful that I had packed a credit card into my survival knapsack before I had been rescued, I awaited the ship's agent, who I was told would drive me to a bank in the centre of Owendo, where I could obtain American dollars.

CREW LIST

Owner: BAYSHORE SHIPPING CO. LTD.			✓ Arrival		Departure		Page No. : 1 of 1

1. Name of Ship MV "BAYNES"			2. Port of Arrival / Departure OWENDO, GABON			3. Date of Arrival / Departure 20 JANUARY 2001	

4. Nationality of the Ship CYPRUS			5. Port Arrived from: MISSISSIPI, USA			6. Nature and No. of Identity	

7. No.	8. Family Name, Given Name	9. Rank or Rating	10. Nationality	11. Date and Place of Birth	SEAMAN PASSPORT
1	ISAKSSON, HAKON O.	MASTER	ICELANDIC	17.10.44 / ICELAND	A274694
2	MARASIGAN, EUGENIO A.	C/OFFR	FILIPINO	08.01.58 / CALAUAG, QUEZON	A488167
3	MONTEJO, ROBERTO F.	2/OFFR	FILIPINO	23.01.61 / BASILAN	A312002
4	GASCON, CONRADO MARTIN A.	3/OFFR	FILIPINO	30.08.73 / ROXAS CITY	A624685
5	PALMERO, JONATHAN C.	A/OFFR	FILIPINO	15.09.69 / NAGA CITY	A645035
6	VOINEA, RADU	C/ENGR	ROMANIAN	26.09.53 / CONSTANTA	8451
7	BAGAFORO, REX A.	2/ENGR	FILIPINO	26.11.63 / BAROTAC, ILOILO	A293661
8	VALIANTIS, MICHALIS P.	3/ENGR	CYPRIOT	22.08.73 / NICOSIA, CYPRUS	707
9	LIGAYO, CARLO ANTONIO Z.	ELECT	FILIPINO	06.06.69 / DIPOLOG CITY	A059452
10	PENDON, JOHN P.	BOSUN	FILIPINO	05.01.69 / POTOTAN, ILOILO	A203348
11	AMPARADO, PAQUITO P.	FITTER	FILIPINO	28.05.60 / ALIMODIAN, ILOILO	A499852
12	BALDEVISO, OLIVER M.	A/B-1	FILIPINO	10.10.73 / D. ILOILO	A185897
13	ORTIZO, EDWIN C.	A/B-2	FILIPINO	08.07.71 / CALINOG, ILOILO	A501566
14	ARGUELLES, JOHN R.	OS-1	FILIPINO	09.11.73 / MALINAO, AKLAN	A314235
15	SIEGA, ERNESTO S.	OS-2	FILIPINO	01.02.73 / MAASIN, S. LEYTE	A592208
16	CAPADOSA, DOMINIQUE H.	OLR-1	FILIPINO	01.12.74 / KABANKALAN, NEG.	A64062P
17	GOMEZ, JIM S.	OLR-2	FILIPINO	31.05.74 / KALIBO, AKLAN	A678718
18	FERNANDO, CHRISTOPHER N.	WIPER	FILIPINO	27.04.71 / ZAMBOANGA CITY	A326527
19	MESINA, EDGARDO H.	C/COOK	FILIPINO	22.04.61 / OLONGAPO CITY	A547742
20	DE ROSALES, CECILIO B.	STWD	FILIPINO	23.08.73 / CANDELARIA, QUEZON	A484285
21	HIGUIT, DENNIS A.	D/CDT-1	FILIPINO	11.12.76 / TIAONG, QUEZON	A427695
22	DIGNOS, ERIC R.	D/CDT-2	FILIPINO	07/03/78 / CEBU CITY	A473196
23	BROADLEY, MICHAEL RICHARD	SUPER-CARGO	CANADIAN	21.09.52 / MONTREAL	VD399999
24	WILSON, TREVOR AMOS	D/CDT-3	BRITISH	03-JUL-1940 / LEICESTER	0105 11272

12. Date and signature of Master, authorized agent or officer   22-01-01

To avoid being imprisoned as an illegal immigrant in Owendo, the author's name was added to the crew-list of M.V. *Baynes*.

Tony, the ship's agent, a native of Gabon, drove his people-carrier to the gangway and I climbed into the cab. With me pretending that I was used to seeing a driver armed with a military pistol, he sped off. With his foot hard down on the accelerator, Tony drove along the hot, dusty road that appeared as if it had been under a recent mortar attack. His eyes were constantly looking away from the road ahead as he nattered away to me. Seeming to aim for every pothole, we bounced our way into town. Rules of the road were non-existent, it was every man for himself as we swerved to avoid oncoming traffic that had strayed to the wrong side.

After mounting the pavement in the centre of Owendo, Tony parked the people-carrier and we climbed out. Feeling safer now, I suddenly became aware of the continuous, deafening chorus of lorry and car horns. Putting my fingers into my ears I turned to my new-found apprentice racing driver and asked, "What else did they get for Christmas?" Not understanding the joke, Tony turned his hands skywards and, shrugging his shoulders, beckoned me to follow him. Dodging between the sea of people on the hot, crowded pavement, we soon reached the bank. This modern, glass-faced financial building that would not have looked out of place in New York had six armed guards standing in a line across the entrance. Each guard was holding a deadly killing machine in the form of a rifle – the type that you would probably see in a war zone on television. To feed this armoury, two leather belts of bullets were strapped across the chests of each one of these guards. As we walked up the marble steps to the bank's entrance two of the guards started to move towards us and shouted something in French to Tony. Grabbing hold of my tee-shirt, Tony said, "Stand still!" During the exchange of words between one of the guards and Tony I soon realised that some kind of identification was required. With a rifle pointing in the general direction of my chest I rooted into my knapsack and fumbled for my passport, thankful it had not been left aboard *Ozama*.

Access to the bank was gained by one of the guards pressing a number code into an electronic lock. On entering the building the relief from the stifling heat was instantly felt with the cooling air-conditioning. A series of glass tunnels had to be negotiated before the bank counter could be reached. Each tunnel ended with a door that was unlocked when the armed guard decided that you were a customer and not a potential bank robber.

Through a narrow slot in a glass shield that surrounded the bank counter I pushed my credit card to a smartly dressed, professional young woman. Not being able to speak French or Bantu myself it was much to my delight that the young woman asked in broken English how she could help. On being told that I needed two hundred American dollars, she casually swiped my credit card through the magnetic slot in front of the monitor. Marvelling at the electronic wonders of global banking, I hoped nothing would go wrong with the transaction, and stood there like a schoolboy waiting to be caned by the headmaster. Gazing intently at the screen that was facing her, she slowly shook her head from side to side. Pushing my credit card back to me through the glass slot she said to me whilst still shaking her head: "Machine no work."

With an expression of disbelief and card in hand I walked over to Tony, who was casually leaning on the end of the counter. "You must give her a present, then machine okay," he told me. The only 'present' I had with me was a twenty-euro note that I had stowed with my passport in the grab bag. An American twenty-dollar bill I had left aboard *Baynes* was also from this grab bag. I handed the euro note and credit card to the girl behind the counter, and the credit card scanning machine was suddenly working again. Instead of two hundred American dollars, though, I would have to take the equivalent in Gabonese francs. "Come back tomorrow and I will exchange," the girl informed me as she counted out a mountain of paper money. This kind of currency, which is unspendable outside its own country, we in the Merchant Navy called *Mickey Mouse* money.

Stuffing the notes into my knapsack and thankful for at least getting this far, we entered the labyrinth of glass tunnels and emerged once again into the dazzling sunlight. As we climbed back into the shipping agent's people-carrier, Tony informed me that he had an appointment to take the vehicle to a garage for repairs to be carried out. It would have seemed a mundane event at first; as events turned out it was anything but that.

We stopped outside the entrance to a huge commercial garage where vehicles of every description were undergoing repairs. To one side of a swing-pole steel barrier that protected this entrance, a guard dressed in a camouflage army uniform came running out of a wooden sentry box as if being chased by a swarm of bees. Screaming at Tony in a language that I did not understand and waving his rifle in the air, he evidently wanted me to get out of the cab. As I fumbled to find the cab door lock to make a quick exit, the ship's agent leaned over to my side of the vehicle and, grabbing hold of my shoulder, said, "You stay in truck." Then, in a fury, Tony continued to confront and hurl verbal abuse in French at his fellow country-man, who was now running to and fro like a tormented caged tiger. The balance of the argument rapidly changed when, with the rifle barrel end resting against my temple, I heard the metallic click of the safety catch being released. The sentry had reached the end of his tether. Terror – pure, unadulterated terror – immediately made me freeze in my seat. After all I'd been through, was it all going to end with an apparent mad-man blowing my brains out? These thoughts raced through my mind as I tried to gather my wits. With my heart pounding so hard that I thought I could hear its beat through my tee-shirt, I pointed to myself and the ground through the side window space. The sentry pulled open the cab door and I scrambled out. Tony carried on shouting abuse at the guard, and with tyres that revolved so fast that they lost traction, took off into the service station.

Not daring to move far from the entrance into which Tony had disappeared in case I missed him on his return, I stood waiting in the scorching sun, thankful for the straw hat that I had bought in Porto Santo. The sentry had returned to the shade of his box where he stood to attention and with rifle by his side waited like a spider in a web for anyone foolish enough to challenge him. (As Tony continued to do two hours later, as he drove out of the compound.)

Driving back to the jetty, Tony informed me that first he had to call at a hotel on the outskirts of the city. A Swedish relief captain who had been staying at this hotel whilst awaiting the arrival of his new command was to be picked up and driven to his ship that had docked that day. The place where the captain was staying seemed to have been built to a standard that had been without limit to the cost. This beautiful glass and blue marble building that soared many storeys skywards took on the appearance of a huge iceberg that was refreshingly in total contrast with the fierce sun that threatened to melt it. The hotel, set in a magnificent tropical garden of palm trees and exotic flowering plants and with the sound of a cascading flow over a waterfall, seemed an idyllic setting of tranquillity. That illusion was soon belied when I spotted the presence of six armed, uniformed guards straddling the entrance to the reception area. Without waiting to be told, I jumped out of the cab. I did not fancy another confrontation or anyone threatening to blow my brains out again. As Tony walked into the hotel to find the captain, one of the guards came towards me. And as if to demonstrate his power, he made it known that he wanted to see some identification. Under whose authority this guard was acting I did not know or care (he had a gun) but after flicking through the pages of my passport he handed it back and returned to his station. After a few minutes Tony reappeared with his charge, who was smartly dressed in white shorts and shirt, with gold epaulettes that denoted the rank of captain.

Three quarters of an hour later the people-carrier arrived back on the jetty and pulled up at the bottom of the *Baynes*'s gangway.

Shaking hands with the Swedish captain and wishing him a safe voyage, I jumped down from the cab. Before driving away, Tony informed me that he would pick me up the next morning at 10:00 to exchange the francs for American dollars. The thought of having to go through all that rigmarole with the bank again was too depressing to dwell on. Just to get away for a while from the sense of being in danger, and the uncertainty of how to react to an officialdom that seemed to be steeped in corruption, was a blessing. As I climbed the gangway clutching my knapsack that was stuffed with Gabonese francs, a feeling of utter relief came over me. Making my way across the ship to the captain's cabin to report the progress regarding my acquiring a visa, I could not help noticing that the cargo hatches were still battened down and derricks not topped. On reaching the upper deck just below the bridge I saw through the open door the Captain sitting at his desk studying a pile of paperwork. Telling me to take a seat he explained that he had had a troubled day himself. The port authority wanted the ship's twenty-thousand-ton cargo of coal to be discharged onto the jetty and left there to await removal by truck. The jetty, which was only supported by wooden piles, would have been in danger of collapsing under such weight. The captain had refused (and rightly so) to comply unless the port authorities signed a waiver note absolving him of any blame should the jetty fail. A stalemate had been reached.

True to his word, Tony at 10:00 the next morning drove his people-carrier onto the jetty and pulled up at the bottom of the gangway.

Climbing into the cab I uttered "Here we go again" to myself and settled down for the bumpy ride along the pothole-strewn road into town.

Retracing our steps from yesterday, and being given the all-clear from the guards, we once again entered the inner sanctum of the bank. The same girl cashier that had taken the 'present' from me was there. I fed the huge pile of Gabonese francs to her through the narrow slot in the armour-plated glass counter shield, and she began counting the notes with the rapidity of a machine. Satisfied everything was in order she exchanged the francs for two hundred American dollars. Folding these into my passport, she pushed them to me along with (much to my surprise) a surplus amount of Gabonese francs. "We buy airline ticket now then see immigration for visa." Tony made it sound so simple.

I had mentally divided my quest to leave Gabon into four stages:

1) bank;
2) buy airline ticket;
3) obtain visa;
4) fly away.

Happy that stage one was now accomplished, I sat in the cab alongside my driver and separated the American currency from the Gabonese. The latter I stuffed into my shirt pocket. The journey to the office of Air France seemed to take forever as we drove at a snail's pace through the city centre in the heat of the midday sun. The incessant din of car horns only added to my wish to be away from all of this. Whilst we were waiting at one of the seemingly dozens of red traffic signals, I turned my head to see on the pavement an old beggar squatting on his haunches. He was blind. A dirty and chipped white enamelled basin that served as a begging bowl was resting on the pavement in front of him. After tapping Tony on his shoulder I jumped out of the cab and, opening the beggar's scrawny hand, thrust into it the bundle of Gabonese notes. This action was not out of philanthropy: it was just that these notes would be unspendable at the place that I hopefully intended to reach soon. The lights had just changed to green as I scrambled back into the cab and rejoined the snail's-pace traffic to the travel agents.

The sales girl at Air France informed me that it would be much cheaper to buy a return ticket to Gabon than a single fare. The logic behind this I could not figure out but I was glad to meet someone who was not trying to rip me off. My flight to Paris was scheduled to take off at midnight that day. To think that in less than ten hours I could be away from this beautiful country that had been sullied and contaminated with the corruption of man. With the airline ticket stowed safely (thank God for credit cards) in a money belt we came out and headed for the immigration office. On reaching the jetty alongside which the *Baynes* was berthed, Tony pulled up outside the building that housed the dodgy official who would issue a visa for a fee of two hundred American dollars.

"Leave the talking to me," Tony said as he opened the door to a small office that had a large fan revolving slowly from the ceiling. Behind a desk sat a fat man in clothing festooned in gold braid that looked as if someone had thrown a pan of scrambled egg over him. After lifting himself from his chair the immigration officer politely shook our hands and, turning to Tony, began an animated conversation in French. Whilst this was going on I made ready my passport and the two hundred American dollars, bribe money. Finally Tony beckoned me to go outside where he would explain the deal reached between himself and the man who had the power to issue the vital visa. The upshot was that for two hundred dollars I could have my passport stamped with a visa that would expire at midnight on that day. So it was that I handed over my passport and hard-earned money for a visa stamp mark that would be valid for about the next eight hours. With slow deliberation the rubber stamp was pressed into the ink pad and with equal slowness a green visa emblem appeared in my passport.

I was filled with mixed feelings of relief and anxiety as stage three of my escape plan was completed – anxious in case the official put some other obstacle in my way.

Stepping outside the office, we noticed that the air was filled with dust from the huge heaps of coal that were being discharged from the holds of *Baynes* and landed on the jetty. A fleet of trucks were taking away this cargo after being hurriedly loaded by a bulldozer. Battling to quickly remove these huge piles of coal that must have put a considerable strain on the rickety jetty, the to-ing and fro-ing of the trucks looked like a swarm of ants attacking a huge liquorice mountain. Later I learnt from the Captain that a waiver note had been signed absolving him from any blame if the quay collapsed or was damaged in any way. Another backhander?

It was whilst back on board the *Baynes* I learnt that after discharging her cargo of coal, she was sailing to another port in Gabon where she would load manganese ore. This cargo was destined for Larvik, where the ship would be dry-docked. When I told the Captain that I would like to send a postcard to him from the U.K. letting him know that I had reached home, he handed to me the ship's agent's address in Larvik, Norway.

Whereas I had first boarded the *Baynes* in mid-Atlantic with little more than the clothes that were on my back, now I had quite a variety of shirts and things that the crew had been so kind as to give me. Looking at these clothes that I had piled in a heap on my bunk, I began to wonder how they could be carried onto the plane, as I only possessed a small knapsack that had sufficed as a grab bag. As if by telepathy the first mate (Eugenio Marasigan, who had picked up my Mayday) came into the cabin and presented to me a luggage case complete with wheels and telescopic handle!

Tony had arranged to drive me to the airport. He would be at the gangway at 18:00. After my packing was finished I still had a couple of hours before leaving the ship. There would be plenty of time to say goodbye. The crew, as I went on deck to meet them, were just closing the hatches after finishing their unloading of coal for the day. I could not leave without thanking each and every one of them. Their coal-dust-blackened faces made the whiteness of their teeth put any toothpaste advert to shame as they told me to wait until they had showered.

The lads had arranged a little impromptu going-away party. And what a good time it was. The laughter and the beer, wine and whisky flowed freely. By the time the Captain came to tell me that Tony was at the gangway I didn't feel like leaving. Stepping from the gangway down onto the wooden jetty, I slid open the side door of the people-carrier and lifted my solitary travel case inside. Finally the Captain shook my hand and wished me farewell, and the waving sea of arms disappeared from sight as we headed for the airport.

Only stage four to complete of my 'escape plan', I told myself as I checked and rechecked the precious visa that was stowed in my money belt. Don't let anything happen now, I prayed as I fastened the seat harness just in case we crashed. My driver, who had his foot hard down on the accelerator, seemed to be steering for every pothole again as we thundered along the highway. (Little wonder the suspension was hammered.) Not wishing to distract Tony from the concentration required whilst driving along these 'every man for himself' roads, I decided to ignore him as he gabbled away. This was entirely the wrong thing to do, for now he took his eyes off the road more often as he turned to see if I had heard him.

The sun had set by the time we arrived at the airport. Stepping onto the pavement I trundled my suitcase through the automatic glass doors and headed for the check-in. Tony followed, and sat down with me on one of the modern settee-like seats. I needed to sort out my airline ticket and passport and an American twenty-dollar bill that I had kept in my grab bag. "Take this," I said, offering the note to Tony (thinking he would bite my hand off), "for the help you have given to me."

Shaking his open palm from side to side and grinning he said, "No trouble, no take." Twenty dollars would probably be a week's wages to him, and his refusal (much to my shame) made me realise that there were good people in Gabon and that they were not all on the make.

The electronic message that scrolled across the overhead monitors told me that it was time to check in for my flight. After I had shaken hands with Tony and thanked him for his help again, he turned and walked back his people-carrier.

In front of the check-in desk a human snake of a queue was rapidly forming. The queue moved at a snail's pace and as I shuffled along with it I could not help wondering about my visa that would expire at midnight. The Air France check-in girl, satisfied that all my documents were in order, quickly encircled my suitcase handle with a sticker and my solitary piece of luggage disappeared on the conveyor. Breathing a sigh of relief, I clutched my boarding card and passport and headed for the departure lounge. An immigration officer, armed to the teeth, stopped me in my tracks and asked for my passport. "Where is your visa?" The visa had been stamped two-thirds into my passport, so its whereabouts was not at first obvious. After I had found the page in question the officer, with what seemed like a look of disappointment, casually handed back my passport.

It was at a quarter of an hour before midnight that the boarding of the plane was announced. The boarding sequence depended on your allocated seat number. Ten minutes to midnight and the next batch of seat numbers for boarding included mine. This is it, I told myself as I hurried to the doorway that led onto the runway. "Visa!" a man shouted at me and I stopped in my tracks. I was beginning to hope that I would wake up any minute and this entire thing about visas would be a bad dream. By the time I had been pulled out of the line of passengers on their way to the aircraft and gone through the visa-showing routine, it was five to midnight.

The giant airliner, a Boeing 747, waited majestically on the runway as her passengers filed aboard. A cluster of arc lights illuminated this beautiful manmade flying machine, revealing the colourful legend 'Air France' painted on the fuselage. Two gangways, one at each end of the aircraft, were straddled by what looked like two lines of ants as the passengers shuffled aboard. Looking desperately at my watch, I saw it was three minutes to midnight as I hurried towards the waiting aluminium angel that would carry me home. As I approached the nearest boarding gangway I was filled with despair as I saw at the lower step a camouflaged figure, complete with machine gun. Was I carrying a banner that I did not know about saying 'Look for a visa'? I thought this to myself as once again I was singled out and pointed to the well-thumbed page that bore the soon-to-expire visa. Satisfied, the guard nodded his head in the direction of the gangway, indicating that I was free to rejoin the boarding queue. Waiting at the top of the gangway was a smartly uniformed and smiling stewardess. After glancing at my boarding pass she uttered, "Welcome aboard." Welcome aboard? I felt as if I could have hugged her in gratitude.

It was ten minutes after midnight and the aircraft was still on the ground. I began to fidget in my seat, half expecting any minute to be escorted off the plane with an expired visa. At last the cabin crew began to close the passenger embarkation doors. Don't let anything happen now, I silently prayed as the locking handles were pulled down into position. Dotted along the aircraft aisles, the cabin crew began to point silently to the emergency exits and demonstrate an escape plan. The only direction of escape that I was interested in at that moment was skywards. This blessed moment came as, glancing through the cabin window, I saw the flashing green light at the end of the wing begin to illuminate the runway as we started to taxi to the take-off position.

With the four thundering engines roaring away, the pilot positioned the aircraft and waited for the control tower to signal to start the ascent. The 'clear to take off' message was followed by the simultaneous release of power and we sped along the runway at an ever-increasing, frantic rate. The vibration of the cabin stopped and started for a second as the aircraft's wheels began to lift. The powerful airflow rushed under the wings and as if in one last desperate effort, the engines roared louder and we were airborne. From above, the mosaic-like pattern of the different-coloured city lights of Owendo reminded me of a doctor's test card for colour blindness. The luxury of such trivial thoughts; such a change and relief from having to think about visas or having my brains blown out. Time to look around at my anonymous fellow passengers strapped into their seats. They too had their stories. Time to think about how many on-board drinks I could buy with my lone twenty-dollar bill. As we climbed higher the manmade land lights gradually faded away and were replaced by the twinkling lights in the night sky. The same starry sky I had looked at in wonder from the deck of *Ozama* only weeks before. The Plough swept past over the starboard wing and as the plane was steadied on course, I knew that we were homeward bound.

And home I reached on 24th January 2001. In a sheep field nestling among the beautiful mountains of North Wales is a tiny cottage, warm and welcoming. This is my home. A home I share with my wife Janet and our cat. As I trundled my trolley suitcase along the narrow lane towards our cottage on that winter's day, the fields were covered in frost. I must have presented a pathetic figure in the way that I was dressed. Although grateful beyond words for the kindness of the crew of the *Baynes* for the clothes on my back, I shivered uncontrollably. The cold north winds that swept down from the Artic Circle cut through the thin cotton of my shirt and trousers. With frozen hands that would hardly unclench, I reached out to open our cottage door. No need, the door flew open and Janet flung her arms around my shoulders, her tears warm upon my neck.

So ended my first attempt to follow in the wake of the yacht *Erma*.

Some time later, a parcel of twenty-three boxes of choco-lates – one for each of the crew of M.V. *Baynes* – was shipped to Larvik, Norway.

PART TWO

Chapter 13

It was to be eighteen months later, in August 2002, that I had enough money to even think about looking for another yacht. A yacht that was suitable to voyage across the Atlantic and hopefully reach Norfolk, Virginia. If possible I wanted to follow in the wake of *Erma*. *Erma* of course was the thirty-six-foot wooden double-ended sloop that had in 1945 carried those brave, desperate souls from Estonia to America. The very epic voyage that had inspired me to try to sail across the Atlantic.

After all the trouble that I had encountered with the drop keel and rudder of *Ozama* I had a good idea of the kind of yacht that I needed. A yacht with a sea-kindly shape, a deep, long keel and a rudder under the counter (stern) and fixed to the keel. The rig, if not junk-rigged, would have to be manageable by a single-hander. A conventional Bermudian rig, then, would have to have roller reefing gear on the foresail. Over the years I had spent too long getting wet on the foredeck, unhanking sails and bundling a heap of sailcloth into the cabin. It was time for a bit of luxury.

Over the past eighteen months I had been looking at many of the 'Yachts for sale' columns in papers and magazines and on the internet. Although I could not afford any of them that would have been suitable, during that time I did acquire a good idea of what looked like a bargain. A small classified advert in a yachting magazine caught my eye. It read:

Trintella 29 for sale excellent condition, recent survey, owner buying bigger yacht, lying Plymouth. £19,500.

This could be the very thing, I told myself as I added the details to the list of possible yachts that fitted in with my requirements and modest budget. In response to those adverts, I had driven to several ports around the country to search for a yacht that would be suitable for my needs. The sea-keeping qualities in the design of these yachts were evident, but all too often the extra work required to bring them up to scratch for an ocean voyage was all too time-consuming and expensive. Being so picky probably put me in the category referred to in those adverts as a 'timewaster'. It could not be helped. At sixty-two years of age I could not afford the luxury in terms of time to take on a prolonged yacht restoration programme – or for that matter the luxury of unlimited funds, as I had a tight budget to stick to.

Incidentally, when restoring a yacht I have learnt over the years to multiply by four the first time-span that you have calculated to finish the project. You will then have a far more realistic idea of when your restoration plan will be completed. This was the outcome I once found out after foolishly thinking that I could emulate Joshua Slocum, who had restored his beloved *Spray* in record time.

As the tick-off marks reached towards the end of my potential yacht list with the crossing off of a wooden Folkboat, I was left with the Trintella 29. As I've mentioned, this yacht was lying at Plymouth. After phoning the owner and asking him many prepared questions, I arranged a meeting with him. From where I live in North Wales the drive down to Plymouth is over three hundred miles. Peter, the yacht's owner, knowing that I was unfamiliar with his home town, asked me to wait for him on the outskirts at a large supermarket. To make things easier I would be wearing a red sun hat.

The drive down to Plymouth was mostly spent with me comparing the time taken to travel by car with that of a yacht.

Ozama adrift in the Atlantic, January 2001.
Rudder lying in cockpit, foreground. Notice Red Ensign flying upside
down as per International Distress Signal.
Photo: Trevor Wilson.

Top: *Ozama* at Barcelona, September 2000.

Right: *Ozama* leaving Gibraltar, December 2001. Handling of single Chinese rig sail is ideal for a single-hander.

Photos: Trevor Wilson.

Top: Rescue ship *Baynes* at Owenda, January 2001, discharging her cargo of coal.

Left: Catching rainwater aboard *Ozama* in the Atlantic.

Photos: Trevor Wilson.

Above: Author with murals of *Ozama* and *Mykon* at Porto Santo.

Below: Replica of *Santa Maria* at Porto Santo, December 2005.

Photos: Trevor Wilson.

Above: A welcome sight – RNLI *Frederick Storey Cockburn* coming to the rescue, 1st December 2002. Yacht *Bowden*.

Below: Calmer waters, Courtmacsherry Harbour.

Photos: Courtesy of Lifeboat Coxswain Dan O'Dwyer.

Courtmacsherry Harbour, County Cork, Ireland, 1st December 2001.
The author being led to awaiting ambulance after rescue by RNLI.
Lifeboat: *Frederick Storey Cockburn.*

Crew List:
Coxswain: Dan O'Dwyer.
Crew Members: Michael O'Donovan. Michael Hurley. Vincent O'Donovan.
Liam Murphy. Conor Dullea. Chris Guy.

auxiliary power. Over the years I have sailed many engineless yachts, which I preferred. But with the growth of crowded marinas these days, some kind of mechanical propulsion is a must unless you have room and energy to carry a sculling oar. One feature of a marine engine that I insist on is that it can be started by a handle. An old-fashioned idea maybe, but in the ships' lifeboats that I've sailed, a few swings of a handle brought to life those little engines when the wind fell away. And who has not pressed a start button at some time to find that nothing has happened?

Peter returned and answered the list of questions that I had written down as I carried out my primary inspection. After the experience with *Ozama* I could not afford to let my heart rule my head and buy the yacht on the word of the seller. Telling Peter that I would buy his yacht subject to a surveyor's report, I handed over a cheque for £100 as a token of good faith and shook his hand.

It was with a happy heart that I drove homeward, feeling as if I owned *Bowden* already. The harsh reality was that there was no place for rose-tinted glasses; first I must contact a yacht surveyor. This was at the top of my 'things to do' list. On arriving home, and before I had even spoken, Janet knew straight away by the look on my face that the yacht-inspection trip had been worthwhile (I wouldn't make a good poker player).

'Yacht surveyors Plymouth' I typed into the search engine on the internet, and a long list of yacht surveyors popped up on my computer screen. Choosing the name of a surveyor at random from this list I picked up the phone. It took about twenty minutes of conversation as I gave details of the thorough survey that I would require to be carried out. *Especially check the rudder and its fastenings*, was one of the instructions that I must have repeated a few times, as the surveyor politely reminded me, probably silently uttering "How many more times?" to himself.

After I explained that, subject to his survey, the yacht was intended to be sailed across the Atlantic, I was promised a full written account of his findings and recommendations. Good to his word, I received the report two weeks later. The summary stated that *Bowden* was soundly built. 'The hull form and the relatively heavy scantlings suggest that this vessel is significantly more suitable for long distance sailing than many younger pleasure yachts.' Apart from several small but important recommendations, the yacht was sound. Picking up the phone I told Peter that if he would make good the standing rigging and halyards he could also make out a bill of sale. He agreed.

The sloop *Erma* and her valiant crew had sailed from Dun Laoghaire for Madeira on 3rd October 1945. This had influenced my decision on this voyage to start it in October, although fifty-seven years later. As it was only the beginning of September, if I looked lively, I told myself, it would be possible to leave Plymouth in four or five weeks.

Having lost all my sailing gear on *Ozama* I would jot down each item that needed replacing as it came to my mind. This item replacement list was growing at an alarming rate. I decided to cut corners on the cost of as many items as I could whilst still retaining their basic function. Out would go famous yachting brand names. Clothing, for instance, that I found usually of good quality was overpriced, usually as a result of being promoted by a sponsored celebrity. Whilst rooting through a rambling kind of shop that sold second-hand ex-army gear I came across a complete waterproof suit that was breathable. The insignia on this khaki suit indicated that it once belonged to a German soldier. Handing over £60, which was a fraction of the cost a 'proper' set of wet weather gear, I thought that I had acquired a bargain. One very important feature of this ex-German army suit that I had overlooked was that the hood was designed to fit over a helmet. This oversight on my part was later to prove a serious error.

The sailing gear was steadily piling up in a heap on the living room floor of our tiny cottage. Each day another bargain would be added to this pile until we had to shuffle sideways to get past it. Promising Janet that there was only one more item to add to this manmade obstruction, I sent away for a parachute sea anchor.

The 5th of September 2002 saw me slowly nibbling away at the heap of accumulated nautical items (that now resembled a small bonfire) as I began to load the car. This 'small bonfire' was going to be temporarily stowed in Peter's house, where he kindly offered to let me stay. I needed a place to live that was near to the boatyard whilst making *Bowden* ready for the voyage. It was on one of those Indian summer days that I drove southwards to Plymouth, constantly shielding my eyes from the sun that seemed to be glued to the car bonnet. Plymouth is well renowned, of course, for the Pilgrim Fathers' voyage to America. The colourful hoardings throughout the city proclaimed that the *Mayflower* had sailed on 6th September 1620 bound for the New World. I had arrived by coincidence on that very anniversary. This important event I could not let pass without finding something out about the ship and its story.

As *Mayflower* would have looked, based on estimates.
Sketch and research: Courtesy B.B.C. Devon.

The *Mayflower* dropped her anchor near Cape Cod on November 11th. This voyage was inspired by the successful establishment of the first permanent English settlement, Jamestown, by the London Company of Virginia in 1607. The ship herself was used as a trader, carrying various cargoes, often wine, between England and other European countries, principally France, but also Norway, Germany and Spain. At least between 1606 and 1622, she was mastered by Christopher Jones, who was Captain on the transatlantic voyage and was based in Rotherhithe, London. It is likely that the ship was broken up for scrap timber in Rotherhithe, the year after Jones's death. The Mayflower Barn just outside the Quaker village of Jordans in Buckinghamshire, is said to be built from these timbers. The *Mayflower* likely had a crew of twenty-five to thirty; however, the names of only five of these are known, including one John Alden, who chose to stay in Plymouth. Details of the ship's dimensions are unknown, but estimates based on its load weight and the usual size of 180-ton merchant ships in the period give her a length of ninety to one hundred and ten feet and a beam of about twenty-five feet. Careful research went into designing the replica. The *Mayflower II* was launched on 22nd September 1956 and resembled its namesake as closely as possible.

Pilgrims' Voyage

Initially, the plan was for the voyage to be made in two vessels, the other being the smaller *Speedwell*. The first voyage departed Southampton on 5th August 1620, but the *Speedwell* developed a leak and had to be refitted at Dartmouth. On the second attempt the ships reached the Atlantic but again were forced to return to Plymouth because of *Speedwell*'s leak. After reorganisation, the final sixty-six-day voyage was made by *Mayflower* alone, leaving Plymouth on 6th September. With the crowding of one hundred and two passengers plus crew, each family was allotted very little space for personal belongings.

At one point, the ship's main beam cracked and had to be repaired using a large iron screw. The *Mayflower* landed at Renews, on the southern shore of the Avalon Peninsula in Newfoundland, where it picked up water and supplies from local fishing families before sailing on to Cape Cod. The intended destination was a section of land near the Hudson River in Northern Virginia. The ship, however, was forced off course by bad weather. As a result of the delay, the settlers did not arrive at the future site of Plymouth Colony until the onset of a harsh New England winter. The settlers had failed to reach Virginia, where they had permission from the London Company to settle. The ship dropped anchor near Cape Cod on 11th November 1620. On 5th April 1621 the *Mayflower* set sail from the Plymouth Colony to return to England, where she arrived on 6th May 1621.

THE PASSENGERS

The one hundred and two passengers on the *Mayflower* were the earliest permanent European settlers in New England. Throughout the winter of 1620-21, the passengers, although living aboard ship, spent time ashore preparing home sites and searching for food. Only about half of the settlers would still be alive when the *Mayflower* left in the spring. Almost half of the sailors had perished also.

On that September day in 2002, as I drove into Plymouth, little did I realise that I would be there for ten weeks, well past the intended sailing date of early October. The recommendations by the yacht surveyor were carried out without too many hold-ups. I had *Bowden* fitted with new chain plates and had all the standing and running rigging replaced. All the electrics were renewed and a wind generator was mounted onto the pushpit. I also had a top-of-the-range roller reefing fitted to the forestay. A wind-powered self-steering gear was also added to the transom. All of these items were costing an arm and a leg but I was in no frame of mind to skimp on these, remembering the ordeal with *Ozama*. One of the last pieces of equipment I obtained was a Tinker Tramp dinghy fitted as a survival raft. Most of the work on the yacht was carried out whilst she was standing in her cradle in the boat yard. It was at the beginning of October that, along with several other yachts, she was craned into the water. Not all the jobs had been completed but they could be easily carried out whilst afloat.

A berth had been secured in the Mayflower Marina. The mooring fees, I was told, had been greatly reduced to a 'winter rate'. This made me feel happy for the first time in my life that summer was over. Tying up alongside my allotted pontoon berth I felt quite pleased that everything had gone without a hitch. This was until I found that I could not turn off the engine that was quietly chugging away. Feeling stupid, I swallowed my pride and asked a neighbour on the next pontoon to help. He tried his best but to no avail – the engine merrily carried on turning. Peter at that time was somewhere in Spain looking at a yacht that was for sale. I sent a text message to him, and he replied with the solution: an obscure switch inside the engine compartment needed to be flicked downwards to cut off the fuel. The marvel of modern-day communication.

Time was pressing and I still had to drive three hundred miles northward to return the car to our home in North Wales. Leaving the cabin keys with a local marine electrician so that he could finish off the new wiring job, I headed homeward. The next three days at home seemed to rush by in a blur, and soon it was time to say goodbye once again. One part of my thoughts was telling me to get back to *Bowden* and the other saying 'stay put'. So it was with mixed feelings that I boarded the train to Plymouth. As I gazed out of the railway carriage window as we sped southward, the beautiful mountains of Wales were in view. I tried to imagine them being under the sea, just like the mountains that I had sailed over in the Atlantic.

As the train journey was to take several hours, I had time to re-read the to-do list and the letter from the yacht insurance company that stated that the new gas pipework needed to be covered in plastic sleeving. They also wanted a small bulkhead in the forepeak glassed to the sides of the hull. It was not structural and had been loosely fitted by Peter to stop the anchor chain from kinking, but the work had to be done. The marine gasfitters and tradesmen were snowed under with work and it was frustrating to have to wait until it was my turn to be at the head of the queue. Frustrating also it was to watch the autumn easterly winds pass me by as I sat moored in the Mayflower Marina.

Eventually the time came when I could sail from Plymouth. It was 15th November 2002, nearly six weeks later than planned. The weather forecast for the next five days was for winds from the northeast, force three to four. Casting off the mooring lines, I felt a huge sense of relief as we cleared the pontoons and headed for the Plymouth Sound. As we steered to the western side of the breakwater I spotted with alarm something ahead that looked like an island. Glancing at the pilot chart that lay in the cockpit did not help, for the 'island' turned out to be a giant submarine.

Clearing the breakwater, I set all sail, the wind being east of north, force four. The mainsail was fitted with a Dutchman's reefing system, one that I had not used before. The basic idea was for the mainsail to slide down onto the boom from lanyards that hung from the topping lift. With this champagne sailing wind there was no need to think of reefing yet. Locking the self-steering gear to the tiller I went below to put the kettle on. The nights were drawing in. The sun set about 17:00, revealing the Eddystone Lighthouse, its beacon arc sweeping in the distance on our port bow.

Bowden raced through the night, sailing full and bye at over six knots through the water. Three o'clock in the morning saw the light of Lizard Point to starboard. This yacht was a thoroughbred, I told myself as she gracefully rode through the moderate sea with the odd phosphorous-sparkling spray breaking over the bow and the trail of her wake shimmering on the black water. Just before sunrise the Bishop Rock light popped up to starboard and by daylight we were in the Atlantic.

The Bay of Biscay can be an unpleasant place at any time of the year, so giving her a wide berth in November seemed a good idea. With this in mind I set a southwesterly course and headed for the invisible line of longitude fifteen degrees west. For the next four days the wind held steady from the north by east, force four. With the day's run from noon to noon averaging a hundred and fifty-one nautical miles we found ourselves about three hundred miles west of Cape Finisterre on 20th November 2002. Glad to have had the good fortune to find ourselves now south of the Bay of Biscay, I set a course for Porto Santo in the Madeira archipelago. *Erma* had called at Funchal on her Atlantic voyage, but after hearing how overcrowded the harbour had now become I decided I'd seek a quieter berth. Just as I was working out the estimated time of arrival at Porto Santo, assuming that these favourable winds held, the wind fell away.

'Don't count your chickens' suddenly came to mind. I climbed into the cockpit and looked in disbelief at the once full sails, now shaking uselessly with every roll of the yacht. After furling the foresail that was chafing on the stays and hardening in the mainsail boom, I went below to make a pan of hot stew. The weather was cold and as I stood shivering in the cabin I warmed my hands on the pressure cooker, such a blessed warm feeling. The ex-German army tank corps suit and woollen jumper that I was wearing kept the wind at bay – it was just my hands and feet that seemed to feel cold. Ladling the piping hot beef and onion stew into a mug I consoled myself with the thought that soon we would be sailing southwards. Sitting in the cockpit with legs stretched out I spooned the hot stew into my mouth whilst at the same time keeping a lookout for any traffic. The limited horizon from our height of two metres above the sea was about three miles. Not a ship in sight.

Looking towards the unseen Cape Finisterre, which lay about two hundred miles to the east, I tried to image the ships that had battled off that Cape nearly two hundred years ago. The outcome of that famous sea battle on 22nd July 1805 between the fifteen ships of the line of the United Kingdom and fourteen French and six Spanish ships of the line prevented the French fleet entering the English Channel. The plan had been for the French fleet to escort Napoleon's army across the Straits of Dover and invade England. I wondered how different our lives would have been today if we had lost the Battle of Cape Finisterre. Those odd thoughts, which would ramble through my mind whilst alone at sea, I considered nature's way of allowing me to 'escape' for a while. Sometimes an escape would occur whilst fast asleep and dreaming of walking through green fields. It was always a shock on waking up after one of these dreams to find that I was at sea.

Finishing the hot mug of stew, I felt warmer. I climbed back into the cabin. The barometer was still steady, so after plotting our position and marking it on the chart, I decided to have a sleep before night fell. It was several hours later that I was awoken by a bleeping noise. In my not fully awoken state I could not figure out where the sound was coming from.

Rubbing the sleep from my eyes I peered around the cabin to find the bleeping was coming from the electronic barometer. A flashing icon displaying a lightning symbol accompanied it. Suddenly I was fully awake and filled with dread as I saw the reading had dropped to 965 millibars. Clambering into the cockpit, I was greeted by a windless sky that was in a totally uniform colour of light purple-pink, as if we were underneath a giant parasol.

Filled with a sense of foreboding I began to prepare for a blow. Holding on the stays I reached the main halyard at the foot of the mast and doused the lifeless sail. With six separate lengths of cordage I lashed the bundle of sail along the boom. The end coils of halyards and topping lift at the foot of the mast were also made fast with a separate lanyard to stop them being swept over the side. The life raft/rubber dinghy that was stowed on the cabin top was also secured with extra lashings. The opening of the chain pipe had been sealed as soon as we had cleared Plymouth Sound, one less path for seawater.

The paddle of the self-steering needed to be lifted up out of the water by removing the sacrificial pin. This was easy to do from a dinghy or when alongside a pontoon, but proved impossible to pull out from on board, as I was pulling it at right angles and could not reach down far enough to pull it out sideways. Launching the dinghy was out of the question for the sea was quite lumpy in spite of having no wind. Next I shipped the special storm door that I had made in Plymouth from a piece of eighteen-millimetre plywood and galvanised bolts. I bolted it into place and unshipped the louvered cabin doors. It now meant that I had to use the companionway as a sort of conning tower: I was to thank God that I did that. No sooner were these preparations finished than, as if on cue from an unseen conductor's baton, the wind came up from the southwest.

An hour later it had reached gale force. The seas also had started to build up and we were taking water over the foredeck. I decided to heave to before night fell and see how we would lie to the expected battering that we were in for. Unfurling the roller reefing foresail to the size of a handkerchief I then lashed the tiller to leeward on a length of stout rubber shock-cord. The mainboom I also made fast either side of the cockpit with an extra piece of cordage. With a tantalising slowness that I was trying to will to hurry, *Bowden* eventually began to turn her bow out of the trough and towards the wind. The windage on her mast was sufficient to give steerage way. She lay at a forty-five-degree angle to the waves and was making about half a knot through the water. The wind had now reached force nine.

Satisfied that there was nothing more that I could do, and having one last look around the horizon for any shipping, I slid open the hatch and climbed down into the 'conning tower'. Making a hot drink was out of the question as it took every effort to hold on to the grab rails. From the waves that were breaking over the yacht a lot of the water was cascading into the cabin from beneath the main hatch, so I stuffed towels beneath it. I also had to drape towels over the companionway stairs, as the stainless steel checkerplate treads were as slippery as ice. Water was starting to fill the bilge. I decided to man the pump once the water covered the cabin sole. To get to the bilge pump I had to go out on deck and lift up the cockpit side-benches to get at it. This required waiting for a gap between waves and then quickly opening the hatch and clambering out.

Hooking my safety harness on to an anchor point in the cockpit I would crouch like a tortoise and with one arm start pumping. It took three hundred strokes to get the water out. As I pumped, more water poured into the opened side-benches. It seemed an endless task as I tried to slam the cover shut as each wave swept over the cockpit. By nightfall the wind was screaming and the whole sea had turned white. Later I found out from contestants of the yacht race to Brazil (Route du Rhum 2002) that the winds I experienced were between seventy and eighty knots. Climbing back into the 'conning tower' I was relieved to see that the water was now not swilling about on top of the cabin sole. With a hand bearing compass around my neck to check the course, I lay down on the starboard bunk. The sound of a rogue wave smashing into the cabin storm door made me sit bolt upright. The door held fast but I dreaded to think what would have happened if the flimsy louvre one had been left in place. Back into the cockpit for more pumping – when was it going to end? In answer, another wave swept aboard as we heeled violently to the onslaught. The safety lanyard on my chest harness pulled tightly against the anchor point, restraining my body as I was knocked over.

I was soaked to the skin by now, as the hood of the army Gore-Tex suit kept being blown off my head, allowing streams of water to be forced inside the jacket. Turning the beam of my head-torch up forward, I was glad to see that the rubber dinghy was still secured. No need to think of conserving the batteries, as the wind generator was racing away. Worried about overcharging the batteries, I had turned on every lamp in the cabin and also had the navigation lights shining brightly. Naively I seemed to derive a childlike comfort from the clearly lit-up cabin which seemed worlds away from what was going on in the darkness all around us.

The welcome sound of air being drawn into the bilge pipe signalled the end of another pumping session. The height of the seas was over ten metres, estimated against the mast height as we fell into the trough.

Those giant waves, white and sizzling, frightened me as they marched in rows towards us out of the darkness. Waiting until we were on top of a wave, I would quickly slide open the hatch and scramble down the 'conning tower' and into the relative safety of the cabin. I was becoming quite adept at this manoeuvre; the hardest part was to keep my feet from slipping off the companionway steps, as the towelling anti-slip cover was always being thrown off. The barometer was rising quickly and I knew things were going to get worse as the eye of the storm moved further away. Water was still being swept over the decks and finding its way into the cabin through gaps in the towelling stuffed around the hatch. Lying down on the bunk I could hear above the screaming wind the sound of bilge water below the cabin sole swilling about with every roll. Thankful that I could have a little rest from pumping, I closed my eyes.

Suddenly I was thrown out of my bunk with such force it was like coming out of a cannon. Everything had gone quiet, the screaming, the battering. Silence. "Christ, she's turned over!" The thought raced through my mind as I hit the teak cabin table. I could hear my ribs breaking and felt an excruciating pain in my left arm. (I found out later that I had three ribs broken and a hairline fracture in the ball and socket joint.)

My head caved in the wooden locker door as I fell downwards from the upturned yacht. A nightmare was beginning. Although it must have been only seconds, it seemed ages before the two-ton keel that was now pointing skywards began exerting its righting motion. Back in Plymouth I had put wooden bungs into the head valves and blocked it off, and was now using the fo'csle as a bosun's store, but now the concertina-style doors had burst open and all my spare kit – sails, clothes, bags etc. – came spewing out. When the 360-degree roll was completed I was thrown across the cabin, smashing into a fire extinguisher. To add to the confusion, white powder was now fizzing out of the extinguisher all over the place and I was choking for breath. With my one good arm I pulled back the hatch and threw the extinguisher into the storm. Just then a huge sea knocked *Bowden* over onto her beam ends and gallons of water poured down through the open hatch. This killed off the electrics, and the lights went out.

It was now 02:00 on day six. I found about nine inches of water over the cabin sole. I forced myself into the cockpit, crouched down and began pumping out. Every time I breathed it was as if someone had stuck a knife in me. After seven hundred strokes of the pump I stopped counting.

By dawn the wind had abated to about force six. The cabin looked as if a bomb had hit it. On deck I examined the damage. The main thing that concerned me was damage to the mast, but thankfully it was in one piece, although the backstay was loose. Renewing the chain plates and stays in Plymouth may have helped. The starboard cockpit dodger had been ripped to pieces but on the portside, where the dodger had held, the stanchions were bent inboard, jamming the sheet winch. The wooden cockpit grating was missing. The £3000 Tinker Tramp sailing life raft had been torn off the cabin top and was jammed between the starboard stanchions and the cabin side. Worst of all, the self-steering paddle, which I had not been able to lift out of harm's way, had been torn off completely and was being towed astern like a drogue. The yoke which held the paddle to the windvane was splayed out and both the main swivel and sacrificial bolt had gone.

With an urgency that made me try to ignore the pain in my ribs and arm, I attempted to repair the self-steering by using a G-clamp to bend the damaged self-steering yoke back into place. I found that a half-inch bolt from the cabin table, which had come apart at the joints following my collision, fitted exactly. The trouble was I had to lift the whole apparatus off the yoke, bolt on the paddle and then try to re-seat it onto a dovetail slide which only had a couple of thousands of an inch tolerance. As soon as the paddle hit the seas the whole apparatus was dragged this way and that and it was impossible to reseat. I therefore lifted it off again, took the paddle off and then re-seated it and accepted it was out of action.

After all of this work I decided to make a cup of tea, only to discover that the cooker's control knobs had seized solid. With the utmost care I used a set of mole grips to try to turn the knobs but failed. I believe the spring gas safety system, whereby you have to push and hold for a few seconds before the gas will stay on, had seized up when the wave hit it. I didn't want to force the knobs open for fear of fracturing a gas pipe. So now I faced the prospect of no warm drinks or food. All my working charts were a pulp on the cabin sole. I sorted some more out from my stores that had not been damaged and decided to set a course for Crosshaven in Southern Ireland.

Chapter 14

Crosshaven lay about seven hundred and fifty to eight hundred nautical miles to the northeast. As I could not handle the mainsail with only one good arm, and the wind from the southwest seemed set to stay there, heading northwards seemed the best choice. Half of the Genoa was unfurled and I could cope with this. With the self-steering out of action an alternative had to be found: this came from the various prepared lengths of shock-cord that I always carry for this very purpose. After putting the wind on the port quarter and fiddling about with shock-cord on either side of the tiller and finally hanging a tin of baked beans off the portside cord, we were steering northeast.

She sailed for hour after hour like this, and I managed to snatch some sleep during the day to be ready for the night, when I kept a full lookout. Sleep did not come easily as my ribs were causing pain and I found out by the blood in my mouth that I had unconsciously been biting the inside of my lip. Strange as it seemed, the pain in my ribs eased when, on lying down, I drew my leg up against my chest. Although devoid of electrical power the wind generator continued to turn round, albeit with two of its blades missing. This unbalanced windmill created such a racket that in desperation I jammed the boathook into the remaining blades.

As the days passed and we sailed further north, the colder

I felt. It was my feet that seemed the coldest, and as every stitch of clothing on board was soaking wet, I cut the woollen sleeves off the jersey that I was wearing and put them on my feet. It was robbing Peter to pay Paul, but I preferred cold arms to cold feet. Sitting in the cockpit during the night I would plan the hot drinks and meaty stews I would have in Crosshaven.

After five days I saw a container ship crossing our bow, heading towards the English Channel. Calling them up on my hand-held V.H.F. I asked them to report my position and intentions to the Falmouth Coastguard. (They didn't.)

The days and nights passed by in attempts to keep warm. Some comfort was derived from the flame of a hurricane lamp that I'd wired to the cooker. After seven days all the paraffin for the lamp was gone. I still had several dry boxes of matches that had been stowed in plastic containers. Carefully rationing them so they would last until I reached land, I allowed myself one box of matches each day. Even at the time I thought I must have looked quite a pathetic figure as I cupped my hands around the burning match. The Christmas story of *The Little Match Seller* by Hans Christian Andersen did come to mind.

On the fifteenth night the loom of a lighthouse popped up and swept the horizon on our portside. One flash every five seconds: it was the Fastnet Rock Lighthouse. The wind was increasing to force six and still from the southwest. I shortened the foresail and set course for the Old Head of Kinsale. At 01:00 the next morning the wind dropped and there was not a breath. The Old Head of Kinsale's light was tantalisingly close as it gave out its identity beam of group flash, two every ten seconds.

It was as if I could almost touch it, though the headland was three nautical miles ahead. Just thirty minutes later the wind came up from the northeast and started blowing at storm force ten. Although thankful that it was not a lee shore, it was with a deep feeling of utter disappointment that I cursed the wind. After completely furling the foresail I hoped that I was going to wake up and all of this was a bad dream.

I was now in fear of being blown back out into the Atlantic, and as I did not want to lose any ground, I decided to stream the parachute sea anchor. The mouth of the sea anchor was about nine feet in diameter so I would need both hands to deploy it and its three hundred feet of fourteen-millimetre thick nylon warp. It had been eleven days since the yacht had rolled over; in this time I had found that I could now use both arms, and my ribs were almost free from pain. I wanted to spend the least time possible on the foredeck to stream the sea anchor, as I could not work there hands-free owing to the violent motion. The plan was first to coil the three hundred feet of nylon warp into the cockpit and then take its end up forward to be made fast onto a swivel-linked anti-chafe chain that would be led through the bow roller fairlead. When that part of the plan was carried out I would crawl aft and deploy the sea anchor from the cockpit. The foredeck was only twenty feet or so from the relative safety of the cockpit, but in the early hours of that Sunday morning, as I shone my head-torch on it and started to crawl forward, it seemed a mile away. Dipping the end of the warp on the outside of the stays, I finally reached the foredeck and hooked myself onto the two wire cables that ran along the length of either side of the deck.

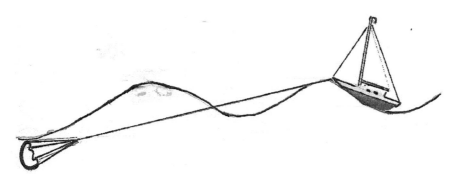

Riding to sea anchor facing oncoming sea.

The crawl back to the cockpit was accomplished between stops, clinging like a limpet onto the grabrail on the cabin top and moving only when on the top of a crest. After bending the parachute sea anchor onto its cable I balanced on the side-benches in the cockpit to throw the whole rope-strewn apparatus into the sea. As I cast it over the side, the wind, which was now blowing at eighty knots, filled the canopy and tore it from my hands. Grabbing hold of the anchor warp as it went flying out of the cockpit, I desperately tried to retrieve the sea anchor: the more I pulled the stronger the resistance became. The sea anchor was now at the end of its three-hundred-foot warp and flying like a kite. The yacht's head was immediately pulled downwind and I was paragliding back into the Atlantic. In those conditions it would have been suicidal to attempt to reach the foredeck and cast free the chain and warp that held the sea anchor. At three knots we were dragged this way and that through the seas, and I held onto the tiller like grim death as I tried to follow the airborne path of the towing kite. Some of the seas we rode over the crests, some we ploughed through, engulfing the yacht. Deciding that hand-steering was futile, I lashed the tiller amidships and found little difference in the yacht's erratic course.

Eventually the parachute sea anchor crashed into the sea and pulled her head to wind, but not before we were knocked onto the beam ends. Water poured down the open hatch to the companionway where I had been standing trying to shelter. Having been knocked flat on my back onto the cabin sole I found myself wedged between the table and struggling to get my head above the water that was swilling over me. Scrambling out of the cabin I began frantically manning the bilge pump in a desperate effort to get rid of the water that was coming on board faster than I could pump.

Now that we were back in the Atlantic and exposed to the uninterrupted three-thousand-mile fetch of the ocean rollers, the seas had increased to a height of twelve metres. To make matters worse the sea anchor did not hold her head into the wind, and we lay broached to in the troughs. It was in this exposed position that we endured three knock-downs. And for the second time on the voyage my safety harness lifeline prevented me being swept overboard with the water as it sluiced over the cockpit.

I could not face the prospect of the yacht being rolled over again. After finding our exact position from my pocket G.P.S. I took the hand-held radio transmitter from its waterproof box and sent out a Mayday message. Less than a mile away and unseen, a French trawler riding out the storm had picked up the Mayday. Not that I knew, for to preserve the battery life I had switched off the radio transmitter. It came as a total surprise when I saw the rust-streaked hull of a trawler bearing down on us.

Her name was *Pluton*. Two of her crew stood poised to throw a heaving line to me and after trying to manoeuvre the trawler to a position to bring me downwind, ran across my three-hundred-foot anchor warp. I watched in helpless horror as *Bowden* was dragged under the trawler's counter, her propeller wildly churning fresh air as it lifted clear of the water. Returning to the sea, the trawler's counter smashed into our foredeck, destroying the pulpit in one fell swoop.

As the trawler swept past our bow and *Bowden* cleared her stern, one of her crew began to hand-signal by mime that they had alerted the air-sea rescue. The Irish Coast Guard helicopter *Rescue 115* was the first on the scene. When it appeared overhead it looked like a winged sycamore seedling being buffeted this way and that as those brave pilots struggled to control their craft in the high winds. The co-pilot signalled to me by holding a radio transmitter into the storm: the voice that came over my V.H.F. radio told me that it was not possible to effect a rescue in those conditions, which was understandable. They had alerted the Coast Guard, and the helicopter would stay overhead and guide the lifeboat to our position.

The sight of that lifeboat struggling towards me from the top of a huge sea and then disappearing into the trough, only to emerge again with an unstoppable determination, I will keep in my mind forever. The lifeboat approached from fifty metres downwind and was skilfully manoeuvred close enough for a lifebelt and rope to be passed successfully. This was a vital step in the rescue, just in case I fell into the water. The lifeboat approached again with the starboard shoulder close enough to the yacht's port beam. Three pairs of arms grabbed hold of me as I made the transfer. This equally important part of the rescue was conducted most professionally and I had full confidence in the crew.

As I was being led down to the wheelhouse I turned my face skywards to my guardian angel that was still keeping a vigil, and raised my two arms in deep gratitude. Before I was taken back to harbour a valiant attempt was made to save the yacht. They picked up the sea anchor warp and started to tow her in. After twenty minutes the warp broke.

Coxswain Dan O'Dwyer was unwilling to risk the life of a crew member in those severe weather conditions by transferring someone onto *Bowden* to secure another towline, which I quite understood.

At 14:30 the lifeboat returned to the calm of Courtmacsherry Harbour and I was back on dry land. Crowds of people were gathered on the little jetty as I was led bedraggled to a waiting ambulance. During the journey to Cork University Hospital all my wet clothes and boots were put into a plastic bin bag and I was wrapped in an aluminium blanket. John and Mary were the paramedics. Both epitomised the warmth and friendliness of lovely Irish people. One of the diagnoses made on that journey was that I had hypothermia. After stopping in a little village, Mary stepped out of the ambulance and returned carrying a tray with a steaming pot of tea and buttered toast. "I'm sure you wouldn't say no to something hot, now would you, Trevor?"

The x-rays at the hospital revealed that three of my ribs had been broken and the shoulder joint had sustained a hairline fracture. During the eleven-day journey my bones had set and by good fortune in the right place. Only the deep yellow bruising surrounded by a black edging that covered the whole of my left side bore testimony to the mishap. Whilst staying at the hospital I had a visit from Michael Hurley, the mechanic and crew member of the Courtmacsherry Lifeboat that rescued me. After letting me know that my wife Janet had been informed that I was safe, Michael presented a bag of dry clothes to me that he and the crew had so kindly collected. The kindness did not stop there for on leaving hospital he drove me to his home in Courtmacsherry, where a lovely hot supper was waiting for us.

In the warmth of their cosy home and sitting around the supper table were Michael and his wife and several friends, and it was late into the night we swapped yarns. I can hardly remember my head touching the pillow after climbing into that warm bed with the knowledge that I need not keep a lookout that night.

The next morning, just before I left Courtmacsherry for Cork International Airport, the local radio phoned to ask Michael if we would give an account of the rescue. I was only too glad to agree, it was such a small request and I knew that I could not ever repay those brave lifeboat men whose forefathers had also saved countless lives over the years. (It was on the 7th May 1915 that the crew of the Courtmacsherry lifeboat, the *Kezia Gwilt*, rowed for over three and a half hours to try to save the lives of passengers on board a ship that had been torpedoed. She was the *Lusitania*.)

When the radio interview was over I went with Michael to say goodbye to Dan O'Dwyer, the coxswain, and thank him once again. With one last farewell wave I then climbed into the waiting taxi that would take me to the airport. As we drove towards the Cork International Airport the driver, a friendly, chatty character, told me about the extent of the havoc the recent storm had caused to his village. Power lines and trees had been blown down, blocking roads, and several local fishing boats had been lost. On this day, however, the sun shone and the wind had dropped. Only the trail of destruction bore silent testimony to how fickle the moods of nature are.

The flight from Cork to Birmingham only took about an hour. As I came away from the plane and once again trod on home soil, I could not help having a feeling of déjà-vu. The only difference this time was that the plane bore an Irish shamrock and I had to travel north instead of south to reach our little cottage.

The transition from being at sea to settling down among the mountains again didn't take long. Sitting in the quiet of our little cottage, I penned a letter to the central offices of the Royal National Lifeboat Institution in Poole, telling of the gratitude I had for the crew of the Courtmacsherry lifeboat.

The letter went on to explain that their help to me continued even when ashore by providing warm shelter and clothes. As Janet carefully folded these clothes and added them to the clothes that the crew of the *Baynes* had previously donated, she jokingly remarked that we would need a bigger wardrobe at this rate.

Her words were to ring true.

The Courtmacsherry lifeboat.
Frederick Storey Cockburn.
Coxswain Dan O'Dwyer.
(Picture by kind permission of Nicholas Leach of R.N.L.I.)

Trent Class All Weather Lifeboat ON-1205.
Length OA: 45' 11"
Length BP: 41' 10"
Beam: 15' 2"
Draught: 4' 6"
Speed: 25 knots
Range: 250 nautical miles.

PART THREE

Chapter 15

My quest to follow in the wake of *Erma* continued, and May 2004 found me in Bradwell-on-Sea in Essex. I had just bought a second-hand yacht that I considered suitable for a transatlantic voyage. This yacht was a Cutlass 27 class and her name was *Mykon*. The insurers of *Bowden* had declared her a total loss and had honoured their part of the agreement and reimbursed the total sum insured. The plan was to sail *Mykon* around the coast in July to Caernarfon in North Wales, where I would spend the winter fitting her out.

My pal Dave agreed without hesitation to crew for me. As I have mentioned, Dave and I have sailed on different yachts together for over thirty years and worked well together as a team. It's important to know your crew fairly well, I think, and to get on well. Whilst respecting the other person's feelings you don't want to be walking on egg shells all the time. There is nothing worse than being at sea aboard a small yacht with a perpetual whinger, as we say on Merseyside. The worst malcontent is a smoker who has run out of cigarettes!

As *Mykon* was standing on the quayside in a cradle, I decided to fit the self-steering gear that had been shipped from its makers in Denmark. The hinged paddle of this self-steering could be lifted out of the water simply by tugging on a lanyard. After the fate that befell *Bowden*'s self-steering, 'once bitten, twice shy' came to mind.

The next six weeks I lived aboard the land-bound yacht, working daily: logging measurements, marking the anchor cable in ten-metre lengths, setting the sails and getting familiar with the reefing system. Time was also spent carrying out all the other little but important details to make her ready for the coastal voyage to her new home.

A very important detail that I was glad I looked for whilst stretching the anchor cable along the quay to check it, was to make sure that the bitter end of the chain could be freed quickly in an emergency. As things turned out the shackle at the end of the anchor cable that was secured in the chain locker was seized with rust and was too big to pass through the chain-pipe in an emergency. With an anchor fouled on the sea bed and a fast-rising tide, too short an anchor cable that's jammed in a chain-pipe is of course a situation best avoided. To prevent this happening on *Mykon* I discarded the shackle from the end of the anchor cable that went into the chain locker and instead rove off a length of nylon lanyard through the end link. The other end of the lanyard was made fast to the eye-bolt in the chain locker. This lanyard was made long enough to allow *all* the anchor chain to travel through the chain-pipe and be accessible on deck. As the anchor chain was only ninety feet long, I would often bend on to it a two-hundred-foot warp. I would then attach to the warp a short length of chain to run through the bow roller. When sailing single-handed I would prepare to drop the hook in plenty of time before coming up to the chosen anchorage. If the water was over thirty feet deep I would flake out all the anchor chain on deck and bend on the warp. The warp was then stowed hand-over-hand to fall as it would into a bucket: this allowed the warp to run freely without fouling. The free end of the warp was then made fast to the Samson post, just in case. I would never forgive myself if I had to watch the shipboard end of the anchor warp disappear below the surface.

With all the preparations finished, the 3rd of July 2004 saw the mobile yacht cradle lower *Mykon* into the water. My pal Dave had arrived and we spent the afternoon working out a sailing plan for leaving the Blackwater River and the first leg of the passage to Brighton. The general plan was to call at Brighton, Falmouth, Fishguard and then the home waters of Caernarfon. Everything being subject to the weather conditions, of course. It was whilst we were engrossed in looking at tide times and plotting distances from the chart of the Thames estuary that a loud rap came on the cabin top: "Happy Birthday, Trevor!" There on the pontoon stood father and son, the previous owners of *Mykon*. "Enjoy this," I heard as I reached for a totally unexpected sixty-fourth birthday present – a bottle of whisky. (Janet had devised the surprise.)

The next day we made ready to leave the marina, and as it was not high water until 13:58 we could do this at a leisurely pace. As I was not familiar with the turning circle of this long-keeled yacht it was decided that we throw a line to the opposite pontoon and pull *Mykon* clear of her berth.

With plenty of time to spare, we walked over to have a yarn with a fellow yachtsman who we had noticed was flying a huge Stars and Stripes flag from the masthead. He had been celebrating early, it seemed, as he raised a glass and proudly declared, "God Bless America". If the sailing weather had not been so perfect we would have stayed in port and gladly taken up the invitation to join the American's one-man party. But 'time and tide ...' so at 14:00 we cast off the mooring lines and headed out of the harbour.

On entering the river we set the main and number one jib. It was a fair wind from the northwest, about force four, ideal to lay the southeasterly course for the Knoll buoy that marked the estuary. Off the starboard quarter a dazzling sun hung against a blue backdrop dotted with fair-weather clouds, adding to this champagne sailing. As I looked astern with hands cupped around my eyes against the sun, there appeared heading towards us a beautiful Thames sailing barge, her huge tan sails powerfully pushing her through the water at about ten knots. The stern chase did not last for very long, and as she overhauled us I could clearly see the mast hoops on the mainsail luff and the massive sprit that held the mainsail. The barge skipper waved to us as he bore away to show us a clean pair of heels. I was glad that our engine had been put to bed as it would have spoilt the moment.

Thames Sailing Barge.
Usually built of wood and eighty to ninety feet in length with a beam of about twenty feet. At the turn of the twentieth century over two thousand were on the register.
Picture: Trevor Wilson collection.

The sandbanks that straddle the Thames estuary looked like the fingers of a giant's hand lying flat upon the chart. Each 'finger' at low water either dried out or had less than a metre of depth. There is a passage through the labyrinth of banks, but local knowledge would be needed to navigate the channels and gullies safely. Not having that local knowledge myself, I decided to clear the banks by steering to the north of them. This involved first steering the opposite course from our destination. Giving the sandbanks a wide berth meant an extra twenty-five miles would be added to the passage, but better that than running aground.

Those Thames sailing barge skippers used to deliberately take the ground on these banks in good weather, and a cargo of sand and gravel or mud would be loaded, to be sold to the building and brick-making industry. (Incidentally, the last Thames barge to trade entirely under sail was the *Cambria*, built in 1969 and for the next twenty years sailed by her owner, Captain A.W. 'Bob' Roberts.)

With the banks cleared in the night, 06:45 the next morning found us abeam of the East Goodwin Light and heading through the Straits of Dover. Many times over the years I have sailed in these narrow waters but never before in a yacht. Ships of every description from all over the world converge in these Straits. I felt like a mouse dodging a cat as I kept altering course to avoid those commercial giants whose sole purpose in life it seemed was to run us down. As these manoeuvres were going on, Dave's head popped up out of the hatch and, handing over a hot dog, he said: "Watch out for the trains – we are sailing over the Channel Tunnel!"

The next morning Brighton lay twenty miles to our west. I had steered close inshore, mainly to keep out of the commercial shipping lanes. This proved to be too close, for we encountered a foul-going tide race off Beachy Head. Our speed through the water was five knots, and after taking several bearings on the Beachy Head lighthouse it was evident that we were not moving over the ground. The solution was to steer further offshore. At 13:00 the entrance to Brighton Marina lay a hundred yards ahead. Dousing the sails I began to prepare for our docking. Not being too familiar with the engine controls or engine I decided to have a practice run before entering the dock. Dave knew even less than me about engines so I thought it best I share what little knowledge I had with him. The saying,

'In the land of the blind the man with one eye is king' did come to mind. (You may remember I said this to another Dave, my deck boy pal on *M.V. Cretic.*) The engine was just ticking over as I went to demonstrate how to put it into driving gear and increase the revs.

The propeller duly started turning and slowly I pushed the throttle lever to full revs. This was followed by a clonking noise coming from the engine controls. I was not unduly concerned about this noise until I found that the control lever had jammed in the full revs position. This was all we needed: a yacht charging around at full speed with an unstoppable engine. With Dave steering the yacht in circles I began desperately to pull on the control linkage until by luck the revs were greatly reduced, although the engine remained jammed in gear and pushing the yacht at two knots. Towing a small sea anchor from the stern reduced this speed to one knot. We headed like this into the marina, with several people on the shore pointing to the strange object that appeared to be following us. Coming alongside a berth that was well clear of any other craft, Dave stepped ashore with two mooring lines and the maverick engine was turned off.

It was the next day that a marine engineer came aboard and after a brief inspection decided that a new engine control lever was needed and that it would take a couple of days for him to obtain one. This suited us fine as the weather had suddenly turned terrible, with heavy rain being driven by winds of fifty knots. A deep depression had swept up from the Spanish coast. The local radio gave out bulletins about the devastation the storm was causing. During the night a drilling platform anchored off the Kent coast broke its moorings and was washed ashore as the weather front hit Southern England. Trees were uprooted. The storm had also battered Brighton's West Pier so badly that it caused a restoration plan to be finally abandoned. A barge anchored off Foreness Point was sunk, and a stranded German yacht off the Norfolk coast was towed to safety by the Cromer and Caister Lifeboat ... the list went on and on. All of these reports made us appreciate even more the sanctuary of this harbour – although I was concerned at the speed with which the weather had suddenly changed. The last forecast we had heard, according to the log book, had been for northeasterly winds force five to six.

'All's well that ends well' is my motto, and by Friday 9th July 2004 the storm was well past. So with the new engine control lever installed we chugged out of the harbour. Once clear of the breakwater we were met by a westerly wind about force three to four. Setting the main and jib we began tacking for Falmouth, which was 193 nautical miles to the west. We first came onto the starboard tack, sailing as close to the wind as possible and hoping that the wind held, a course that would bring us to the Cherbourg Peninsula was laid. Setting the self-steering gear was a pleasure, as it meant being free from constantly looking at the compass and being stuck to the tiller. There have been times in bad weather, and before I could afford a wind self-steering system, when I had been hand-steering continuously for over thirty hours. With this new mechanical crew member I always made the yacht steer herself as soon as it was practical. Hour after hour the wind vane nodded this way and that, constantly correcting the course without complaint. Before the novelty of the self-steering wore off I would feel quite guilty about leaving it to steer without a relief, and wondered if it wanted a cup of tea or something.

We resumed the watch-keeping duties, which were two hours on and two hours off. The stand-by man usually did the cooking and kept the watchman supplied with hot drinks. On that Friday afternoon Dave, who was in charge of the cooking, put a pan of water on the stove to boil. This was in readiness for the mackerel to be caught when the fishing lure was towed. In the month of July the waters around the coast were teeming with shoals of hungry mackerel and it was rare to have to wait more than a few minutes before they had been hooked on the silver lure. We had a strict rule to only catch the amount of fish that we could eat at one meal and not to needlessly kill them. The mackerel would be gutted, washed in the sea and plunged into the boiling pot for about five minutes. It would be difficult to taste a fresher fish, and with a dash of vinegar it made a meal that was absolutely delicious and never to be found ashore.

The next day found us a few miles to the north of the Cherbourg Peninsula. The wind was holding from the west and Alderney in the Channel Islands lay ahead. Time to bring *Mykon* about to the port tack on the next leg to Falmouth. After we were sailing on the new tack I reset the self-steering vane and went below to work out the e.t.a.

Before I had time to begin any chart work I was stopped in my tracks by the flogging sound of the foresail as we had luffed up into the wind. The self-steering control paddle had snapped off and hung useless in the water on the end of its lanyard. Heaving the paddle on board I found that the aluminium casting that formed one part of the hinged joint that enabled the paddle to be lifted clear of the water had fractured. The old faithful and reliable lengths of shock-cord sufficed as a substitute for the broken self-steering, and after fiddling about with different tensions a reasonable course was held. If the wind had been abaft the beam the shock-cord would not have coped and it would have been hand-steering.

As I sat in the cockpit on my watch I had time to reflect and compare the cheap piece of elastic with the brand new top-of-the-range self-steering unit that I had paid over £2300 for and whose work it had now taken over. After telling myself that worse things can happen at sea, I tried to shake off the feeling of disappointment and promised myself it would be sorted in Falmouth, which lay ninety-five nautical miles to north of west of us.

As night fell so did the wind, until I had to start the engine – which in itself made the steering shock-cord redundant. The vane self-steering, even if it had been working, would also have been out of work. Oddly enough I felt slightly better now.

20:15 on Monday 12th July 2004 saw *Mykon* tying up alongside a pontoon in Falmouth Harbour. After spending the last three and a half days on passage we both agreed that the next port of call should be the alehouse. Outside the docks we walked along a narrow cobbled street lined with old-fashioned houses, some with overhanging top storeys that jutted outwards at different angles. If Long John Silver had suddenly appeared, complete with peg-leg and parrot, he would not have looked out of place on this quaint and unspoilt waterfront. The nearby pub we called into, appropriately named the 'Chainlocker', with its original creaky wooden floors and huge wooden beams supporting low ceilings, had mercifully been left untouched by modern design 'experts'.

I tried to imagine whose footsteps must have walked on those pitch-pine floors over the centuries. If only walls could speak. It was the eight-gun topsail schooner HMS *Pickle* that in 1805 arrived in Falmouth bringing news of Nelson's death at the Battle of Trafalgar. Her crew may well have supped in this very tavern. The pub this night, however, was filled with the noisy, friendly chatter of folk who were glad to be on dry land, and to have a chance to speak to another human being that was not a crew mate. However well you get on together on board, I think it's good to listen to a different voice for a change. I am sure seafaring makes people – myself included – appreciate being on the land more. Not having to worry about the weather or tidal streams for a while, and swapping yarns over a pint all made that first venture ashore at Falmouth well worthwhile. To the accompaniment of "Time Gentlemen Please!" which the pub landlord must have bellowed umpteen times, we finally made our way with the rest of the crowd into the now lamp-lit cobbled street.

Wishing our new-found friends goodnight we headed back to *Mykon*. I could hardly keep awake. It was in that mood of contentment that my head touched the pillow and I went out like the proverbial light.

Early the next morning, and with all the signs of the weather set fair, I sat bleary-eyed in the cockpit, drinking a cup of tea. It was whilst sitting there and quietly watching the world begin to stir that I was rewarded with an unexpected and magnificent sight. A fleet of twenty or so Dragon class yachts were leaving the harbour under sail. These beautiful engineless yachts moved through the water in unison with the grace of swans. Popping my head into the hatchway I told Dave (who was busy cooking breakfast) about the rare sight that I was witnessing. Hurrying into the cockpit, Dave stood gazing in amazement at the sight. Just as I was thinking nothing could add to this perfect start of the day, the waft of frying bacon came drifting out of the cabin.

I was going to be busy that day so I appreciated the good start I'd had. My main task that day was to begin to find a way to make good the broken self-steering gear. The start of resolving the problem came about after I had phoned Denmark, where the makers were situated. I was informed that only a mile away from the docks was an agency and workshop that specialised in that make. This was their sole agency in the U.K., which made being in Falmouth better still. It was nearly a week later that, good to her word, the agent who with her husband ran the self-steering unit workshop arrived on the jetty where *Mykon* lay. In one hand she joyously held aloft the new replacement part that had just been flown in from Denmark, and her other hand was holding onto her toddler son. After inviting them on board Dave put the kettle on and fished out the most respectable teacup we had for our guest. A cup I joked that least resembled having been used to bail out the bilges. Her toddler son was content with tackling a banana whilst at the same time exploring the cabin. It was during this happy gathering that I learnt that the hinged facility on this self-steering unit was not recommended for yachts going deep sea.

A substitute for the hinged joint on the self-steering was a heavy-duty aluminium sleeve, which was manufactured for the very purpose and was more reliable. I decided to have the hingeless version of the steering paddle – although it meant the paddle could not be lifted clear of the water, it was less likely to snap off.

The next day was Tuesday 20th July 2004 and *Mykon* was ready for the next leg of her voyage. A fresh southwesterly breeze was blowing outside the harbour so we hanked the number two jib to one of the twin forestays and put a single reef in the mainsail in readiness for the head-wind that we would meet when out of the protection of the breakwater.

Over the week we had made friends with John and Penny, a local couple whose yacht was berthed nearby. It was they who wished us fair winds and a safe voyage as our mooring lines were being taken in. The fresh southwesterly wind that had headed us and kept us busy as we tacked out of the Falmouth Bay faded away to nothing as we reached the open sea. Reluctantly we started the engine and stopped it after two hours when the wind came back. This engine stop-start routine carried on until we rounded Lizard Point and the wind sprang up from the west. With the self-steering gear now back in service the watchkeeper would now have only to concentrate on sail trimming, keeping a lookout and calling for cups of tea.

Our position the next day, twenty hours after the leaving of Falmouth, was five nautical miles to the north of our old friend the Wolf Rock. The Wolf Rock brings to mind an incident that happened to me one winter's night over thirty years ago. I was one of the crew on passage from Cork to Rotterdam aboard a small coasting oil tanker. The beam of the Wolf Rock awoke me from my bunk as it shone through my cabin porthole. Scrambling from my bunk I rushed up to the wheelhouse. There, dead ahead, white breakers could be seen pounding on the Wolf Rocks that lay less than five hundred yards away. Grabbing the wheel from the deck boy I swung it hard to starboard. The second mate (who had been fast asleep on the chart room table) came rushing into the wheelhouse shouting, "I wasn't asleep! I wasn't asleep!" The lighthouse and rocks could be clearly seen through the darkness as they swept past our portside. Ronnie the deck boy, who had been on the wheel when this near-miss happened, had never been to sea before and had only worked on the Liverpool landing stage tying up the ferry boats. The poor lad had steadfastly held the course he had been given five hours earlier.

More than thirty years on, as the Wolf Rock came on our quarter, a northerly course was struck for St David's Head on the coast of Pembrokeshire in Wales.

Psychological, of course, but now that *Mykon* was on the opposite side of the coast to that of Bradwell, I felt that we were homeward-bound and had that happy feeling. On the merchant ships we called that sense of being nearly home 'The Channels'. The wind's strength had now fallen to force three and backed to the south, so we were now running free. I decided to try out the cruising chute, one of the many sails that came with *Mykon's* wardrobe. These spinnaker-like sails are cut so they can be set without a pole to boom them outboard. Handy when single-handed. The only drawback about running free was that the self-steering could not maintain the course, so it was hand-steering. A small price to pay for the extra two knots we now gained, which would push us clear of the shipping that had converged on the Bristol Channel.

It was during that night's sailing that all the electrics decided to pack in. A powerful torch was always kept handy in the cockpit so I was not unduly worried about not having navigation lights. I think it is important to carry a back-up for all electrically operated units where possible. As I have mentioned, an old-fashioned sounding lead and a Dutchman's Log to calculate the ship's speed through the water are just two of the reliable items I never sail without. Now that the

L.E.D. readout log and echo sounder were out of action it was a comforting thought not to have been solely dependent on them. And of course there was the starting handle for the engine. So it was we sailed through the darkness accompanied by that lovely tune on the radio that precedes the B.B.C. inshore shipping forecast at about one o'clock in the morning, the tune appropriately called 'Sailing Bye'.

Before the daylight reappeared the beacon light of the Smalls Lighthouse, which marks a cluster of rocks off St David's Head, Wales, popped up fine on the starboard bow. It was in the Smalls Lighthouse that in 1801 a tragic event happened when one of the two keepers died. The surviving keeper, fearing he might be accused of murder, did not commit the body to the deep. Instead he put it in a box that he made from some of the woodwork in the lighthouse. This box he then lashed to the lantern rail and awaited the usual relief boat to arrive that would succour the distressed survivor. After this incident it was decreed that three keepers should be appointed to every lighthouse.

With the sun climbing above the horizon *Mykon* passed the Smalls. The wind was holding steady from the south and the lighthouse disappeared below the horizon. By noon a ninety-degree course change to the east as we headed for Fishguard meant that the cruising chute that had been pulling like a workhorse throughout the night was now redundant. With the wind now on our starboard beam (a soldier's wind) the self-steering took over and gave us a blessed relief from hours on the tiller. The sun was shining, we had a fair wind, Fishguard lay only a few miles ahead ... what else could complete such a happy end to the second leg? Just as I was thinking 'nothing' the electronic readout on the instruments lit up. Had the warmth of the sun dried out a vital connection? I did not know. Whatever caused the electrical restoration was then a mystery to me, but as I pressed the start button the little diesel engine sprang to life and we chugged into the protection of the Fishguard harbour.

Fishguard is a busy ferry port for the Stena Line that runs to Rosslare in County Wexford in Southern Ireland. To the south of the harbour, in a tiny inlet, several yachts and small craft lay bobbing up and down on a trot of buoys. The chart informed us that this area dried out at about low water, which was not suitable for *Mykon* with her long keel.

It was whilst chugging around the harbour looking for a safe place to moor, clear of the ferries, that a familiar put-put sound of the old faithful Seagull two-stroke outboard motor was heard. Looking astern we spotted a man in a small dinghy making his way across the dock. He would know where we could berth, so pushing the tiller hard down we gave chase. After a few minutes of the dinghy altering course in an effort to avoid us the man realised we only wished to communicate with him and not run him down. Coming up to the dinghy I put the yacht's engine out of gear and the man switched off his put-putting outboard motor. Before I had a chance to speak, the friendly middle-aged man with a weather-beaten face and a sun-faded fisherman's smock wished us good day and asked how he could help. Pointing to a Stena Line ferry that was berthed against one of the harbour walls he informed us that we too could tie up along that wall, provided of course we kept well clear of the commercial traffic. "I'll come over to help you in a minute or two to give you a hand with the mooring lines, there's quite a big rise and fall here," he casually said before deftly tugging on the starting cord of the little Seagull engine and put-putting away.

Whilst Dave hung on to the steel ladder that was recessed into the harbour wall and held *Mykon* steady, I climbed the ten feet or so up on to the quay with two mooring lines in hand. Good to his word, the man who had been in the dinghy reappeared and took hold of the mooring back-springs and ran them along the quay. To help further he pointed out two discarded heavy-duty snatch blocks lying on the quayside, once used by the local commercial fishermen. These heavy snatch blocks were ideal to lower along the mooring lines, keeping the tension on them as the tide rose and fell. These weights are called 'angels'.

Stuart was the name of the helpful Good Samaritan, and we learnt that he was a member of the crew of the Fishguard R.N.L.I. lifeboat. Housed on top of the slipway was the lifeboat; she had been purchased entirely with funding by the young viewers of 'Blue Peter'. The Lifeboat was appropriately called *Blue Peter V11*. Still continuing his help by pointing out a nearby freshwater tap, Stuart, who was now ready to drive home, offered to give us a lift into town, which was about a mile away.

On reaching the town centre we both thanked the kind stranger for his help. Stepping out of the car we were greeted by the lovely aroma of fish and chips wafting through the air. Sitting on a nearby wooden bench we both enjoyed a simple paper-wrapped supper that we had just bought from the chippie. After the three days that it had taken us to reach here from Falmouth this meal seemed to taste better with the thought of not having had to cook it or wash any dishes afterwards. And what better way to round off the evening on our brief run ashore than to call in at the local pub for a chat and a pint or two?

Walking the mile or so back to where *Mykon* lay berthed was a welcome change from the naturally restricted space of a yacht.

The sun had just dipped below the horizon by the time we climbed back down the ladder to our little floating planet. Switching on the cabin light just long enough so I could find a box of matches, I lit the oil lamp to save the battery power. Dave opened two cans of ale from the pack we had just bought and we sat yarning about the different merchant ships we had sailed on. It's not unusual for some folk, after having a few drinks, to sing. Dave doesn't: he produces a battered harmonica and gives out a tuneless rendition of songs that probably would have been heard during World War Two. To the reedy sound of 'It's a Long Way to Tipperary' I pulled the hood of my sleeping bag over my head and slept soundly until 05:30 the next morning.

It was just after 05:30 that the BBC gave out the shipping forecast, and as we intended to sail that day on the last leg to Caernarfon, I didn't want to miss this all-important information. Poking one arm out of my sleeping bag I fumbled about to put a stop to the tin alarm clock that was rattling merrily away on the chart table. The forecast given for the Irish Sea that day was west to southwest three to four, becoming five to six occasionally, seven in the north. Strong southwesterly winds at the Caernarfon Bar would have made it untenable for a small yacht to cross in safety. I decided therefore that Holyhead on the western coast of Anglesey, with its deep approach channel, would be the next port of call. Dave was standing over the stove quietly making a pot of tea, his harmonica sticking mercifully silent out of his shirt pocket. When the tea had brewed we both sat in the cockpit and watched life begin to stir across the harbour. It was as we sat there in silence drinking our tea that a shrill whistle 'chi-keeeee' filled the air. To our amazement, there on the stern mooring rope, only six feet away, was perched a small, plump, colourful bird with a disproportionately large head and long dagger-like bill. It was a kingfisher with beautiful iridescent electric-blue plumage on its crown and wings, and orange-red on its breast. Not daring to stir or make a sound lest we frighten away our colourful visitor, we looked on at the wonderful once-in-a-lifetime sight that we had been privileged to witness. After a few minutes the kingfisher disappeared into a hole in the side of the harbour wall. I had always thought these birds lived near fresh water – wrong again!

Kingfisher.

With the tea finished and our feathered friend gone it was time to think of the last-minute things needed before we sailed away. Fresh bread, milk, eggs, bacon, orange juice were jotted onto a list. The local shops had closed by the time we had reached town yesterday evening, so I was delegated to walk into town and collect these perishable items whilst Dave filled the fresh water containers from the lone tap on the quay.

Walking past the now empty berth that the Stena Line ferry had occupied the night before explained *Mykon* rolling about in the early hours when the ferry had moved away from the quay and sailed for Rosslare.

It was nearly two hours later that I returned with the bag of shopping, as I spent some time sitting on a bench in town reading the morning paper. After reading about all the seemingly out-of-control fighting and turmoil that was going on all over the world, I was thankful that I could return to a relatively simple world aboard *Mykon*.

Author returns with the shopping. *Mykon* at Fishguard, 24th July 2004.
Photo: Trevor Wilson.

Whilst I prepared the yacht for sailing, Dave started to fry eggs and bacon. These fried breakfasts were out of the question at sea, so we regarded them as a bit of a rare luxury. A suitable situation really, as this kind of diet is not high up the list on the healthy eating chart. It was whilst eating our late breakfast that a Stena Line ferry docked, dwarfing *Mykon*. A couple of hours later, at about 11:30, the same ferry headed out to sea with *Mykon* following as a duckling would follow its mother.

Once clear of the protective mole, we were met with a west-southwesterly wind about force four, ideal for our course towards Holyhead, which was eighty-six nautical miles northwards. Bringing *Mykon*'s head into the wind I set the main and the Genoa that I had hanked to the forestay (whilst Dave had been cooking the breakfast) and laid a course that would bring Bardsey Island off the starboard bow. The engine was doused. Now there was only the sound of the hull cutting through the water as *Mykon*, heeling gently, lifted up her skirts and ran for home.

It was not long before a school of dolphins joined in the race and frolicked and played all around the yacht. Racing ahead then turning on the proverbial sixpence and then racing back again. Although we were sailing at a respectable 6.1 knots through the water we were no match of course for the dolphins that could easily have doubled our speed. Any previous thoughts we had about catching a mackerel or two for dinner were put aside just in case we accidentally snagged one of our waterborne playgroup. What would be wrong with beans and sausages anyway?

Dolphins playing around *Mykon* in Cardigan Bay.
Photo: Trevor Wilson.

The wind, which had held steady from the west-southwest, by evening had started to veer to the west and gradually increase to force five. Not wishing to be shortening sail in the dark I changed the Genoa for a number two jib and put a reef in the main whilst we still had daylight. We could always shake it out if the wind fell. After altering course to bring the yacht's head a few more degrees to port to allow for the extra leeway caused by the wind shift, I said goodnight to Dave; *and* to the dolphins that were still playing their chase game.

It was nearly midnight when I stirred from my sleeping bag. I'd been nearly four hours off watch. It was not like Dave to let me sleep in. Climbing into the deserted cockpit I could just make out the shape of Dave in the darkness lying on the foredeck, looking over the side at the dolphins. The darting black silhouettes of these graceful sea mammals now contrasted with the brilliance of the luminous phosphorescent streaks that cascaded from their backs as they arched out of the wave tops.

The Bardsey Island lighthouse was also shining to starboard, giving out an identifying group flash five every fifteen seconds. With forty miles to Holyhead, at this rate we should be there at 08:00 in the morning. By the time Bardsey Island was abeam the wind had other ideas and fell light, and the dolphins swam off. The shipping forecast still gave winds of six to seven from the west so I left the reef in the main and started the engine. Chugging away into the night and with little wind, I was thankful that I had given Bardsey Island a wide berth. There are treacherous currents that sweep around its coast. Bardsey was the name given by the Norsemen – Ynys Enlli is the true Welsh name, which means appropriately 'island of the great current'.

The wind did eventually come back and at 11:45 we tied up at Holyhead. We had sailed a total of 901 nautical miles from Bradwell-on-Sea and it had taken twenty-one days.

Chapter 16

Three days after docking at Holyhead it was Wednesday 28th July 2004, and the strong southwesterly winds had blown themselves out and shifted to the northwest. An ideal wind to sail *Mykon* around to her new home port of Caernarfon, which lies on the banks of the Menai Straits; about eighteen nautical miles away. Dave had by this time returned home to where his own yacht was moored on the River Mersey. My new crew member was my wife Janet, whom I persuaded after much coaxing ('press-ganged' – her words) to enjoy a pleasant sail around to Caernarfon. The winds held fair and the sea calm. The next day found *Mykon* moored in the Victoria Dock, Caernarfon, and Janet once again hurrying for dry land and vowing 'never again'.

The long list of yacht modifications and improvements that would be needed to prepare for the Atlantic crossing was headed by 'avoid the need to hank sails to the twin forestays by installing a roller reefing system'. It was this reefing system that I decided to have fitted at Caernarfon and try out on the Isle of Man run. In the month of October the sailing season in these northern waters is coming to an end. I would have to look lively to prepare the yacht if the planned single-handed run to the Isle of Man was to happen before the bad weather set in. The local yacht riggers and sailmakers are kept fairly busy all the year round, but during the sailing season the demand for sail and rigging repairs peaks. By the middle of August the riggers measured *Mykon*'s mast for the roller reefing system and the sailmaker began cutting a new foresail.

The total cost of the modifications to *Mykon* and equipment that I would need were going to be almost as much as I'd paid for the yacht. This had been taken into account in a deliberate budgeting plan that I had devised when seeking out a suitable vessel for an Atlantic crossing. The reasoning was: if I could buy a yacht for roughly half of the insurance money received for the loss of *Bowden*, the remainder could be used to make good the long list of preparations and new equipment that would be needed.

On the *Bowden* I had a top quality roller reefing system fitted – a Furlex – which never once failed and got me safely back home. 'Proof of the pudding' as the saying goes, so that was the one I ordered for *Mykon*. Having the roller reefing system fitted meant sailing along the Menai Straits to the tiny harbour of Port Dinorwic where the riggers had their workshop and the use of a waterside crane. Port Dinorwic lies about three nautical miles to the northeast of Caernarfon. It was on a swinging mooring trot just outside the Port Dinorwic lock gates that I had secured a place for *Mykon*; handy, as it turned out, for the rigging shop. These swinging moorings have to be vacated towards the end of October before the winter bad weather sets in, when a more sheltered berth has to be found.

On Saturday 24th August 2004, however, the summer was still with us and *Mykon* entered the harbour lock gates. The arrangement had been for the riggers to begin work on fitting the roller reefing at the start of the Monday after the weekend. Having the yacht moored outside their workshop in readiness seemed to make sense. After flooding the lock chamber, the harbour master opened the inner gate and waved us through. The road bridge spanning the harbour swung open and *Mykon*, with engine quietly chugging away, headed for the vacant berth under the jib of the dockside crane. Leaving *Mykon* securely moored to the dock wall, and with all the fenders that I could gather hanging over the side, I headed for home.

The next few days, I promised myself, would be spent with Janet and walking along the lanes and grassy bridleways that criss-cross the beautiful Welsh mountain landscape where our tiny cottage lies. There would be times when I was on the ocean and far from land that I would long for the sight of a tree or a meadow. On board *Mykon* I had attached to the bulkhead above the chart table an ear of corn picked from a field in Bradwell-on-Sea. Several coats of clear varnish ensured that this simple souvenir of terra firma did not fall to pieces. I have noticed on many yachts that a framed picture – usually of a seascape – adorns the cabin bulkhead. Each to their own, but the last thing I want to look at whilst at sea is a picture of it, when all around you can see the real thing. Absence makes the heart grow fonder, I think, for I seem to appreciate more not just absent friends but the sights and sounds of the land.

The sound of a telephone ringing doesn't necessarily come into my list of favourite sounds, but a phone call from the riggers informed me that the roller reefing gear, complete with the new foresail, had now been installed. I had timed the drive back to the dock where *Mykon* lay so I would reach there in the correct time slot, as the lock gates of the harbour could only be opened an hour or so either side of high water.

With the all-clear message from the harbour master I cast off the mooring lines from *Mykon*. Heading towards the swing bridge that had started moving to its opened position, temporarily stranding a small group of people on either side of the harbour wall, I increased the engine revs. Fifty yards before reaching the swing bridge the water was suddenly clouded with debris and black ooze as the yacht's keel became stuck on an underwater mud bank. At full revs, the propeller turning first ahead and then astern, I tried to free the entrapped keel, but it was hopeless. The only outcome from the wild thrashing of the water was to bring more particles of mud and waterlogged twigs and leaves from the bottom of the harbour. To make matters worse the temperature gauge started to rise at an alarming rate, indicating that the cooling system was being clogged as the polluted water was being drawn into the engine. Switching off the engine, hoping it would cool down enough so that I could reach my mooring, I threw a rope to the harbourmaster who was now standing on the quayside. The group of people who had been patiently waiting for the swing bridge to close came hurrying to help. After making fast my end of the tow-rope to the Samson post, the harbourmaster with four helpers who would have been a credit to a tug o'war team dragged *Mykon* clear of the mudbank.

Restarting the engine, I headed past the bridge and entered the locks, where I stopped the engine once again as I waited for the water levels of the locks and Menai Straits to coincide. After reaching the mooring, which was mercifully only a few minutes of engine running-time away, I set about unblocking the cooling system. Four hours later, after I had renewed the engine cooling water filter and dismantled and flushed clean the piping of mud and bits of twig, the temperature gauge read normal. Later I learnt that the lock gates to the harbour were in need of repair and water was leeching out at such a rate that some yachts inside the marina would take the ground at certain times of the tides.

It was on 2nd September 2004, four days after the new roller reefing had been fitted, that Janet donned sea boots and lifejacket and made her way to the water's edge at the bottom of the Port Dinorwic slipway. We were sailing to the Isle of Man. I held the fibreglass yacht tender as steady as possible as Janet stepped tentatively aboard, and sitting down on the after thwart she held tightly onto the gunwales. Knowing Janet's fear of the water I had spent some time to explain to her in detail how the transfer from the dinghy to the yacht would be carried out, and tried to reassure her that everything would be alright. Sitting on the amidships thwart of the dinghy I took hold of the oars and, gently dipping the blades into the water, pulled away from the shore.

It was an idyllic setting as we glided through the green water, passing a vacant mooring buoy being used as a perch by a group of cormorants that gave out a chorus of indignant squawks as we passed by. The weather forecast had been good: winds of south by west force three had been predicted. As I rowed towards where *Mykon* lay moored I tried to ease any fear Janet had by reassuring her that there was simply nothing better than messing about in boats. I was beginning to sound like Ratty out of *Wind in the Willows* by Kenneth Grahame. Though from the expression on Janet's face, Mole was not convinced. The transfer from the dinghy to the yacht went smoothly, and whilst Janet made herself at home in the cabin and lit a cigarette to calm her nerves, I started to get things ready for sailing.

The timing for leaving the mooring is important, as a rock-strewn channel in the Menai Straits known as the Swellies has to be negotiated to reach the open sea. In the pilot book it advises that two hours before high water at Liverpool is the best time to navigate this passage. With the yacht's tender made fast to the mooring buoy I cast off the head rope, and *Mykon*, with tiller lashed slightly to port and engine turning the propeller at low revs, swung gently towards the Swellies. It was 10:50. (Incidentally, these precise times and details are obtained from the rough log books and letters that I would post home from time to time.) Breathing a sigh of relief after negotiating the Swellies, I unfurled the new foresail. The wind was on the quarter, making this an ideal time to try out the new roller reefing.

A few days before sailing I had bought an extra hand in the form of an electrically powered automatic steering arm that I would use when the engine was running and recharging the ship's battery. With the wind-filled foresail pulling us through the water, aided by the engine turning the propeller at half revs, and with a fair tide, we were making six knots over the ground. Some of the fairway buoys are a mile apart, which gave plenty of time for the tiller auto-steering arm to respond to the slight course changes required as we headed for the open sea. Janet, after convincing herself that the sole purpose of a yacht was not to drown its occupants, began to relax and climbed into the cockpit to watch the slowly changing scenery as we sailed along the beautiful Anglesey coastline.

At 13:20 we had reached the open sea, the engine was turned off and the electronic steering unit stowed away. With the foresail still drawing well I set the wind vane self-steering gear and left the mainsail lashed to the boom. Sailing under a single sail was in order to deliberately slow down the yacht's speed, to ensure that we did not arrive at Douglas (which was sixty nautical miles away) before daylight the next morning. Steering north-northwest at a gentle, unhurried speed of just over three knots, *Mykon* ploughed towards the Isle of Man, which was as yet out of sight below the horizon. Fair weather clouds that resembled a flock of sheep were dotted about the clear blue sky, and the warmth of the early autumn sun completed these perfect sailing conditions.

Perfect, that was, with the exception of a heavy groundswell that we met in the relatively shallow water near the land that we were sailing away from. Until we reached deeper water the groundswell caused the yacht to roll in an uncomfortable manner, and Janet, who until then was beginning to show signs of enjoying herself, became sea-sick.

Remembering the times as a deck-boy when I was sea-sick, and how lousy it made me feel, I asked Janet if she wanted to return home. Shaking her head from side to side, she reached for the cup of fresh milk that I had just poured for her and uttered, "I'll carry on." Thankfully, after two hours we reached the deeper water and the groundswell disappeared. Janet's sea-sickness gradually disappeared as well and she began to feel better after having a bowl of hot soup that I coaxed her to take.

By 19:30 the sun had gone to bed and so had Janet, who slept soundly until about midnight, when I heard her voice coming out of the darkness of the cabin asking, "Do I need to have a passport to fly home from the Isle of Man?" After reassuring her that she didn't need a passport I tried to change the subject by pointing out that a white light flashing every five seconds had popped up; the Chicken Rock.

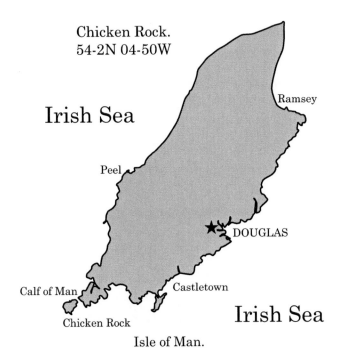

Chicken Rock.
54-2N 04-50W

Irish Sea

Ramsey

Peel

DOUGLAS

Calf of Man

Castletown

Chicken Rock

Irish Sea

Isle of Man.

The Chicken Rock Lighthouse lies at the southern tip of the Isle of Man. It always brings a smile to my face when I recollect an incident that happened to me just off Chicken Rock over forty years ago.

It was during daylight hours in the month of February that we were on passage from Carrickfergus in Northern Ireland to Avonmouth. I was on the wheel at the same time as a small coastal tanker called M.V. *Argosity* of 877 gross tonnage belonging to F. T. Everard & Son. A southeasterly gale had sprung up and was throwing the ship about like a cork (as we were in ballast), when the chief engineer stepped into the wheelhouse. The skipper, who had been looking out of the wheelhouse door with some concern at the east coast of the Isle of Man which was to our lee, turned to the engineer with a questioning look. "We'll have to stop the engine, one of the pistons is cracked."

"I can't – not with that lee shore!" the skipper yelled back, pointing to the coast that was becoming more obscure in the bad weather.

"Okay, but you will have no engine left in twenty minutes from now," the engineer answered back in a fairly matter of fact voice that seemed to be out of place considering the potential mess that we could be in.

"How long will it take then?"

"If all hands help I could have the piston taken off in an hour," the engineer told the skipper. With that the engine telegraph in the wheelhouse was moved to the 'Stop Engine' position.

After the ship had lost steerage way she fell into the trough of the heavy seas and began rolling violently. The rolling was so bad that Carlos our cook was thrown backwards out of the galley followed by a huge pan of rice that had been cooking on the stove. Carlos was a Greek Cypriot who, although usually good-natured and friendly with everyone, had a very short fuse and could be easily upset. Running into the wheelhouse, Carlos, who was now covered in boiled rice, began shouting like a man possessed at the skipper. "Look what you done to my good jersey I had for Christmas," and added in a ranting afterthought: "My girlfriend she knitted this for me!" Carlos was livid and, stripping off his rice-encrusted jersey, threw it wildly at the skipper. The jersey missed its intended target and hit me in the face before wrapping itself around my head.

Carlos ran out of the wheelhouse followed by the skipper's threats, that were carried away, unheard, by the wind.

It would have been like a scene from a comedy film if the situation that we found ourselves in had not been so bad. Out of the total of nine crew members, eight of us, including Carlos the cook, piled down into the engine room to help remove the damaged piston. The skipper remained on the bridge, keeping an eye on the lee shore that was then about three nautical miles away. Under the supervision of the chief engineer we rigged chain blocks to lift the broken piston clear of the crankshaft. The piston with its con-rod was about ten feet high, with a piston diameter of two feet or thereabouts, resembling a giant version of one that could be found in a car engine. The violent rolling of the ship hindered our efforts as we struggled with guy ropes to steady the swinging piston unit when the massive nuts that held it to the crankshaft were released. To make matters worse, every twenty minutes or so the skipper's urgent call could be heard from the voice pipe that linked the bridge with the engine room. "How long are you going to be?" he asked, as if his question would speed things along.

The skipper's question was followed by a report of the distance our powerless ship was being swept towards Chicken Rock. After one and a half hours the damaged piston had been removed and secured in a cradle that had been specifically designed for it. On hearing of this progress the skipper shouted down the voice pipe: "Okay chief, start her up!" You could almost hear the relief in his voice.

"I can't! Not until we list her to port, to bring one of the two pistons to top dead centre." Running up the steel ladder from the engine room I made my way with another A.B. to the starboard well deck, where we began to open the discharge valve that would allow hundreds of tons of water ballast to be transferred from the starboard tank to the portside tank, causing the ship to list to port. Even in ballast the freeboard of our ship was only about four feet in the well deck.

Whilst we waited for the list to develop, which seemed to take forever, we sheltered on the flying bridge from the seas that were sweeping across the decks. The ship was listing to an alarming angle of about forty-five degrees when above the noise of the gale we could hear the massive air compression units being opened in the engine room which began to push downwards the two remaining pistons. Silently willing the ship's engine to start, I closed the water ballast transfer valve to stop the ship listing further. A black cloud of diesel smoke came suddenly pouring out of the funnel to be swept horizontally away by the wind. Two muffled bangs followed as the ship's engine roared to life. We were underway again! The skipper, who was on the wheel, turned the ship's head into the wind, affording shelter to us as we re-trimmed the water ballast. The white tower of the Chicken Rock lighthouse, discoloured by a black tidemark, could clearly be seen about a mile off our starboard quarter, defiantly warding off each wave as they crashed against its stout base.

Much to the relief of everyone on board, the *Argosity*, now with its engine power reduced by a third, began with a tantalising slowness to pull away from the lee shore. We resumed normal watch-keeping duties and headed for Avonmouth, where a replacement engine piston was installed. Incidentally (this may be of interest for marine engineers), the make of the ship's engine was a Doxford, built in Sunderland.

Carlos the cook had quietened down by nightfall when I knocked on his cabin door and handed him his rice-covered woollen jersey. "I do not want it anymore, it spoiled now, always there will be rice in wool, you take it." I didn't mind a few grains of rice and I wore the jersey when on watch. (The predictions Carlos made, though, turned out to be true. Months later and after several washes I would not fail to find bits of rice embedded in the jersey's cable stitchwork.) *Argosity* progressed southward and the light of the Chicken Rock dipped out of sight.

Over forty years later aboard the *Mykon*, the sight of the Chicken Rock light appearing on the horizon brought some comfort to Janet, who was understandably feeling nervous in an environment that she considered alien. The sun would be rising about 06:30. I altered course slightly in order that the nearest point of land on the Isle of Man would be seen when daylight appeared, hoping this would make Janet dispense with any thoughts of passports and of flying home. By daylight Douglas Head lay ten nautical miles to the north. The features of the Isle of Man could be seen clearly now and resembled a giant green and gold patchwork quilt dotted with miniature white cottages that stood out in the early morning sun. The wind was still from the southwest force three, and we skirted along the coastline, standing about a mile off shore. With a fair wind and a flooding tide that was carrying us swiftly towards our destination, I decided to contact the Douglas harbourmaster for docking instructions. This was the very time that the onboard V.H.F. transmitting radio, that had been working okay until then, decided to pack in. This reinforced my belief that perhaps there was something true about Sod's Law after all. I was not unduly concerned, as I had sailed to Douglas many times before and knew that the harbourmaster's office was only a ten-minute walk from where we could berth for a while alongside the dock wall outside the marina.

Half a mile before we reached Douglas Head, the buoyed channel for the Douglas harbour began. I started to prepare for docking. The engine was fired up and the lone foresail, that with a fair wind had pulled *Mykon* sixty nautical miles to our present position, was furled in a twinkling of an eye. I never failed to appreciate the ease with which I could now reef or furl that foresail. As one by one I was making fast a row of fenders to either side of the yacht, Janet, whose spirits had suddenly been raised by the thought of being on dry land again, threw a fender towards where I stood on the side deck. Before I could catch the sausage-shaped missile the wind blew it into the water, followed by the cries of Janet: "Leave it, leave it!" After telling Janet not to lose sight of the fender that kept disappearing in the trough of the four-foot wavelets, I set about to retrieve it. Grabbing hold of the boathook and at the same time disengaging the electronic tiller steering unit, I took over the helm. After four futile attempts at circling the seemingly mocking floating sausage, I managed to twist the boathook around the fender's lanyard and haul it on board. Janet was furious that I had apparently wasted so much time on retrieving the fender until I pointed out that it could have been a man overboard.

The tide had not yet flooded the lock entrance to the marina by the time we arrived in the outer harbour. After spotting against the dock wall a conveniently berthed Customs Patrol launch I steered *Mykon* alongside her and tied up. Whilst Janet, happy now that she was surrounded by the sights and sounds of the land, set about cooking breakfast, I headed for the harbourmaster's office. After I had explained that our radio didn't work, the harbourmaster said that if the yacht was outside the lock gates at 12:45 he would let us in. The lock gates were duly opened and we headed towards the last barrier that would prevent us from reaching the marina: a massive lifting road bridge that had begun to open on our approach, quickly causing a tailback of road traffic. A uniformed marina official who was standing on one of the pontoons called out to us the identification number of the berth where we should dock, and after pointing to where it was located, met us there and helped us to tie up. "We have just sailed from Caernarfon!" Janet exclaimed proudly to our uniformed helper, who after a couple of seconds of silence replied: "There's main electrics available if you want to pay extra for it."

Over the years of sailing to Douglas I've met some interesting characters, and one of them is a black and white duck that lives in the harbour and spends most of its time scrounging food from visiting yachts. We have christened him the 'Douglas

Duck'. This duck would not be out of place in a Walt Disney cartoon, for after he has 'adopted' a yacht that feeds him he will chase away, regardless of size, any other duck or swan that dares to approach his floating pantry. If his quacking is ignored he will hop uninvited on board and have a root around the cabin for food. Although it had been over ten months since visiting Douglas aboard my pal's yacht *Elsue*, as I stepped onto the pontoon from *Mykon* the 'Douglas Duck' appeared and ran excitedly in circles around my feet, quacking loudly as if it was glad to see me again. Janet fell about laughing at his antics and this made up for the lack of the fanfare that I think she had expected on our arrival.

Paying a visit to *Elsue* 2003.
Photos: Trevor Wilson.

The Douglas Duck 2004.

We stayed at Douglas for five days, and during that time I had the chance to show Janet the lovely places on the island that she had heard about so many times. There is an old-fashioned 'Puffing Billy'-type steam train that runs on a narrow gauge track from Douglas to Port Erin in the south. We would catch this train, and from the swaying carriage window the unspoilt pasture and heath land was a sight to behold as we were trundled along the track on our mini journey. (The Isle of Man is only about thirty-three miles long and thirteen miles wide.) The long and urgent-sounding shrill of the train's steam whistle when a bend or level crossing was approached echoed to the sounds of a bygone era on the mainland.

The port of Ramsey on the northeast coast of the island was also one of the numerous places we visited, and it was there I came across a local works that specialised in the installation of maritime electrical equipment. The next day saw a brand-new V.H.F. transmitting radio installed on *Mykon*. Bill Bevan, the marine electrician who ran the Ramsey-based company, had installed the radio, and being aware that we must leave the island before the autumn gales set in, gave us priority by putting on hold the job he was doing at the time. A more conscientious tradesman I could not hope to find, a rare thing these days. I promised that I would return to Ramsey early the next summer, when I would engage his services for a complete renewal of the yacht's electrics and to install a Rutland 913 wind-powered generator.

The weather forecast was for a southwesterly wind four to five on the afternoon we let go the mooring lines and headed out of the harbour. All thoughts of passports and of flying home were now put aside by Janet as she lit a cigarette and waved farewell to the uniformed marina official who had been more interested in supplying electricity than in her epic voyage from Caernarfon. The autumn nights were starting to draw in. Three hours after sailing for home, darkness fell, and from our starboard quarter the beams of several lighthouses silently marked the now unseen island. The wind was as forecast, southwesterly four to five, until around midnight when it suddenly backed to the southeast, increasing to six as it did so.

This sudden wind shift caused the main to gybe and me to curse myself for not keeping my wits about me. Standing on the new tack, I deep-reefed the mainsail only to find it was still too much sail to carry in the wind that was now gusting to force seven. The mainsail was doused and under the shortened foresail only, we sailed through the night towards the Menai Strait. Two important weaknesses in the sailing rig had been revealed in that sudden blow. These weaknesses, that would be added to the winter's 'to do' list, were:

1) The roller reefing on the mainsail involved taking the sail slides out of the mast track, which was fiddly and time-consuming. I had this system replaced with single-line slab-reefing where the sail slides could be left remaining in the mast track when shortening sail.

2) An extra set of reef points to be sewn into the main in order to balance the sail area in strong winds. I was to be very thankful for this when on the Atlantic crossing.

Daylight found the southeasterly wind having eased to force three and *Mykon* riding to her anchor off Puffin Island, waiting for the floodtide. We had been on passage for almost twenty-four hours when we finally picked up our home mooring buoy at Port Dinorwic, and as the night was falling decided to stay aboard until the morning. When the kettle started to whistle merrily away on the stove I made two hot whisky toddies, and as we sat yarning in our oil-lamp-lit cabin I thought perhaps Janet could get used to this after all.

Chapter 17

The winter of 2004 found *Mykon* berthed in the shelter of the Victoria Dock at Caernarfon, where I set about carrying out all of the items on the 'to do' list that would be needed for the Atlantic crossing. Engineers, sailmakers, riggers, stainless steel suppliers, were all in turn contacted until, by the time I had to leave the dock in the spring, only two items remained unchecked on the list. The two items were the complete strip-out of the yacht's old electrical wiring and the installation of the Rutland 913 wind-powered generator.

At the end of April 2005 I sailed *Mykon* (alone this time) to Ramsey in the Isle of Man, where Bill Bevan's maritime electrical expertise allowed me to tick off the remaining items. It was the start of June before I could return to Port Dinorwic, owing to the bad weather that accompanied the series of lows that seemed to be endlessly sweeping across the Irish Sea.

Monday 11th July 2005 found *Mykon* at last ready to sail on the first leg of her transatlantic voyage to Norfolk, Virginia, where the *Erma* had sailed to all those years ago. Third time lucky? The past few weeks had been spent rowing out to *Mykon* with the rigid dinghy laden with ex-army kitbags that were full of food, plastic boxes containing charts, and the hundred and one other things I would need when away from the land. Two hundred litres of bottled drinking water, weighing as much as two heavy crew members, had been stowed whilst

Having electrics renewed at Ramsey, Isle of Man.
Photo: Trevor Wilson.

alongside the wall at Ramsey. The amount of drinking water I had been consuming, noted from previous times, was three and a half litres per day. In the flexible plastic main tank was a further forty litres of drinking water that I had dosed with purifying tablets.

Incidentally, when I ran out of these water purifying tablets I dosed the forty litres of water with one tablespoon of household bleach – a tip learnt from a fellow voyager. I'm still here, but as they say on TV, "Don't try this at home!"

As the food, water, stores and equipment were being stowed I would log into a notebook that I'd entitled 'Where is it?' the exact location of every item. This notebook saved lots of head-scratching and rooting around unnecessarily for something whose location you had once been certain you would not forget.

Besides having tinned food, plentiful supplies of pulses, lentils, peas, brown rice, sunflower seeds and dried apricots were included. A powdered mixture called Complan, which is rich in essential nutrients and only needs water stirred in to make an emergency meal, was placed in the grab bag. Although Complan has a pleasant enough taste I hoped that I would not have the need to sample it.

The weather forecast, of course, was the deciding factor for the day on which I would sail away. For the 11th July 2005, northwesterly winds force three to four were predicted, ideal for heading southwards. It was in the surreal atmosphere of that early morning time that I rowed the inflatable dinghy out to *Mykon*. There was not another soul about and only the sound of the oars dipping into the water disturbed the stillness of a world not yet awake. Climbing on board *Mykon* I lifted the rubber dinghy onto the foredeck. In order to have one thing less that could be swept over the side, I deflated the dinghy and stowed it below deck, in the forepeak.

The very act of stowing the dinghy like this brought home to me that I had now severed an umbilical tie with the shore. The thought of the unknown adventure that lay ahead only made me keener to set out.

However keen I was to leave, the start of the ebb tide at midday was the deciding factor. The morning was spent making cups of tea and making ready the self-steering gear, the sails, sorting out the Irish Sea charts, re-checking the G.P.S., making sure that the transmitting radio still worked, and every item that I could think of that would lead to a smooth departure.

At the turn of the tide and the start of the ebb *Mykon* swung around on the mooring buoy and into the northerly wind. With the mainsail set and swinging idly on its slackened sheet I let go the mooring and motored clear of the yachts that lay tethered nearby. With a wind of three to four on the starboard quarter the foresail was unfurled, the engine doused and we stood on towards the Caernarfon Bar and the open sea.

After all the months of preparation this was *it*.

Chapter 18

Along the Menai Straits we followed the channel buoys, and passing the control tower of the Victoria Dock at Caernarfon, I called out for a radio check. Mark, the dock master, who had obviously received my radio message, confirmed all was loud and clear, and wished me good luck. I promised that I'd bring a parrot back for him. Little did I realise at the time that I would be lucky to bring myself back.

After passing through the funnel-like gap at Abermenai Point at the estuary of the Menai Straits we followed the buoyed channel that led to the Caernarfon Bar. Once clear of the Bar I set the Aries self-steering, and with the wind still in the northwest, headed towards Southern Ireland and the Atlantic. Under full rig and with the foresail unfurled to the size of a Genoa, *Mykon* gracefully sailed through the water at five and a half knots, the land gradually disappearing in her wake. Before the land disappeared altogether and I lost the mobile phone signal I called home to Janet to let her know all was well, but even as I spoke the signal faded away and I lost contact. It was to be twenty-eight days later that the signal was recovered – in the Azores.

At the time of leaving Caernarfon I had not decided on a specific first port of call in the Azores group. I headed for the middle of the archipelago where, depending on the prevailing conditions at the time, I would make my final choice. The

169

sailing plan I had devised was to arrive in Norfolk, Virginia in nine months' time – in May 2005, before the hurricane season started. In the meantime I would follow the Mid-Atlantic Ridge that meandered down to the Saint Peter and Paul Rocks and beyond. That was the plan, and it meant I could visit ports that I had never been to when in the Merchant Navy.

On that first day of sailing we were clear of the Caernarfon Bay by the time the sun had dipped below the horizon. Off the starboard quarter the beam of the South Stack lighthouse swept its silent warning. The twinkling shore lights gradually faded away, leaving just a faint orange smudge on the skyline, and we were in the Irish Sea. Before settling down in the cockpit for my night-time lookout duties, I put on extra warm clothing: woollen jersey, sea-boot socks and hat. I find that in these coastal waters the nights always feel cold even during the summer. The experience I had on board *Bowden* when I had hyperthermia also probably concentrated my mind on keeping warm.

That night I also had to concentrate on the traffic that criss-crossed this busy stretch of water. A trawler that appeared ahead and was slowly dragging its nets over the seabed in a huge circular sweep really kept me on my toes – I kept altering course to avoid him as he seemed intent on scooping me up with the rest of his catch. With a sigh of relief, I saw the trawler's stern light hold steady until it was just a harmless white dot on the horizon. Time to put the kettle on, and in the luxury of an electric cabin light, now that the wind-powered generator was merrily whizzing away. After making a cup of hot Bovril I took it into the cockpit and sat in the shelter of the canvas spray hood. With my back resting on the cabin bulkhead and legs stretched out I watched the luminous phosphorescent wake that looked like the tail of a comet following *Mykon*. I found that gazing into the yacht's bubbling wake had a mildly hypnotic effect on my concentration – the same as you might experience when looking into the glowing coals of a fire in a hearth.

This would not do at all in these busy waters, so standing upright astride the cockpit side-benches, where I could see all around the horizon, I started singing so that I would not nod off. Singing? Probably a debatable term. One of the joys of single-handed sailing: there is no one to suffer my out-of-tune renditions, except the fish perhaps.

The sound of that lovely tune 'Sailing Bye' that precedes the B.B.C.'s inshore shipping forecast came floating out of the cabin and put a stop to my croaking. It was at 00:48 every morning that these forecasts were given out, and I would listen to them intently, hoping the word *gale* would not be mentioned too often. As things turned out the forecast for the next twenty-four hours for Tuesday 12th July 2005 was for favourable winds still from the northwest three to four. Through the darkness the silhouetted curvature of both sails could be seen drawing beautifully with the silent power that can only be found in a wind-driven vessel. The conditions were ideal, and heeling slightly to port *Mykon* sped through the night. At this rate we should be south of the Tuskar Rock, off the Irish coast, by the afternoon. I wanted to make as much westing as possible to avoid the unfavourable conditions usually found in the Bay of Biscay.

In making this westing I had of course to allow for the Rennell's Current that runs at a rate of one to one and a half knots northwards along the southeastern Irish coast. This current, incidentally, has its origins in the Bay of Biscay and sweeps up past the Isles of Scilly before heading along the St George's Channel.

It was James Rennell who first studied and recorded this current that bears his name. His final and most important work, *Currents of the Atlantic Ocean*, was published posthumously by his daughter Jane in 1832. He was married to Jane Thackeray, a great-aunt of the novelist. The nave in Westminster Abbey is his final resting place. Seamen of today the world over owe a debt of gratitude for the work of James Rennell, who was a pioneer of oceanography and lived from 1742 to 1830.

The allowance that I had made for this current was justified when, twenty-six hours after sailing from Caernarfon, the Tuskar Rock stood five nautical miles to the north.

I was now starting to feel in need of a good sleep, having, with the exception of a few cat-naps whilst in the cockpit, been awake all night on lookout duties. To make sure that these cat-naps did not last too long I copied a trick learnt from a fireman when I was working aboard a tramp ship. I would grasp in my hand a large spanner which would clatter to the deck if I nodded off too deeply. The waters that we were now in were not as busy as the Saint George's Channel that we had sailed through during the night. I decided to have a series of daytime one-hourly intervals of sleep in my bunk. If I am deprived of sleep for over thirty-six hours I find that I start to see things that are not there. (It happened on a coaster once when I was on the wheel one night and saw privet growing up the side of the binnacle.) After setting the alarm clock to go off in an hour and having one last look about the horizon, I curled up on my bunk. I didn't bother with the civilities of getting undressed for bed as I reasoned it was wasting sleeping time.

As soon as my head touched the kitbag of dry clothes that I used for a pillow, I drifted off into a deep sleep. It only seemed like ten minutes before the annoyingly tinny rattle of the alarm clock brought me back to life. It was so tempting to have just a few more minutes' sleep, but rules are rules, as the part of my brain that dealt with running a tight ship told me. Climbing onto the steps that led to the cockpit, I gazed aft with squinting eyes. Less than a hundred yards away and heading for us was a ship. Suddenly I became wide awake. What was happening? The grey warlike-looking ship had the legend P31 painted in black on her bows, and with my very limited knowledge of naval vessels did not mean a thing.

Nipping smartly back into the cabin I took the hand-held transmitting radio from its rack. Returning to the cockpit, with my heart beating like mad, I tried desperately to sound casual as I called out over the radio: "P31 ... P31 ... yacht *Mykon* ... yacht *Mykon* ..."

Obviously they could see my every movement from their bridge, and a reply came back immediately. From the conversation that followed I learnt that the P31 had picked us up on their radar screen from several miles away and decided to investigate. I also found out that the P31 was an offshore patrol vessel belonging to the Irish Naval Service. The captain of the P31 spoke in a polite and friendly manner as he asked me a series of questions regarding my identity and the name of my vessel, my last port and where I was bound etc. Satisfied that all was in order, the captain wished me good luck, turned his vessel about and soon disappeared over the horizon. After having a quick look around for any other shipping I reset the alarm clock and climbed back into my bunk.

Offshore Patrol Vessel P31, met off Southern Ireland.
Photo: Trevor Wilson.

The barometer was holding steady and the fair weather continued. I could not believe my luck – the wind was still from the north, blowing at about force three. By Friday, four days out, this fair weather had carried us to a position seventy-five nautical miles south of the Fastnet Rock light. We were now over a relatively shallow area of water known as the Labadie Bank.

To our portside several rust-streaked Cornish trawlers with identification lettering PZ (Penzance) painted on their sides were busy harvesting the abundance of fish that fed there. Just to see Labadie Bank on the chart reminded me of a time I was in Newlyn, Cornwall. We were sheltering at Newlyn during a spell of bad weather when I was crewing aboard a friend's yacht. It was in a dockside pub that we were having a friendly yarn with a local trawlerman who told us that they had been fishing over the Labadie Bank and caught a crab that was three feet wide. We fell about laughing and my beer spilled over the table on hearing this unexpected revelation. Much to my shame, the trawlerman's words turned out to be true, as we read in the local paper that indeed a three-foot crab had been caught on the Labadie Bank and landed alive at Newlyn and then taken to the Newquay Sea Life centre. Here I was, eight years later, sailing over the very bank where the giant crab had been caught, and I was trolling a silver fishing lure over *Mykon*'s stern. It didn't take very long before two mackerel, having mistaken the flashing lure for a meal, had been hooked and hauled into the cockpit. With my quota of the fishing harvest boiling merrily away on the stove, I wound in the hook and line, hoping that I was helping in a very small way not to over-fish our fast-diminishing shoals.

By Monday 18th July 2005 we had been at sea for a week and the fair winds had held long enough for us to reach the position forty-eight degrees north and fifteen degrees west (these positions are derived from letters I sent home and are only approximate). Although we sailed from the relatively shallow water of the Continental Shelf and into the deep water of the European Basin I still felt uneasy about having to cross the latitudes of the Bay of Biscay. Over the many times that I have crossed the Bay, be it in the summer or winter, the weather has always been bad, although some people have told of it being like a millpond when they crossed.

The barometer was starting to fall and I was beginning to feel chilly. Was a cold front approaching? I could not receive the B.B.C. shipping forecast now that we were out of range of the signal, so I relied on local signs in the sky and the barometer, or 'the liar' as seamen of old would call it. With the wind backing from the northwest to west by north and gradually increasing in strength, I suspected that we were in for an unsettled spell. From the cockpit, and in the twinkling of an eye, I shortened the foresail to the size of a number two jib; the joy of roller reefing. Two reefs were then tucked into the main. During the winter months of preparation for this voyage, I had lazy jacks fitted so as to stop the mainsail being blown away from the boom when reefing: this was to be worth its weight in gold. The mainsail was also fitted with three single-line slab reefing points controlled at the foot of the mast, which was stepped on the cabin top. I did not really mind the weather changing, but felt grateful for the settled spell that had held for a whole week. After all, I told myself, the weather was only doing its own thing and no one had forced me to sail into the Ocean. Under this shortened rig and increasing wind *Mykon* skipped happily over the seas that had started to build up and headed towards the Azores. I felt happy too, knowing that I could reef the main still further with the extra reefing point that the sailmaker had sewn in.

After the disastrous consequences that followed the roll-over on *Bowden* I had fitted webbing straps to each of the bunks on board *Mykon*. Now at least I could lash myself into the bunk and not be thrown about like a pea in a whistle if the worst should happen. Before nightfall the main was deep-reefed and the foresail shortened even further as the wind had backed to the west and was now gusting to seven. The moon, big and bright, had just started to climb over the horizon, revealing masses of white and grey clouds scudding rapidly eastwards. Water was now sweeping along the sidedecks, and although most of it fell back into the sea over the top of the three-inch 'bulwark' the rest of it remained swilling fore and aft owing to the totally inadequate one-and-a-half-inch diameter scuppers. A small blip in the otherwise sea-kindly design of the Cutlass 27.

Another fault in the design of the yacht was revealed that night when water began to pour into the cabin from the fore end and sides of the sliding hatch. The sliding hatch needed a garage (horrible word) to deflect the seas when they mistook *Mykon* for a half-tide rock. My sleeping bag was soaking wet by the time I had found a plastic cover to try to protect the bunks from a further drenching. Bolting the stable door after the horse had run off would have been an appropriate adage for my pathetic actions.

By midnight the wind was gusting to gale force, causing the weather stays to give off a high pitched 'singing' sound as they vibrated under the strain of the deep-reefed main. The 'singing' sound travelled down the stays to the oilskin locker in the cabin amidships, which amplified it as a soundbox on a guitar would. It was as if I had my own personal choir on board.

Climbing into the cockpit and hurriedly closing the sliding hatch, I snapped my safety harness hook onto one of the anchor point eye-bolts. Standing astride the side-benches and holding onto the sprayhood rail for balance, I directed the beam of my head-torch forward and searched for anything that was amiss. Everything seemed okay. The size of the fully reefed main, with its large black identification lettering, almost sitting on the boom was ample for these conditions. In the shelter of the Caernarfon harbour when I first set the mainsail to see how it looked with the additional reef, the reduced sail size looked too tiny. Crossing the Bay, however, in this blow, the fully reefed sail looked massive although it was only forty-five square feet. The sea had now stabilised into huge water mountains and occasionally only the top of the mast showed above the foam. Watching *Mykon* with her sea-kindly hull climb to the crest of these waves and then slide down the other side with the grace of an expert Alpine skier, I gave silent thanks to the designer of this noble craft.

Satisfied that *Mykon* could look after herself for a while, and after having one last look around the horizon, I went below to put the kettle on. The cabin storm door was bolted into place after me. It was quite a balancing act trying to fill the kettle using only one hand whilst holding onto the grab rail with the other. What I needed was a webbing cradle that I could hook onto the stove front so that I could work hands-free. I promised myself that when the weather calmed down I would sort out some webbing and rig this extra hand. Although the stove was gimballed and fitted with high fiddles I always secured the kettle or pans on to it with shock-cord.

Sitting on the cabin sole, out of reach of the mini-waterfall that kept cascading through the gaps in the sliding hatch, I put my hands around the hot mug of Bovril that I'd just made. The warmth from the mug penetrated my cold fingers and I derived a simple pleasure from the very thought that I had made a hot drink in those conditions, when the wind was howling all about us. With the Rutland generator whizzing round like mad in this near-gale, I had switched on all the cabin lights, the masthead tri-light and the telltale compass light in an effort to stop the main battery from over-charging. Lying down on the weather bunk, which was soaking wet, I secured myself in with the two nylon webbing straps that I had fitted during the winter. Hoping these straps would not be put to the test, I lay awake on the bunk, and now and again glanced at the telltale compass that was bolted onto the cabin sole.

The multitude of sounds that could be heard through *Mykon*'s hull as she ploughed on through the night at four knots were interrupted by brief moments of relative silence when the height of the waves became higher than the sails. I prayed that we would not be rolled over. The pointer on the clinometer indicated that we were heeling at fifteen degrees to port: at this angle the lee decks would be just above the water. I had made it a rule of thumb that if the angle of heel went over fifteen degrees I would further shorten sail. Just as I was willing *Mykon* to carry us further away from the Bay of Biscay, the weather side of the hull resounded to a mighty crash, as if someone was trying to stove in the ship's side with a tree trunk. Plates, cups, plastic containers of tea and sugar, and all the navigating paraphernalia from the chart table rack went flying across the cabin as over we went.

I struggled to free myself from the straps that held me fast in the bunk. We were on our beam ends, we had been knocked down. Gripped by fear, I flung open the sliding hatch and, fumbling about for the cabin roof grabrail that was now pointing towards the unseen horizon, I pulled myself into the cockpit. The crosstrees had just started to lift out of the water as the massive weight of the deep keel began its righting motion. A split-second assessment told me that the mast and sails were still attached to the yacht.

Totally ignoring everything else I unlatched the self-steering and pulled the tiller frantically to windward. The sails gave out a mighty whip-cracking sound as they filled again with the wind that had now reached gale force. Sitting on the side-bench, my legs were shaking with fear as we gathered way again and I eased the bows off the wind. As each minute passed with an agonising slowness and a semblance of normality ensued, I kept repeating, "Thank you God, thank you God." The water in the cockpit was six inches deep and it was painfully slow before the self-drainers emptied it back into the sea. These one-and-a-half-inch diameter self-drainers are far too small in my opinion and would be more suitable for empting bathwater.

By daylight the wind had eased to force five and had backed to the south. I made my way to the mast, carefully holding onto the stays and grabrails as I went and shook a reef out of the mainsail. Immediately our speed increased to five knots and we gradually began to leave the Bay in our wake. Having been kept busy most of the night following the knockdown, I was ready for my bunk, but first there was the cabin to put in order.

Cups, plates, cutlery and numerous other items had been thrown out of their racks and the navigation instruments had found their way inside the stove grill. In the to-do book I jotted down 'zigzag shock cord to be fitted over the galley shelves'. Satisfied that everything looked shipshape, I climbed into my bunk and after covering myself with the driest part of the sleeping bag, I went out like the proverbial light.

Five hours later I was woken by the long, strident note of a ship's whistle. It was a warning coming from a French tuna fishing vessel – the one long blast meaning 'T' of course: 'Keep clear of me; I am engaged in pair trawling'.

Deep-sea tuna fisherman.
Photo: Trevor Wilson collection.

We passed well clear of the stern of the tuna fisher but close enough to see the trolling lines bearing hundreds of silver lures being slowly pulled through the water. Never having tasted fresh tuna, I began to wonder if I too could catch one. Apart from a few mackerel that I have caught for my dinner I am not an expert angler by any stretch of the imagination, but reasoned that to catch a fish the size of a tuna would require a fairly large lure. This was a problem, as the only

lures I had in my fishing kit were relatively small. It was whilst
rummaging through a shopping bag of tinned food looking for
a suitably sized tin that I could fashion into a lure that the
penny dropped. The bag itself! It was a green cool-bag from
the Asda supermarket, lined with a silver metallic coating.

After cutting out a shape that resembled a nine-inch-long
fish that had a silver-coloured body and a green tail I secured
it around a length of monel wire bearing a large hook on one
end. The trolling line was a two-hundred-foot length of orange
'crab line' wound onto a wooden spool. As I watched the lead-
weighted fishing line run swiftly out from the stern the silver
lure disappeared under the water. After holding the trolling
line in my hands for twenty minutes and having no sign of the
homemade lure appealing to a tuna, I decided to rig a hands-free
fish-biting indicator. This Heath Robinson type of fish-biting
alarm worked like this: a matchstick was held across a small
shackle with a loop of the trolling line. The weight of a caught
fish snapped the match stalk and dragged a saucepan clattering
along the side-bench. Five minutes after setting this indicator,
the saucepan went flying onto the after deck with an alarming
din. A bite! Standing on the side-bench I grabbed hold of the
fishing line and, hand-over-hand, started to haul it in. The
excitement began to build up as I could feel that I was dragging
something heavy through the water. The retrieved fishing line
began to rapidly fall into a heaped pile in the cockpit. Twenty
feet from the stern I could see just below the surface a silver
flashing shape. As I brought the silver flash alongside I could
make out the shape of the biggest fish that I had ever caught
in my life. Bending over the side and hauling with both arms
I heaved on board a three-foot tuna.

Such a beautiful fish it was, too: large, streamlined and
deep-bodied, its eyes were really big, and not unlike you would
see on a rag doll in a toy shop. The tuna's colourings were a
dark metallic blue on the back with a silver-coloured belly, and
an iridescent blue band ran along each flank. The pectoral fins

were very long, reaching as far back as the second dorsal fin and coloured yellow. I know fishermen exaggerate about the size of the fish they catch, but this one must have weighed twenty pounds. Not having any weighing scales I tried to compare the weight of the tuna to something that I was familiar with, and that was a twenty-pound bag of potatoes. There, flopping about on the cockpit sole, was my dinner – as it turned out, dinner for the next eight days. Taking a large galley knife I swiftly ended its distress. The tuna steaks were cooked immediately in the pressure cooker, and each day I would try to concoct a different recipe: tuna steaks with vinegar, curried tuna, pasta with tuna and so on. It was delicious.

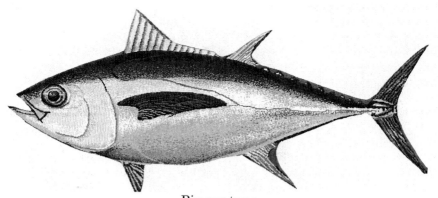

Big-eye tuna.
Sketch: Trevor Wilson collection.

The French tuna fisher disappeared over the horizon and, unknown to me then, it was the last sign of human life that I would see until I reached the Azores in just over two weeks' time.

The barometer had been slowly rising all through the day and the wind had fallen to force three, still from the south. After shaking all the reefs out of the main and unfurling the rest of the foresail, we stood on course under a blue sky and calm sea; what a difference a day makes. My mood had risen with the barometer and I set about doing one of the numerous jobs listed in the to-do book. The woodwork surrounding the galley shelves was duly drilled, making a series of holes, and a length of shock-cord rove through in a zigzag fashion. Now at least the cups and plates and all the other bits and bobs would be held fast in the bad weather.

One job out of the way, now I would not feel guilty about relaxing in the cockpit for an hour or two, reading and trying to fathom out the plot in a paperback copy of *Vanity Fair: A Novel Without a Hero* that I'd bought in a charity shop. As with the pictures of trees and fields etc. that I chose to have in the cabin, it made a refreshing change from the sea that surrounded us. Before I settled down in the cockpit I had hung out my wet sleeping bag and clothes to dry in the hot sunshine: it made *Mykon* resemble a floating laundry. By the time the sun had gone down all of the laundry was dry – and what a joy it was that night when I snuggled down inside a sleeping bag that didn't literally feel like a wet blanket.

It was early the next morning that I was woken by the piercing *eeyah* cry of a noisy flock of sea birds (identified later from my *Sea Birds of the Ocean* tea towel as Great Shearwaters). The otherwise calm sea was alive with activity. Hundreds of small silver fish were frantically leaping out of the water as they were being chased by giant tuna that could be clearly seen devouring them. The poor small silver fish (probably young pilchards) were in a terrible dilemma: if they stayed in the water the tuna got them. If they jumped out of the water or swam too close to the surface the hungry Great Shearwaters dived with folded wings and took them. They had Hobson's choice, doomed whatever action they took. These Shearwaters had a wingspan of about three feet and had been following *Mykon* for a few days. I noticed how elegantly they flew, dipping from side to side on stiff wings with very few wing beats. Their flight was powerful and direct, with wings held stiff and straight. They were to follow *Mykon* all the way to the Azores, settling in noisy flocks on the surface of the sea whenever we were becalmed. I was beginning to wonder if they thought that we were a giant marine bird, for as soon as the 'wings' of *Mykon* filled they took to the air and continued following us.

These birds were going to spend plenty of time just bobbing about on the water, as we had sailed into an area of high pressure (Azores High) and were to experience extremely light winds for the next seven days. We hardly had steerage way and I was mindful of the North Atlantic Drift that was setting us in a south by east direction at a rate up to one and a half knots. After about twenty-four hours of light zephyrs the wind fell away altogether and we were left totally becalmed. Even the absence of a sailing wind was not all bad, for the ocean was transformed into a world of profound tranquillity. A massive, smooth and waveless swell moved with a silent gentleness which in itself made you feel at peace with the world. It made me think of the poor souls in the cities who daily commute to work on crowded trains, to face a stress-filled environment in offices, banks, shops and the like. I was indeed fortunate to find myself in a totally different world.

I couldn't spend all day daydreaming. I told myself that Saturday morning that it was time for my weekly routine of 'lifeboat drill', engine run for twenty minutes and haircut. It was 23rd July. My 'lifeboat' was a six-man life raft that I had bought from eBay. Before I had sailed I had this top-of-the-range life raft serviced by its manufacturer in Birkenhead. The 'lifeboat drill' involved dragging the valised life raft from under the quarter berth and heaving it onto the cabin step and then into the cockpit. To familiarise myself with its deployment I pulled away a Velcro flap to reveal the end of the painter that would have to be made fast to the yacht should the life raft have to be thrown into the water. In broad daylight and in calm seas the deployment of the life raft seemed naively simple on these practice drills, though I realised it would have been time well spent should an emergency arise.

The second part of my Saturday routine involved running the engine for twenty minutes, to prevent it seizing up, and if becalmed, the added bonus of charging up the battery. The Bukh diesel engine used less than a litre of fuel per hour when run at half throttle and I carried enough fuel to run it for twenty-four hours.

The third part, as I've mentioned, was my haircut, and it always brought a smile to my face when I thought back to Mike the Frenchman in Porto Santo.

That smile on my face was soon to be replaced by an expression of agony. For it was whilst the engine was undergoing its test run that I stood peering over the transom to check that the cooling water was flowing properly. Whilst looking over the side I noticed something that looked like a light blue plastic bag fouling the self-steering paddle. Clearing the paddle would have to wait until I had a haircut, in keeping with the Saturday routine. I could easily have poked the obstruction clear with the boathook (whatever possessed me not to?) but instead I reached over the side and, plunging my hand below the surface, grabbed hold of the 'plastic bag' only to have an excruciating pain shoot up my arm. I had grabbed hold of the tentacles of a Portuguese Man o' War. Holding tightly onto my wrist with my left hand I did an involuntary dance in the cockpit, screwing my face up in agony. It was as if my hand had been stung by a swarm of angry bees. The throbbing pain seemed to be travelling up my arm and interrupted my train of thought as I desperately racked my brain for a remedy. Scalding hot water! That was it. I remembered when working down the West African coast on board a tramp ship that the deck boy had been stung by a Portuguese Man o' War off Freetown. The First Mate administered this treatment to the poor lad by immersing his stung foot into a bowl of extremely hot water. The deck boy had lived to tell the tale.

Lighting the stove and filling the kettle with one hand was a feat in itself, but waiting for the water to boil seemed to take forever. I do not know to this day if plunging my swollen hand into that almost unbearably hot water resulted in a cure, but the red welts and the swelling and pain did eventually disappear. Applying ice to the area of the sting is also a fairly effective way to suppress the pain according to the latest medical research. Ice works by constricting the blood vessels and so reducing the flow of toxins to the brain and other parts of the body. Even if I'd known this information then, the chances of obtaining ice were virtually zero.

Sea turtles are immune to the poison of the Portuguese Man o' War and they are an important source of food in their diet. Ironically, sea turtles often mistake discarded plastic bags for this part of their diet and consequently choke to death, a sad legacy of man's pollution of our planet.

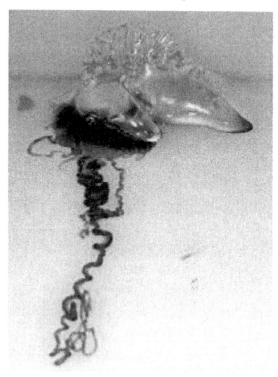

Portuguese Man o' War.
Photo: Trevor Wilson collection.

A strict self-imposed rule that I stuck to was to bring ashore any plastic waste, packaging etc. There always seemed to be a skip or dustbin where I could put these bags of rubbish. As the weeks at sea rolled by, the forepeak would look like someone had been grocery shopping for a large family as these rubbish-filled plastic bags piled up. Although sometimes these stowed bags became a nuisance, I consoled myself by regarding them as extra buoyancy. Empty food tins filled with seawater I threw into the sea, reasoning that they will in time degrade. And I have thrown the odd message in a bottle overboard but have never received a reply from any of them; although I have always promised the finder five pounds sterling. I have a cutting from a local newspaper that tells of a message in a bottle that had been floating in the ocean for thirty-four years. The barnacle-encrusted bottle had been picked up on a north Cornish shore by a local woman while beachcombing in January 1990. The bottle contained a 1956 shilling and the address near Durban of the schoolboy sender, Ryan Smith. Coastguards believe the bottle had travelled hundreds of thousands of miles after getting caught up in a complex series of currents that took it around the world. It is believed that the bottle may have reached the Indian Ocean before being swept towards Japan, then bobbed across the Pacific and travelled on north of Australia. According to a computer-induced tracing, the bottle may have passed Durban again going south of the Cape of Good Hope, eventually meeting the Gulf Stream, which swung it towards the Cornish coast. Perhaps there is hope for my messages in bottles after all.

It was to be two days of drifting before the wind increased from nil to force two. Although it was on our nose from the southwest, at least we were sailing through the water at two and a half knots. As the powerful North Atlantic Drift had set us to the east of our course line for the Azores, I came about onto the port tack and, close on the wind (what little there was), steered west-southwest. The flock of Great Shearwaters that had adopted *Mykon* suddenly realised that we were sailing away. They took to the air in a noisy chorus, only to settle on the water about half a mile ahead, waiting for us to catch up with them. The sea was calm and reflected the vivid blueness of a sky dotted with a few grazing sheep. All we needed now was a little more wind to complete a perfect day.

It was Monday 25th July. We had been at sea for two weeks and were roughly halfway to our destination. Our position was easily derived of course from the G.P.S. readings. In keeping with my not wishing to being totally dependent on anything electrical, I also carried a sextant, just in case the powers that be decided to switch off the G.P.S. facility. It was a plastic sextant and I was very much a novice in its use, in fact I had to keep checking the instructions from a *Teach Yourself Basic Astro Navigation* book. Fifteen minutes before ship's noon I would take a series of sun sights and take the same number of sights until fifteen minutes past the hour. These sights would be jotted in a note pad and an average altitude derived. Some of the sights even I could see were way out of true, probably the result of bringing the sun down too erratically. Being a novice at astro navigation I found this was the most accurate way to obtain a reasonable altitude of the sun with which to obtain our latitude. The longitude was found by the *equation of time* method, which is simply converting the difference in time that you are from the Greenwich meridian into degrees of arc at your local noon. Professional astronomical navigators would probably cringe at the simplicity and crudeness of this way of obtaining longitude, as there are far more complicated and accurate ways, involving trigonometry. The simple method that I used was sufficient for my needs, the average error of the sextant-derived position being twenty nautical miles when compared to the true position derived from the G.P.S., the nearest to our true position I have ever obtained being six nautical miles. I was very pleased with that.

The daily noon positions were marked into an A5 book of graph paper that I used as a plotting chart, the scale of the Admiralty charts being far too small of course. I only used the Sun and Polaris, but would gaze at the night sky at the mass of stars and planets, and be filled with wonder and admiration of the early seafaring explorers that used them as signposts to find their way across the oceans. 'Twinkle twinkle little star, how I wonder what you are ...' words I learnt at nursery school over sixty years ago, words that were only words *then*. Now the childlike simplicity of those very words took on a breathtaking poignancy as I too looked into the silent night sky and asked myself the same question. Being alone at sea, I find, gives you time to think. It puts things into perspective and makes you aware of just how really unimportant some of the things are that we worry about in our daily lives ashore.

The winds had held light and still from the southwest for the last three days, but we had made just over two hundred nautical miles of westing, which put us back on the rhumb line for the Azores. Our position, incidentally, was not far away from where in July 1969 an abandoned trimaran was found by a passing merchant ship. The trimaran was called *Teignmouth Electron*. Its owner was Donald Crowhurst, who was an English businessman and amateur sailor, who died whilst competing in the *Sunday Times* Golden Globe Race, a single-handed, non-stop, round-the-world yacht race. The voyage had been virtually doomed to failure from the outset. At the time the forty-foot *Teignmouth Electron* was a new and unproven design. However, to comply with race rules of leaving not later than 31st October 1968, Crowhurst had sailed from Teignmouth on that day with many of the preparations unfinished and untried. Some of his spares and supplies were also left behind in the haste and confusion to meet with the deadline. Donald Crowhurst had entered the race hoping to win the cash prize from the *Sunday Times* to help his failing business venture. The prize was £5000, quite a considerable sum then; the equivalent to about £60,000 in 2005. To improve safety, Crowhurst had planned to fit an inflatable buoyancy bag to the masthead, activated by sensors in the event of a capsize. This idea was going to be a part of a business venture on his return but was never implemented through lack of time.

Early in the voyage he encountered a leaking hull, the first of many problems that would arise as the voyage progressed. Crowhurst then secretly abandoned the race whilst reporting false positions in an attempt to appear to be still circling the globe. He was in fact sailing erratically about the South Atlantic, and at one period called at a small fishing port on the Argentinean coast (contrary to the rules of the race) to make repairs to his trimaran.

Most of the voyage was spent in radio silence, although his assumed position was being plotted by the race organisers using the false data that Crowhurst did transmit. One of the false claims he sent was to have sailed 243 nautical miles from noon to noon: this would have been a record day's run at the time if it had been true. By December 1968, Crowhurst, based on his reports, was being predicted worldwide as the likely winner of the race, although Francis Chichester, who was on the race committee, publicly expressed doubts about the supposed progress.

The deception by Crowhurst was also to have devastating repercussions on one of the other competitors in the race. Nigel Tetley was also sailing the same class forty-foot Piver trimaran. On hearing the false progress reports Tetley pushed his vessel to virtual destruction, and on 30th May 1969 had to abandon ship. It is almost certain that had Crowhurst finished the race his deception would have been exposed. His log books would have been closely examined by experienced sailors such as Chichester.

The last entry Crowhurst wrote in his log book was on 29th June 1969. It is assumed he then committed suicide by jumping overboard and drowning. The condition of the trimaran did not indicate that it had been damaged by a freak wave or run down by a ship or that Crowhurst had accidentally fallen overboard. Two navigational log books and one radio log had been left on board which revealed his true navigational course during the voyage and the state of his mind that led to his demise. The true winner of the race was Robin Knox-Johnston, who unselfishly donated his winnings to Donald Crowhurst's widow.

Nigel Tetley was awarded a consolation prize, and the money went towards building a new trimaran. He too committed suicide for reasons unknown a year later. For a brief period the *Teignmouth Electron* was put on display to raise funds for Donald Crowhurst's family, although this fundraising effort was stopped at the request of his widow.

Eventually the *Teignmouth Electron* was shipped to Jamaica, where she was restored by the new owner who offered pleasure cruises aboard her. After being re-sold to someone who ran a scuba diving business on the island of Cayman Brac, the trimaran was badly damaged in a hurricane and today lies rotting in the sand dunes on that island.

I tried to imagine how terrible it must have been to be alone at sea for all of those months for the tortured soul of Donald Crowhurst, knowing that on reaching land, his self-woven web of deceit was bound to be revealed. Such a sad tale, and so in contrast to the contentment that I felt all these years later as we sailed near to where the *Teignmouth Electron* was found abandoned.

One part of the contentment I felt was that I'd finished eating that tuna fish I had caught eight days ago. After the first four days I was beginning to lose my enthusiasm for eating cooked tuna but could not bear the thought of throwing good food over the side. Thursday 28th July was a tuna-free day, and curried tinned chicken and rice could not have tasted better. Although I tried to eat as healthily as I could manage aboard a yacht, every day I continued to take an 'over-fifty' vitamin tablet and a swig of cod-liver oil. The habit of taking cod-liver oil was a legacy from when it was supplied free by the government to children during World War Two. The fresh oranges were starting to go bad, although they had only been on board for three weeks. I cut out the mouldy bits and ate the rest, peel and all. In fact during the next week I was eating four or five mutilated oranges per day in an effort to consume them faster than they could deteriorate. I told myself that it was a scurvy-prevention measure. One of the signs of having scurvy is that your teeth start to become loose. A tooth in the front of *my* mouth was becoming loose, although this was not caused by the lack of vitamin C but old age. "Long in the tooth, shrinking gums and all that. Your teeth are okay," the dentist said, "but your gums will have to come out." An old Christmas cracker joke that was now ringing true. Always mindful of eating healthily so that the one-man crew didn't become laid up, I always tried to eat well, starting by having a good breakfast, usually porridge with dried fruit.

The routine before breakfast, though, was to pump out the bilge, which took about twenty-five strokes of the handle in calm weather. The water was coming into the bilge from a slight drip around the prop shaft; it was a job that I had overlooked before I had sailed. An electric bilge pump that would automatically activate when the bilge-water reached a depth of ten inches had been fitted before I sailed. An extra hand-operated pump – a Whale Gusher 10 that was identical to the one in the cabin – I had installed in the cockpit. This cockpit-situated pump proved invaluable during bad weather.

Another important reason that I regularly hand-pumped the bilge was to stop the automatic pump kicking in, as it took quite a heavy strain on the ship's single battery. Whenever possible I stuck to a self-imposed shipboard routine, as I found that I was less likely to overlook something important in the running of the ship.

It was on Friday 29th July, when I was kneeling in the cabin, engrossed in the pre-breakfast bilge-pumping routine, that I casually looked up at the sky through the door opening. My eyes focused on a huge anvil-shaped cloud sitting on the horizon. It was a storm cloud of course, and it looked not unlike the mushroom cloud following an atomic bombing. Hastily finishing off the bilge-pumping I sprang to my feet to see that the barometer had fallen rapidly in the last hour. Usually a blow does not last too long when the barometer falls quickly like that, which was a comforting thought. The wind had veered to the west and was only blowing at force four, as I fully reefed the main and shortened the foresail.

To an onlooker this may have seemed like taking caution to the extreme, but I told myself that it would be easier to shake the reef out than put one in during a blow. At the time of reefing, the sun was shining and the sky was mostly blue; everything looked quite peaceful except for that weird-looking cloud. It was the faint sound of distant thunder rumbling away that gave an inkling of what was to come. The first signs were a grey blanket of cloud being pulled low over the sky as insidiously as a lighting technician in a theatre would change a scene from a colourful summer's day to one of twilight. I felt as if I could almost touch the low ceiling of cloud with an outstretched arm. Tiny spots of rain began to fall and the wind momentarily died away as if waiting for the cue from an unseen conductor's baton. Then the raised baton must have come down with a fell swoop, for all hell suddenly broke loose. In what seemed to be only seconds the wind reached force seven and the heavens opened up. Taken by surprise by the rapid onslaught, *Mykon* heeled alarmingly to port.

Strangely enough I didn't feel frightened this time: not out of bravado, but after experiencing the last knock-down I had more confidence in the yacht's ability to cope with this sudden attack. Usually a heavy sea accompanies a blow but surprisingly the wave height remained quite low. It wasn't very long before *Mykon* responded to this unusual combination of sea and wind and took off like a startled fawn. We were flying along at 6.7 knots; the fastest speed of the voyage to date. It was exhilarating to watch how momentarily in the sudden gusts – which were now reaching gale force – we would quickly come hard onto the wind. The Aries self-steering with an equal response 'up-helmed' and brought us off the wind again. That self-steering could steer consistently better than any helmsman.

The mainsheet was bar-tight and I anxiously looked for any potential weak points, as the wind was now gusting to nine. Once again I gave thanks to Bill Dawson, the local sailmaker who had sewn in the triple-stitched extra set of reef points and extra strengthening patches on the mainsail. Just as I was deciding to douse the main altogether, the wind eased off to seven. The heavy rain was bouncing off the cabin roof, and from below it sounded as if we were under a waterfall. I had gone below to take off my soaking wet clothes, and change into something more suitable for the sudden change in the weather. I had been caught off-guard. A six-inch depth of rainwater, constantly replenished by the downpour, remained swilling about in the cockpit. The undersized self-drain valves could not cope with such a heavy volume. Sheltering under the sprayhood, I sat in thought, gazing at all the good drinking water that was going to waste, literally down the plughole. How could I collect it?

The strong winds lasted until nightfall, when they began to ease and the barometer began to rise sharply. I am always wary when the barometer behaves like this, for usually it foretells a stronger blow. By midnight the wind had veered to the northwest and returned with a vengeance. Nipping smartly to the after deck, in the beam of my head-torch I reset the self-steering vane. The new wind direction had put us on a broad reach, making it easy for the Aries to maintain our course in seas that had now become confused in the sudden wind shift. After deciding that *Mykon* could look after herself for a while, I waited until we had reached the top of the wave and climbed into the cabin.

After bolting the door into place I hurriedly closed the sliding hatch lid, shutting out some of the noise that was going on all around us. Water was still finding its way into the cabin through the gaps in the sliding hatch, though now I had plastic sheets draped over the bunks, and this did help to keep my sleeping bag relatively dry. The next trick, I told myself with an air of determination, was to put the kettle on and make myself a large hot toddy with whisky and boiling water. I had discovered early on in the voyage that extra grab rails were needed in the cabin, especially around the stove area. As a temporary measure, onto the wooden partition that housed the galley I had clamped a steel G-clamp. This makeshift grab handle was invaluable during bad weather. I became quite adept at measuring out a single cup of water to tip into the spout of the whistling kettle, lighting the stove, and pouring the boiled water into a mug, all with one hand. After wedging myself into the pilot seat and drying my face on the tea towel, I held the mug of hot toddy with both hands and, being careful not to scald my lips, slowly sipped the heart-warming drink. Life wasn't too bad, was it?

It was about one o'clock in the morning as I sat, quietly listening to the myriad amplified sounds from inside the hull as *Mykon* ploughed on through the darkness and bad weather. Bad weather that I hoped would blow itself out by daylight, for now it was Saturday, lifeboat-drill day etc. Irrespective of the weather I would only put off the weekly haircut, which could wait. The reasoning behind keeping to the lifeboat drill routine, of course, was that in the event of having to abandon ship, the conditions were most unlikely to be in fair weather.

As things turned out, I did manage to cut my hair that day, for by the time the sun had started to pop up, the wind had

eased to five. Strapping on my safety harness I made my way
to the mast and shook out one of the reefs. Looking around the
horizon from beside the mast, I saw a promise of fine weather,
such a contrast from the battering in the night. If it hadn't
been for all the bilge water that I had to pump out I would
have thought it had been a dream. Looking at the now almost
benign sea brought home how I must never take its mood for
granted, as it could change from being a playful kitten to an
enraged lion in the twinkling of an eye. And change it did: by
noon I had shaken out the remaining reefs in the main and
unfurled the foresail to the size of a Genoa. We were sailing
full and bye.

Four hundred and seventy-five nautical miles ahead lay
the archipelago of the Azores. If we could have sailed as the
crow flies we would have reached the Islands by now, as we
had already sailed thirteen hundred nautical miles over the
ground. It was now time to decide on which island and harbour
I should head for. The navigation charts I used were British
Admiralty, most of which were second-hand. These charts bore
the stamp marks of various Liverpool shipping companies that
sadly are no more. Most of the world's shipping now sails under
flags of convenience – usually Panamanian or Monrovian. In
the winter, before sailing away, all of the second-hand charts
had been taken to Liverpool to be corrected; coincidentally
by their original makers. I did have some brand-new charts
though, and the archipelago of the Azores was one of them.
With the exception of the navigation chart being currently
used, all of the others I had rolled up and stowed inside a
length of rigid plastic piping.

This piping, which I had bought from a builder's merchant,
was sold as four-inch diameter soil piping. After I had cut it
to the width of a chart and pressed a plastic blanking cap on
each end it became a watertight chart container. The contents
of each container were identified by the wording on it in C.D.
marker pen. I would have preferred to stow these charts flat,

but there was not enough room on board for that luxury. When I had finally managed to stop the Azores chart from trying to roll itself back up again, I spread it out in the cockpit. The last time I had spread this chart out was on the bedroom floor of our cottage. Bearing testimony to this were the many paw prints left behind by our Persian cat Bramble, who had walked all over it as I was planning the voyage. Seeing these paw prints brought a smile to my face, and at the same time I suddenly felt homesick, although the feeling soon passed.

Praia da Vitória on the Island of Terceira was to be our first port of call. Although we had not reached the co-ordinates on the large scale Azores chart, I folded it to fit into the pilot desk and carried on to plot our position in the graph-paper book. It was to be two days later, on 1st August, that I could dispense with using graph-paper and begin to plot our position on a real chart. In those two days we had sailed two hundred and two nautical miles over the ground. The weather had held fair, with a wind from the northwest at force three. The bad weather that we had previously encountered only made me appreciate this good spell more. As if to share my joy, a pod of dolphins suddenly appeared. I counted twenty of them. These were bottlenose dolphins, ranging from eight to twelve feet long. They seemed to be smiling as they raced along the side of *Mykon*, sometimes actually touching us with a gentle brushing motion.

Not wishing to let the chance of company go begging, I cupped my hands to my mouth to communicate with them. After I called "Hello dolphins, I am so pleased to see you!" they seemed to welcome my mid-ocean conversation and became even more animated and rolled over several times, so I added: "Thank you for allowing me to be in your home." After all, it's where the dolphins live; we belong on the land and really shouldn't be there at all. We are only guests and on their sufferance. That's the way I see it, anyway. Making my way to the foredeck I hung on to the forestay and sang at the top of my voice "Hey Jude". Immediately the dolphins responded by leaping high out of the water and spinning several times, as if they were dancing. And amid the white water as the dolphins splashed in the sea, a chorus of squeaking followed. It is experiences like this that cannot be bought and in my opinion are treasures.

Bottlenose dolphin.
Photo: Trevor Wilson collection.

The family of Great Shearwaters that had adopted *Mykon* glided overhead. Their piercing cries of *eeyah* added another dimension to the activity already surrounding the floating village. As the barometer slowly rose higher, the northwesterly wind, with an equal slowness, began to fade away. Our speed through the water fell from 4.2 to 2.2 knots that day. The dolphins lost interest at our slow speed and soon disappeared, racing ahead of us to reach a destination that only they knew about.

By Wednesday 3rd August the wind had disappeared altogether as another Azores high pressure system dominated the area. We were now 168 nautical miles from Praia da Vitória. It was during this period of calmness that whilst sorting out the contents of my odd shackle box, I discovered two stainless steel eye-bolts. After drilling through a bulkhead and the wooden stove surround, I used these eye-bolts to secure a webbing belt cradle that would leave me hands-free when cooking in the bad weather.

In the conditions that prevailed at the time there was certainly no use for a restraining webbing belt around the stove. We only had light zephyrs of wind that changed direction throughout the next forty-eight hours and brought us to within ninety-six nautical miles of our destination by evening on Friday 5th August. There was still enough drinking water on board to last a further three weeks, so I was not unduly concerned about the extra time it had taken to reach this far. However, I was concerned that Janet would be worried, as I had told her that with good winds the passage should take about two weeks. I was hoping that she had been looking at the Atlantic weather maps on TV, which would explain the reason why I was overdue.

By 01:00 on Saturday morning, the zephyrs of wind increased slightly, bringing our speed through the water to two knots. After adding on the fair-going current we were moving at 2.75 knots over the ground. In these ghosting winds I found that it's vital to move about the yacht with an extreme gentleness – almost as if I were walking on egg shells and trying not to break them. Any sudden or clumsy movement would disturb the hull's shape as it was presented to the water, and immediately speed would be lost. Hence, that day the lifeboat drill and haircut were carried out in slow motion.

With the Saturday jobs out of the way, I fished out the pilot book and studied the approach and docking instructions for Praia da Vitória. I was starting to get the 'Channels'. By that evening we were only thirty-six nautical miles from our destination. Ahead of us the sinking sun was leaving a deep blood-red smudge on the horizon. In a vain hope that I might see signs of land before the sun finally went to bed, I stood on tip-toe on the side-benches and looked ahead. On the horizon, and standing out distinctly against a backdrop of the red sky, was what looked like a lump of black coal. It was the island of Terceira. A sudden thrill coursed through my blood as I stood gazing at the silent testimony of land. I could easily imagine how those early Portuguese explorers must have felt on the first unexpected sighting of these islands. The land soon disappeared from view with the last fading embers of the sun, but I had seen the island long enough to know it was not a mirage.

It was in a happy frame of mind that I put the kettle on and began to run through my mind the preparations that would have to be carried out for docking. The first job would be to retrieve the chain that lay at the bottom of the chain-locker, unshackled from its anchor. The opening to the chain-pipe had been blocked off with rags. It had been nearly a month since I had used my mobile phone, so I put it on charge, just in case I was lucky enough to receive a signal when off the coast. Sitting at the pilot desk in the glow of the cabin light, I wrote another page in my letter home to Janet. These letters were a journal of the voyage and – unknown at the time – would serve to recoup detailed information, dates etc. in compiling this book.

Owing to the close proximity of land, I stood watches of one hour on, one hour off. As the night wore on the weather gradually began to change, and by daylight the sky was grey and overcast, and it was raining. The wind was still light and now coming from west by south, although I did begin to feel concerned as the barometer was falling.

The island of Terceira lay out of sight, ten nautical miles ahead. Among the preparations for entering port, I got ready the Portuguese courtesy flag, which I set from the starboard crosstrees (prematurely, as events turned out). Six fenders were also laid on the cockpit sole, along with the four Terylene mooring ropes that I had taken from the side-bench locker. By 10:00 that Sunday morning of 7th August, the island of Terceira reappeared. Even through the drizzle I could clearly make out buildings, cranes and other shore features. The G.P.S. told me that we were four nautical miles from the harbour: after sailing for over nineteen hundred nautical miles I regarded this short distance as being as good as being there. Bringing the yacht's head into the wind (what little there was) I furled the foresail and, uttering a silent prayer, pressed the start button that thankfully brought the Bukh diesel engine to life. With the propeller turning at half revs and the electronic steering arm engaged to the tiller, I nipped smartly to the mast and doused the mainsail.

The red and white beacon that marked the harbour entrance could be seen in the distance off our port bow as I made fast the fenders and hung them over the side. To starboard, an old pirate lookout tower stood clearly visible on top of a hill. The sight of this tower only added to the feeling of already reaching land. Unlocking the steering arm, I took over control of the tiller. We were chugging merrily towards our destination at three knots. The totally unexpected events that happened next could have been devised by some evil monster from the pages of a Boys' Own adventure book.

Hurtling down the side of a low mountain ridge, a violent offshore wind suddenly stopped us in our tracks. The shallow water was turned into a mass of white confusion. The ten-horsepower diesel engine was totally overpowered by this sudden onslaught, and we were being blown back out to sea. The fenders were swept back on board as they swung on their lanyards. With her sails doused and engine overwhelmed by the strong blow, the yacht was out of control.

Concentrating on the sole act of unfurling a very small area of foresail, and to the exclusion of any other thoughts, I eased away the furling line. With just a rag of a foresail set, our head was immediately turned away from the wind, which had now reached force seven, and we ran offshore into deep water. The engine, which had only been running a few minutes, was switched off. With the foresail set, the violent rolling eased and I felt safer now that we were back in deep water. It was time to gather my wits, think clearly and devise a plan of action. The very thought of sailing all this way only to have it end in disaster I could hardly bear to think about. This was the first time in my life that I had experienced such a rapid and vicious change of wind strength. Fearing that there was worse to come, I decided to set the trysail, which was much smaller than the fully reefed main. The trysail that I had bought second-hand from the sailmaker back home had an area of just over twenty square feet. This sail ran up an extra mast track that the riggers had fitted before we sailed away. Each Sunday had been the day that I had practised setting this boomless trysail, a practice that I was now thankful for. With the trysail set slightly to the weather, the jib backed, and the tiller lashed to leeward, we became hove to. By late afternoon the winds were gusting to force nine and the strong coastal currents were setting us slowly southwards.

As the night fell, Praia da Vitória had disappeared from sight and the shore lights of Angra do Heroísmo that lay on the southern tip of Terceira could be clearly seen off the port bow. Two black lumps of rock sticking out of the water to a height of about eighty feet could also be clearly seen silhouetted against the shore lights. These rocks, I found out from the chart, were called Dos Hermanos (Two Brothers). By midnight the wind had eased to force six, making the small trisail ineffective as a driving sail. Still wary of the rapidity of the wind increase that day, I decided to wait until daylight before piling on any more canvas. The low sky cover had dissipated during the night, and by morning only the few fair-weather clouds that were remaining floated high in the light blue sky. The wind was still from the west by south and blowing fresh as we stood on the port tack. It would have been far easier to bear away from the wind and head for the marina at Angra do Heroísmo, which was only three nautical miles away. With the original destination of Praia da Vitória being so tantalisingly close yesterday, I was determined that this should be our first port of call.

After working out a sailing plan to reach our destination, I struck in pencil the tacking courses required on the chart. Next I set the mainsail deep-reefed and left the trisail lowered in its own sail track in readiness lest the wind should suddenly decide it wanted to blow us back out to sea again.

Satisfied that *Mykon* was making good progress in the headwinds, I went below to make some porridge and a hot cup of tea. It was whilst waiting for the kettle to boil that I disconnected my mobile phone from its charging rack. Standing on the top cabin step, phone in hand and with my head and shoulders protruding from the hatch lid, I tapped out the overseas telephone number for my home. I had to keep ducking below as the odd wave cascaded over the cabin top. It was with utter amazement that I could hear the phone giving out its calling tone. Immediately I nipped below and turned off the stove: breakfast could wait.

"*Hello?*" said a quiet female voice.

There was a deep poignancy in this apparently simple question. In the nanosecond delay in the caller receiving my reply I could sense an unspoken expectation of the answer to her question being received with either deep joy or deep sorrow.

"Janet, it's me – Trevor! Everything's okay. I'm off the coast of the Azores." I hurriedly blurted out this information in case the phone signal was suddenly lost.

"*Trevor! Thank God!*"

For the next half-hour we chatted away, interrupting each other with a barrage of questions. We were as excited as two lost souls who had just rediscovered each other after many years instead of twenty-eight days. 'Absence makes the heart grow fonder' certainly rang true. The sounds of the waves pouring over the cabin top and *Mykon* ploughing through the water were being amplified by the mobile phone microphone. My cursing was also being amplified as my sleeping bag became increasingly soaking wet with every sea that found its way onto my bunk. Having a wet sleeping bag was a small price to pay, though, for making contact with Janet. That unexpected phone call had been a surreal experience for Janet; for a few moments she had been transported from our little cottage among the Welsh mountains to the sounds of a yacht many miles away on the high seas. After promising to call home as soon as we docked, I returned to cooking my porridge.

I spent the rest of the morning making preparations for docking, having ready the ship's papers, passport etc. The courtesy flag was still flying. The mooring lines and fenders I decided this time to leave stowed in the lockers until we were actually inside the protection of the harbour walls. Superstition, I know, but we may have tempted providence last time by preparing for docking too early.

It was in the early evening that *Mykon* rounded the outer breakwater at Praia da Vitória. Once inside the outer harbour I could see the mastheads of several yachts sticking up over the top of the inner harbour wall that protected the marina. Approaching with the utmost care I looked for a gap in the wall, but I could not see any entrance to the marina. Several times I came about and searched in vain. The whole length of the wall ran from the beach and ended at the side of a hill. Obviously there must be an entrance, I told myself, unless a helicopter had lifted the yachts over the top of the marina wall. The answer to the puzzle was revealed when a speedboat went roaring by and disappeared from sight behind the beach end of the wall.

Following in the wake of the speedboat I found a twenty-foot-wide channel that led to the marina. On reaching a pontoon that supported a large sign with the word 'Reception' painted on it I was met by the harbourmaster. Pointing to a vacant berth next to a yacht flying the German flag he said that he would meet me there.

Actually there were three people to welcome us as *Mykon* gently brushed her fenders alongside the pontoon. We were soon tied up with the help of these kind strangers. Thrusting a plastic gate pass into my hand, the harbourmaster disappeared, saying that I should report to his office in the morning. I felt elated to have reached our destination, even though it had taken longer than expected. We had been twenty-eight days on passage and although the distance from Port Dinorwic is thirteen hundred nautical miles, we had sailed one thousand nine hundred and nine nautical miles through the water.

Chapter 19

The first thing I wanted to do now that I had reached the shore was to have the luxury of a hot freshwater shower. I had managed to keep a set of clothes clean and dry by wrapping them in a plastic bag. Stepping onto the pontoon, armed with soap and towel etc., I took my first faltering steps towards the shower block. Faltering steps? I could hardly walk straight or balance without immense concentration.

Feeling like a much older version of a new-born gazelle on the savannas of Africa I lifted each foot clumsily before me. It was with some relief, then, that I spotted a Red Ensign poking out over the pontoon. It belonged to a yacht called *Matuta* from Conwy, a port not far away from my home port of Caernarfon. This would be a chance to talk to a fellow countryman and at the same time rest and regain some of my composure that was being lost with my stupid-looking walk. Cupping my hands to my mouth I called, *"Matuta!"* From the open hatch of the yacht's companionway, two heads popped up. "Hello, I'm from that British yacht over there," I said, pointing to *Mykon*, adding: "I'm from Caernarfon."

"That's great," the man and woman – both in their thirties – said almost in unison. They both stepped onto the floating pontoon, causing it to sway very slightly.

The events that happened next should have been recorded on video. The slight movement of the pontoon caused me to lose my balance, and with both arms flailing like a demented windmill, I fell into the dock. The first sounds that reached my ears when I surfaced were howls of laughter as the couple doubled up in convulsions. I felt such a prat swimming around holding a bag of clothes in one hand. The couple, who reached down to pull me out of the water, could hardly do so for laughing. Tears were running freely down their cheeks as they pulled me onto the pontoon. I tried to continue the conversation as if nothing had happened, but every time I looked at the couple, the air was filled with uncontrollable laughter. Laughter is the best medicine, so the saying goes, and once I had sorted out another set of dry clothes and showered I too saw the funny side of my impromptu ducking.

Sounds of electric guitars, castanets and trumpets wafting across the harbour from a group of players on the esplanade only added to the joy I felt when embarking on that first run ashore. In fact the music seemed to lend a festive atmosphere to the waterfront as I headed for town with a wallet full of wet euros. The very narrow streets were teeming with throngs of happy and excited people, many of them waving bottles of wine or lager in the air. The crowd seemed to be heading in one general direction: up a fairly steep hill which wound its way past unevenly built houses and shops. Had it not been for the blue and white ceramic street signs and house names that were displayed on the stucco walls, this narrow street could have come out of a Dickens novel. Rows of colourful bunting were strung in a zigzag fashion across the street between the upper storeys. Music was blaring from amplifiers that had been fixed to balcony railings. As the merry crowd made its way to the top of the hill (and the town square as things turned out) further revellers joined in the throng. I found myself in the middle of it, with no other choice than to go with them. As I shuffled to the top of the hill among the happy crowd, I caught a glimpse of a red-tailed firework snaking into the air. As we all gazed skywards, a deafening explosion surrounded us as the rocket cascaded into a shower of brilliant colours. The crowd immediately broke into a chorus of singing and cheering and began waving rainbow-coloured parasols in the air. With a sudden urgency the crowd swept forward, taking me with them as they went.

The tightly packed crowd suddenly fanned out in all directions as we emerged from the narrow lane into the town square. Running towards us from the opposite lane was a screaming bunch of men being chased by an enraged bull. I turned to run, but was hemmed in by the cheering crowd who seemed to think it was quite normal to be gored to death by a manic bull with a fifty-foot rope around its neck. The crowd that was being chased by the bull collided with 'our' crowd, and parasols were raised in an effort to ward these invaders away. It began to look like a battle scene from the Wars of the Roses. The noise was chaotic and exciting, and strangely enough I began to enjoy myself now I accepted that I couldn't turn back. One of the drunken revellers ran at the bull with a plastic chair. The enraged beast, after snagging one of its horns into the chair, sent it flying and then turned to attack its tormentor. The drunken man, who had now been deprived of his protective chair, turned to run away. Too late. One of the bull's horns caught under the leather belt of the would-be escapee and lifted him bodily into the air. The crowd went hysterical as the bull charged towards an old gnarled olive tree that stood in the centre of the square and rammed into it, battering its unwelcome rider, who fell to the ground.

Another firework snaked into the air, followed by an enormous explosion. Almost immediately another enraged bull ran into the square from a side lane. It became apparent to me that this rocket-firing was a signal that another agitated bull was being released to run amok in the street. One of the revellers in our crowd opened his parasol, stepped forward and began to taunt the new arrival with it. I do not know

if animals can communicate with each other but *both* bulls
suddenly turned on this new tormentor, who swiftly turned
on his heels and began running back towards us. Both bulls
were in hot pursuit. The crowd, immediately sensing danger,
turned in unison like a shoal of sardines trying to escape
a school of hungry tuna. Terrified people, myself included,
scrambled to escape into the funnel-like entrance of a side lane
that led to the beach. Several of the crowd who had stumbled
to the ground were left to their own fate. It was every man
for himself. People who were on their balconies and well clear
of the pandemonium that was going on beneath them were
shouting and laughing. Eventually we reached a slipway to the
beach and, still following the crowd, I ran into the sanctuary
of the sea, the bulls halting at the shore line.

This was the second time in a space of a few hours that
I had soaked a clean pair of shorts and shirt in seawater. It
would have been pointless going back aboard to change, as
I had no other dry clothes suitable for this hot climate. The
bulls were causing havoc about a hundred yards away when
I made it to an open air bar and bought an ice cold bottle of
lager with a wet euro bank note. Sitting under the bar awning
I quietly watched the sun go down. I had had enough excitement for one day.

It was with utter contentment that I laid my head down
that first night in the sanctuary of a harbour: to be able to
sleep without wondering about the weather or the amount of
sail that we were carrying. Joy, unadulterated joy!

During my stay I got to know quite a few yachtsmen and
women and we became very friendly, swapping yarns and
friendly banter. My German neighbour, Werner, whose yacht
shared the other side of the pontoon finger to *Mykon*, was my
contemporary, and we soon became good friends. Werner,
who was born in August 1940, was one month younger than
me, and I used to jokingly tell him to have respect for his

elders. We would sit over a glass of whisky or schnapps some evenings, and to hear his experiences of the war in 1944 were fascinating, as they were told through the eyes of a German infant.

Werner was from Hamburg, and remembered how his mother took him into their cellar for protection during the heavy bombing raids that we rained down on that port with its vital docks and submarine pens. I too would relate some of the things that I could remember: the droning noise of German planes that flew over the skies of my home in Leicester; the smell of the plaster from the walls of houses bombed to heaps of rubble; the Mickey Mouse-shaped gas masks we had to carry to school. There was not an iota of animosity between Werner and me when we discussed the war – in fact it made us more thankful that we had both survived to tell the tale.

Werner's yacht, the *Kathinka F.*, was made of steel and nearly forty feet long. He had recently arrived in Praia da Vitória after a single-handed non-stop passage of one hundred and seven days from Natal in Brazil. Natal, by coincidence, was one of the ports I would be bound for.

During the month that I stayed in Praia da Vitória I explored the island as much as possible on foot or by local bus. The villages that I passed through stood as if time had passed them by. The out-of-plumb whitewashed cottages with their pan-tiled roofs and small chapels with ornately decorated façades all added to an as-yet unspoilt quaintness. In sharp contrast to these villages, I came across an American air base in the northeast corner of the island. This explained the Stars and Stripes that I saw flying from newly built properties that I had passed on my mini excursions. As a courtesy formality I was flying the Portuguese national flag at *Mykon*'s crosstrees. When I discovered that the Azores did indeed have a flag of their own, I promptly bought one and flew it under the one I already had flying. Incidentally, the buzzard-like bird depicted on the flag is a goshawk; *acor* in Portuguese because it was mistakenly thought by the early discoverers to be a common bird on the archipelago. Owing to the wonders of modern technology we now know that this bird never existed on the islands. The bird most likely seen by the early explorers was indeed a sub-species of the buzzard that is common here, namely the *Buteo buteo.*

Azores Flag.
Trevor Wilson collection.

I could not leave the island without paying a visit to Angra do Heroísmo, the capital. The bus ride to Angra was a lot less eventful than the unplanned night sighting that I had of the town lights, when *Mykon* was blown down there. It was whilst I was in Angra that I came across a shop that specialised in all the paraphernalia required for home brewing. From this shop I obtained an assortment of items: plastic tubing, brass spigots and miniature stop valves etc., which proved suitable for making a rainwater-catching device on *Mykon*. Such a simple device that actually worked![1] The installation was to prove invaluable at a future date when I was worrying

---

1   Details of rainwater catcher in back pages of book.

if the drinking water was going to last. The cost of groceries on the Island was relatively cheap, especially tins of tuna. I love tuna, so I stocked up with an extra fifty tins of it, and as an added bonus the pull-off tin lids were oval shaped; an ideal shape to make fishing lures.

When I returned to the marina that evening, Werner announced that he had decided to sell his yacht and give up sailing. It was not a sudden decision, his wife in Hamburg had been ill for some time. The next day I helped him to bring his yacht to the boat lift, where she was brought out of the water and lowered into a cradle on the quayside. Finally I helped him to unship the mast. During the last week before I sailed away I would see Werner hammering and scraping away at the many coats of paint that had been below the water line. The bare metal of the hull that was revealed was absolutely sound, with only a few minor rust marks. Epoxy tar resin paint that he had applied many years ago had kept the metal hull in such a pristine state. I made a mental note of this excellent metal-protecting paint – although *Mykon*'s hull was constructed of G.R.P., her engine bed was of metal.

Three o'clock in the afternoon on 8th September 2005 saw *Mykon* singled up to one head and one stern line, and ready to leave harbour. Several of the *to-do in port* jobs had been ticked off as completed, and the drinking water replenished along with food stores that I had consumed to reach Terceria. Among the extra food stores that I ought to mention were tinned tomatoes. The canning process does not destroy the vitamins, and I found it the height of luxury to eat the tomatoes uncooked by spooning them straight from the tin. I bought fifty small tins of tomatoes before sailing.

A little congregation of about ten people had assembled on the pontoon to see me sail away. After they cast off the two remaining ropes and *Mykon*'s engine slowly pulled us stern-first away from the pontoon, the air was filled with a chorus of hand-held fog horns. The little group of friends that I had come to know in port also shouted good luck messages and the one last message that stuck in my mind was from Werner: "Gott be wit you my friend!"

Author inspecting work on Werner's yacht at Praia da Vitória.
Photo: Trevor Wilson collection.

Chapter 20

O nce clear of the breakwater I fully set the main and foresail and doused the engine. With the northeasterly wind blowing at force three I set the self-steering and stood on for Porto Santo in the Madeira Islands.

Porto Santo Island is another peak of the underwater mountain chain and part of the Atlantic Ridge that we were following. Although I had enjoyed my stay in Praia da Vitória I was glad to be back at sea once again. For the next day or so I would have to keep my wits about me as two islands of the Azores archipelago lay in our path. I had decided to sail to the west of these islands, Sao Miguel and Santa Maria, and once clear I would steer a more easterly course. The south-setting Azores Current had to be taken into the reckoning, for if we were swept past Porto Santo there could be no turning back. It was to be after two days that the lights of Vila do Porto, the capital of Santa Maria, were spotted off the port bow and we altered to an easterly course. The weather by this time had turned miserable, the sky overcast, and a steady drizzle made visibility poor.

Several lights of trawlers that would suddenly appear out of the gloom kept me on my toes. I could snatch only a few minutes' sleep at a time until we had cleared the fleet. Once well clear of the islands I settled down to a fairly orderly shipboard routine. The routine, as usual, was fairly simple: carry out any maintenance work until noon, then have a relaxing treat in the afternoon, either writing letters home or having a read, or anything else that took my fancy. If we were clear off the shipping lanes I would get my head down at night time, the strict rule being that if at any time I should wake up, I would go out on deck and have a look out.

It was in the early hours of one morning whilst on passage to Porto Santo, when I was snuggled down in my sleeping bag, that my brain flickered into semi-awakeness. "Do I have to go into the cockpit and have a look out?" was the question one part of my mind was asking. The answer came as "No, stay put." It was so tempting to stay in bed. "Rules are rules," I told myself, hauling myself into the cockpit. Focusing my sleep-filled eyes to starboard I could make out a white light about six miles away. Plenty of clearance. Casually turning my head to look forward, I froze on the spot.

Less than five hundred yards away and dead ahead were one red and two white lights! It would have been pointless to alter course, for we would just clear the ship's stern anyway. But then I watched in horror as the ship altered course to port and came down our port side. Its black silhouette could be seen clearly, and in the lamplight of a doorway I could see a ship's crew member smoking a cigarette. The noise from the ship's engine was plain to hear as we passed in the night. I did shine my torch onto the ship's bridge, pretending that I was just drawing attention to our presence, and it was quite normal for a yacht to stand on. The ship soon disappeared over the horizon and we were alone again, but my heart was beating like mad.

I went below and made a hot drink, and taking it into the cockpit I sat thinking about the close encounter. If I had stayed in my bunk I would not have known of the closeness of the near miss. The incident concentrated my mind on finding a solution. The solution came from the pages of a yachting equipment catalogue that I had on board. A relatively new piece of electronic kit called an Automatic Identification System (A.I.S. for short) would sound an alarm if any ship came within an eight-mile range. The visual detection range of any ships by this A.I.S. was sixteen miles, and was displayed on a radar-type screen. The ships had to carry an A.I.S. system themselves in order to be detected. On 1st January 2006 (in about three months' time) it would be international law that commercial shipping had to carry this equipment. The price of this electronic lookout was relatively cheap at £210 sterling. After jotting down all of the details, I promised myself to order an A.I.S. over the phone when we arrived at Porto Santo.

After we had been at sea for five days, the weather suddenly brightened up and I set about carrying out one of the many jobs from the to-do list, which seemed to be growing longer each day. The job in question was to secure extra elastic shock-cord ties around the foot of the mast that would hold in place the ends of the reefing pendants, allowing each one its own individual tie. These ties would stop the tail ends of the reefing pendants being swept over the deck and fouling the jib sheets in bad weather. It was whilst standing at the mast that I noticed that something in the water had fouled the self-steering paddle. We had sailed over a ten-foot length of ship's mooring rope. Taking the boat hook I dragged the heavy rope (which had a diameter of about four inches) into the cockpit. Both ends of the synthetic rope showed signs that it had had parted under an immense strain. There were signs also that it had been in the water for a considerable time, for along its entire length lived a colony of miniscule marine life – plankton and barnacles, and a crab. The crab, which had a body about the same size as a doughnut, fell off the rope and scurried under the steering compass in the cockpit.

After returning the piece of rope to the sea I reached under the compass to officially welcome on board the new passenger. The shell of the crab was in the shape of a queenie scallop, fan shaped and a yellowy colour with purple dots.

The crab's legs were also purple but with black tips. Its mouth, which seemed to be continuously opening and closing, was situated between its eyes. When the inspection and welcome on board talk were over I decided to call my new friend Horace. Reasoning that crabs eat fish, I opened a tin of sardines and laid one in front of its pincers. Immediately the sardine was seized and Horace began to devour it. I decided to feed our new friend at exactly the same time every twenty-four hours, which would be at 17:00 ship's time. In the cockpit I had a small plastic bucket on a lanyard which I would drop over the side and scoop up seawater. In an effort to make Horace feel at home, throughout the day I would pour a few bucketfuls of sea water onto the cockpit sole, the self-drainers having been plugged. His self-selected home was in the shade under the compass. Although I seldom felt lonely whilst at sea, I would not turn away any chance of the company of another living thing, and I used to have quite long discussions with Horace, albeit one-sided. I know of an outcrop of rocks on the shore at Porto Santo, and informed Horace that I would drop him off there to live. Over the next few days, with a regular feeding of sardines, my little crab friend began to lose his shyness and would emerge from under the compass and crawl over my bare feet as I sat in the cockpit. I was very pleased with the trust that he had in me, now that he realised I was a source of food and not the other way round.

It was on the eve of docking at Porto Santo that I thought it would be a good idea to treat Horace to a chunk of tinned tuna instead of sardines, a sort of going-away treat. The weather was starting to deteriorate, so keeping a supply of seawater in the cockpit for him was not a problem. As the night was drawing in I fully reefed the main and to help counteract the increasing heel, set about shifting heavy bags of food and five-litre bottles of water to the weather bunk. The wind was still in the northeast, which gave us a 'soldier's wind'. Happy that it was an easy course for the self-steering gear to cope with, I went below to cook my dinner, consisting of instant potatoes and the remainder of the tin of tuna that I had opened for Horace.

The wind that had been gusting to force seven during the night had eased to four by daylight. "Time to shake the reefs out," I told myself, sliding open the hatch. The big yellow morning sun sitting on the horizon silently foretold a fine weather day. What could possibly spoil such a lovely start to the day? The answer came as I stepped into the cockpit. Horace was dead. The huge chunk of tinned tuna, half devoured, remained held in his pincers. A sad end, really, to what was supposed to be his going-away treat.

I'm afraid to say that my sympathies for Horace quickly faded away when it occurred to me that I had been eating this tinned tuna for several weeks. With my miniscule knowledge of Portuguese I could make out from the label on the tins that the tuna should not be given to infants. Well, that counted me out. It was some time later that I found out that owing to the pollution of the oceans, the accumulation of heavy metals – mainly mercury – was finding its way into the food chain, and in particular via the Albacore tuna. In England many years ago mercury was used in the hat-making industry to form the different shapes. Apparently mercury affects the brain, hence the term 'As mad as a hatter'. Hmmm?

After reassuring myself that all was well I made my way to the mast, and as I stood on tip-toes, the black shape of Porto Santo met my eyes. The northern tip of the island, with its outcrop of rocks that reminded me of the Needles off the Isle of Wight, stood fine on our starboard bow. If the wind held we would be off the harbour entrance by nightfall. Outside the harbour I knew that there was a suitable anchorage with a good holding ground of sand. I had the choice then, to either anchor and wait until daylight, as I had done with *Ozama*, or enter in darkness. It was nearly midnight when the red and green beacon lights that marked the entrance to the harbour could be identified against the backdrop of a kaleidoscope of confusing shore lights. The nearer we came to the harbour entrance, the more plainly objects could be distinguished. Deciding that it would be safe to enter I doused the sails and, with the diesel engine ticking away, headed for the middle of the gap between the red and green lights. It was five minutes to midnight when I dropped the hook inside the harbour, in the last few minutes of Sunday 18th September.

Chapter 21

Through the semi-darkness I could see the masts of many yachts that lay alongside the marina pontoons. Very different from the last time I was here in Porto Santo with *Ozama*, when only three foreign yachts occupied the harbour. It was whilst surveying *Mykon*'s new surroundings that I saw lying against the stone wall of the inner breakwater a medieval sailing ship. It turned out that she was a replica of Christopher Columbus's old ship, the *Santa Maria*. By good fortune I had arrived at Porto Santo during the annual Christopher Columbus festival week.

Satisfied that we were anchored safely, I climbed into my bunk and after saying "Goodnight, *Mykon*, well done girl," fell into a deep sleep.

As I was rowing ashore the next morning in my two-man rubber dinghy, I looked with pride at *Mykon*, now lying quietly at anchor in silent gracefulness. Who would have thought that she had struggled so gallantly since sailing from Port Dinorwic and through all kinds of weather to bring us here?

On reaching the shore I lifted the dinghy onto the concrete slipway, and with the ship's papers headed for the harbour-master's office. The harbourmaster was the same person who had cleared *Ozama* almost five years ago. I was flattered that he remembered me after all that time. He mentioned that I had asked him about the radar buoy that marked the summit of the underwater mountain that lay halfway between Gibraltar and here. With the yacht's clearance completed and the marina fee paid in advance (it's cheaper this way) I made tracks for the shower block. As I stood looking in the mirror, a smile came to my face when I remembered this was the mirror where Mike the French yachtsman had discovered that his locks had been hacked off.

The first place I headed for after leaving the shower block was along the quay wall. Hundreds of murals depicting the names of the visiting yachts were painted on this wall, and you will remember I painted one for *Ozama* when I was here last time. Owing to the shortage of space remaining on the quay wall, some of the yachts' names had been painted over by new arrivals. I was delighted to see the mural for *Ozama* had not been painted over, as it had been there for almost five years. Before sailing from Porto Santo I added a mural for *Mykon* directly above the one for *Ozama*.

The painting on the wall was of course a piece of trivia: there were far more important things on the to-do list to sort out. Top of the priority list was ordering an A.I.S. from the mail order store in the U.K. I arranged with the store for the unit to be posted to my home. Janet was flying out to Lanzarote and I hoped that she would not mind packing the A.I.S. unit (which was the size of a portable radio) in her suitcase. Incidentally, when phoning home I found it many times cheaper to buy a phone card at the local post office and make calls to the U.K. from a phone box. Unlike in the U.K. I did not see a single public telephone box that had been vandalised. The streets were also litter-free, making me wonder where we had gone wrong back home.

It was along these streets that I would trundle my shopping trolley from the little supermarket in Cidade Vila Baleira, which was a good half-hour's walk from Porto de Abrigo, the harbour. The road into town ran alongside a beach of golden sand, and often on my return trips from town I would leave my laden trolley on the almost deserted beach and have a swim. It was perfectly safe to swim in these waters, the only obstruction being an outcrop of black rocks. Pity Horace never made it; I am sure that he would have been happy among those rocks, his intended new home.

It was from this beach that a re-enactment of Christopher Columbus's landing of 1492 took place. What an enjoyable night it was too. Crowds of local people dressed in fifteenth century costume gathered on the beach and promenade to watch the *Santa Maria* (the replica of course) appear out of the darkness and drop anchor about two hundred yards from the water's edge. In the glow of the oil lanterns, the ship's gig boats could be seen being lowered into the water. One by one, the crew and passengers – all dressed in period costume – then climbed down rope ladders into these boats. Once the passengers were settled on the thwarts the crew manned the three sets of oars and began to row ashore. Two rows of beacons made of straw and sticks that had been staked out on the beach to guide the gig boats clear of the rocks were then lit by a flaming torch. It all looked very dramatic as each gig boat touched the ground on reaching the shallow water and the crew jumped over the side to carry the lady passengers onto dry land. Music then filled the air; music in keeping with the medieval atmosphere was played on traditional instruments. A group of dancers cavorted around the landing party as they went in single file to a rostrum where stood a welcoming gathering of local dignitaries.

Dozens of little market stalls had been set up around the beach, selling locally produced embroidery, jams, wine and cake etc. In one of the stalls a Madeira cake that was in a sealed tin caught my eye. I bought it for the time when we would be celebrating crossing the Equator. A marquee had been set up on the beach as a beer tent, and it was in there that I met one of the crew of the *Santa Maria*. I learnt from him that the original ship was affectionately known by her sailors as *Marigalante*, literally 'Dirty Mary' (a euphemism for a prostitute). Of the three ships that Christopher Columbus used on his first voyage across the Atlantic – the *Santa Maria, Niña* and *Pinta* – the *Santa Maria* was, at seventy feet in length, the largest, and although the slowest, became his flagship. On completing the Atlantic crossing the *Santa Maria* was wrecked off Haiti on 25th December 1492. It was on a Saturday night that the Christopher Columbus festival took place, and as I had decided to sail from Porto Santo the next day it rounded off a very enjoyable week there.

During the week's stay I had tried in vain to exchange an empty gas bottle, as there was not a single one available. One of the girls in the marina office explained that there was a commercial war going on between two different bottled gas suppliers, and the supplier with the most clout would only import large domestic gas bottles, too big for a yacht. The next intended port of call on my itinerary was supposed to be Puerto Naos in Lanzarote. Because I did not like the idea of not having a spare bottle of gas, I decided to sail to Machico first, on the main island of Madeira, to buy one.

It was a pleasant day's sail round to Machico, and as an added bonus I tied up alongside a Dutch yacht that belonged to two yachtsmen that I had made friends with in Porto Santo. The two Dutchmen were sailing around the world in a thirty-six-foot ketch as a part of an organised flotilla. They themselves were rafted up next to a seventy-foot schooner that belonged to an American. And a friendly soul he was too. No sooner had I returned aboard *Mykon* with my full gas bottle than he knocked on the cabin roof with an invitation to come and join him and the two Dutchmen for a drink. I didn't need asking twice, and filling my Asda shopping bag with bottles of beer, I went aboard the schooner. It was so interesting to listen to other people's stories and their different experiences at sea. The laughter went on late into the night at our little impromptu party; it was if we had known each other for ages. It was like ships passing in the night, though, for by the time the respective crews had stirred to see in the new day, *Mykon* was heading out to sea.

A fresh northeasterly wind met us as we cleared the harbour, and I tucked a reef in the main to stop the lee side being constantly awash. The sea was relatively smooth considering that the wind was blowing at a good force five. A low-lying peninsula, Ponta do Rosto to the north of us was probably acting as a natural breakwater. About ten nautical miles to the southwest lay Funchal. It was at this port that the *Erma* had called almost fifty years ago to the day, to replenish the food and water for the sixteen souls on board before her epic voyage across the Atlantic. About twenty nautical miles ahead of us lay a string of bleak, uninhabited islands appropriately called Desertas Islands. These high and long rocky islands are barren of soil, and apart from a few non-native rabbits, goats and rats brought there by the early Portuguese sailors, nothing else lives there. With the wind's strength steadily increasing I decided to pass the islands to the south, as I did not wish to have those desolate rocks as a lee shore. The course I set stood us a mile off the chain of islands, and through a pair of binoculars I scanned the bleak landscape for any signs of life. I could not see a living thing, not even a tree. I tried to imagine the scenario of a shipwrecked sailor being washed up on these Desertas Islands. It would have been a cruel twist of fate. There was a sinister atmosphere about those lonely islands and I felt happier when they disappeared below the horizon. With *Mykon* flying along at 6.2 knots and night falling, I went below to make myself a hot whisky toddy as a reward for clearing the islands – or anything else that I could think of that deserved rewarding.

Once we were clear of land, the mobile phone signal disappeared and contact with home ceased. In order to compensate for this lack of conventional communication, I carried out a routine that involved sending a vocal message home. At precisely the prearranged U.K. time of 20:00 I would look towards the direction of our cottage in the Welsh mountains and shout something like, "Janet, it's me – Trevor! Everything is okay. Goodnight, love!" There were times when owing to bad weather or handling the ship I missed 'calling home' at the prearranged time, and although I would send a similar late message home, I somehow sensed that it was not being received. I would not blame you for thinking that the mercury-polluted tuna had begun to take effect on my brain, but I did really feel a positive sense of having sent a message home. Telepathy – who knows?

Now that Horace had gone, I reverted to talking to the yacht again. In fact, whilst at sea, every morning on waking I would say, "Good morning, *Mykon*," but not before I first thanked God for seeing me safely through the night.

In the middle of that particular night the wind decided to gust to force seven, causing me to curse and scramble on deck to fully reef the main. It was my own fault for not reefing down before I turned in. With a beam wind I could reef on the run, simply by easing off the main sheet, which of course saved time at the mast. Incidentally, to work hands-free at the mast I would steady myself by slipping my bare feet under the cabin-top grab rails. I did design an adjustable stainless steel foot clamp to be fitted either side of the mast, but that job remained unfinished in the to-do book. As events turned out, I did not have to go to the mast until reaching Puerta Naos, as the wind remained constant in direction and strength. I am not a racing man by any means, but I was impressed by how *Mykon* was cutting through the water at 6.8 knots. Taking into account the natural southerly-setting drift of the Canary Current and the leeway from the northeasterly winds, I set a course close on the wind until we were sailing full and bye.

In order to check that we were keeping to the north of the Canary Islands, I would plot our position every three hours instead of the usual single noon-to-noon plot. The stretch of water that we were sailing in crossed the South America-to-Europe shipping lanes, so during the night I only slept in two-hourly intervals. When I did get my head down I would light the new lantern that I had bought in Porto Santo and hang it from the backstay. This new warning light, which ran on paraffin, was an over-two-hundred-candlepower pressure lantern. The near miss with the ship when sailing from the Azores did concentrate my mind on making our presence known to night traffic. This bright, all-round white light on the backstay did not conform to the official shipping regulations, but I think it is more important to be seen.

When I was on lookout duty when working on merchant ships I never ever caught sight of a yacht's navigation lights until we were almost running the yacht down. The only lights from a yacht that did attract our attention was when a powerful torch was shone from the yacht towards the ship's bridge. Shining a torch on a yacht's sails doesn't work either. From a ship the illuminated sails look just like another white breaker on the sea's surface. In my opinion the worst condition for a yacht to be spotted at night, is when the moon is shining brightly. Any white light displayed from the yacht, be it a torch or lantern, seems to be lost among the moon's reflection on the water.

Whenever I saw the moon at sea my thoughts would often drift to Joshua Slocum aboard his beloved *Spray*, and how clever he must have been to find his way across the oceans using lunar astronomy. To make Joshua's navigation even more astounding, he only possessed an old tin alarm clock that had the minute hand missing, although I think perhaps Josh was just being mischievous when he wrote that. Even so, to navigate by lunar calculations is far beyond my capabilities, and I am filled with admiration for anyone who has that skill.

The moon was still shining when the northern shore lights of Lanzarote popped up over the horizon. Once we were well to the east of this northern headland I altered course to run parallel to the coastline. This new course gave us a following wind. So with the fresh wind still coming from the northeast I doused the mainsail and ran free. As I was unfamiliar with the harbour at Puerta Naos, I did not want to arrive there during the hours of darkness. The wealth of information I gathered from a book called *Atlantic Islands* by Anne Hammick proved invaluable to me when trying to work out the best approach to these ports. At daylight, with the sails doused and the anchor made ready, we chugged into the inner harbour, passing huge merchantmen and passenger ships moored alongside the breakwater of the outer harbour.

The inner harbour was fairly crowded with mostly local fishing craft. Only a few yachts lay at anchor. As I passed one of the yachts, a man on board pointed to a nearby white buoy and said, "Pick that one up, the owner's gone away."

Chapter 22

The passage from Machico to Puerta Naos had taken sixty-seven hours, and we had sailed three hundred and fifty nautical miles over the ground. I was very pleased to know that *Mykon* had been averaging 5.2 knots fully reefed. The run of one hundred and twenty-five nautical miles measured from noon to noon was the furthest we had ever sailed in one day. A rough rule of thumb that I reckon on is a more realistic average of three knots that *Mykon* will sail through the water.

As I've already mentioned, the journey is more important to me than the destination, and the arrival I look on as a kind of bonus. This time, however, I was keen to make harbour so that I could arrange a flight for Janet, so that we could spend a holiday together. As things turned out, the only flight available was seven days after I had docked at Puerta Naos. It was during this time that I had the good fortune to make friends with a fellow yachtsman, Trevor Rishman, who was the kind stranger who had pointed out the spare mooring that we were now lying on.

Trevor, who was about the same age as myself, had made Puerta Naos his home, and had been living aboard his yacht in the harbour for a number of years. One evening whilst we sat in *Mykon*'s cabin, swapping yarns over a drink or two, I mentioned how the water during the bad weather would cascade into the cabin through the gap surrounding the sliding hatch. "What you need is a garage. Leave it to me, I'll sort it out for you," Trevor casually said.

Good to his word, four days later *Mykon* had a garage made from G.R.P. installed. And a better job I could not wish for. Trevor had been a professional boat-builder and had at one time owned his own company. I offered most willingly to pay for his excellent work but Trevor said, "No, I've enjoyed the challenge," adding: "Just pass a good deed on to the next stranger on your travels." Over the years I have always been aware that there is a brotherhood among seafarers, whatever their nationality. If only a fraction of Trevor's philosophy could prevail, the world would indeed be a better place.

A friend of Trevor's, a Polish yachtsman called Matt who also lived afloat, unwittingly taught me a lesson in etiquette that makes me cringe with embarrassment when I think about it. I had invited Matt and Trevor on board *Mykon* for a drink one night. Two dinghies duly arrived with my guests, whom I welcomed on board. I had spent the afternoon making a space for them to sit by throwing everything off the port bunk into the forepeak, and they made themselves at home. This is where I showed my lack of social graces. Matt handed to me a jar of olives which I stowed in my food locker, thinking that they would come in handy for Christmas. Several days later Matt invited onto his yacht three Polish friends and Trevor and myself for a get-together. Not wishing to arrive empty-handed, I brought a bottle of brandy and a jar of courgettes, thinking that he would stow the courgettes away as I had done with his olives. I could have died with embarrassment when Matt took the courgettes and poured them into a coconut shell so that everyone could help themselves. The other guests had brought Polish dishes that were laid out for everyone. And I had stowed away that jar of olives that Matt had brought. My face has gone red just writing these words.

Those feelings, however, paled into insignificance when I discovered that during the night fifteen drowned bodies had been washed up on the shore near Puerta Naos. Apparently the coastal police had intercepted a boatload of would-be illegal immigrants who had jumped overboard in an effort to escape arrest. To bear testimony to the trafficking in human cargoes, at the low water mark in the harbour, several crudely made open wooden boats lay moored. These engineless boats, which are about twenty-five feet in length, had been towed from as far away as Mauritania before being intercepted off Lanzarote. It was whilst talking to a captain of one of the coastal patrol vessels that I learnt that often these engineless boats are cast adrift many miles offshore by the owner of the towing vessel, leaving the poor wretches to their own fate. Hearing stories like these makes me appreciate just how lucky I am. All that I had to be concerned about that day was catching the bus to the marina at Puerto Calero to the south of the island to secure an alongside berth for when Janet arrived.

Janet stayed for three weeks, which sped by all too quickly. We explored the island by bus, reaching the summit of Montanas del Fuego on one of the days. We could feel the heat of the volcano through the soles of our sandals as we looked out on what could have been a lunar landscape. It was a very relaxing holiday, and Janet even took a turn at steering *Mykon* along the coast to visit Trevor and Matt at Puerta Naos. It was ironic that during our coastal trip – when I had an extra pair of eyes (Janet's) as a lookout – the newly installed A.I.S. sounded its alarm to tell us a ship was approaching. Not only did the A.I.S. warn of a nearby ship, but gave its course and speed through the water and the ship's name. Although it was not a substitute for keeping a lookout, with this new installation I slept more peacefully.

It was from a peaceful sleep that on the morning of 26th November I was awoken by the sound of a dinghy bumping alongside *Mykon*. Trevor had rowed across to wish me luck, as I was sailing for the Cape Verde islands that day. Everything had been stowed the night before in preparation for leaving, and as I was on a mooring buoy it was simply a matter of letting go.

During the time I was at Puerta Naos I had bought a stock of things from the supermarket to celebrate Christmas, which included a leg of smoked pork. Matt, who had been to Cape Verde several times, had warned me that the groceries there were quite basic and very expensive. I had heard stories from quite a few yachtsmen that it was best to keep on good terms with the beach children on Cape Verde, who offered to keep a safe watch on your dinghy. Not wishing to have my beached rubber dinghy slashed to pieces – as I had heard could happen – I bought a few bribes. I had stocked up with colouring books and crayons, small stocking-filler toys and packets of sweets etc., hoping that these would suffice. My reasoning was that it would be cheaper to buy a few toys than a new dinghy. As things turned out I found that the beach children were not miniature gangsters at all, but friendly and helpful, pulling my dinghy beyond the high water mark in my absence.

Whilst I cannot vouch for the other islands, I found that on Sal the people, although desperately poor, were most welcoming and friendly. Perhaps I am lucky, for on my travels the people I have met have always seemed to be friendly. And the people that I had met in Puerta Naos were no exception, as the new garage on *Mykon*'s sliding hatch bore testimony.

Chapter 23

Although I had enjoyed my stay at Lanzarote, I was glad when we cleared the breakwater of Puerta Naos and stood out to sea. Our destination lay about a thousand nautical miles to the south-southwest: Sal in the Cape Verde islands.

The wind was from the northeast at about force three and held steady for the next two days until we were south of the Canary Island archipelago. It was at this point that the wind faded away to a zephyr and steerage way was lost. Being clear of the land, I wasn't unduly concerned – at least the Canary Current was taking us towards our destination, although only at about one knot.

It was whilst we were becalmed that the A.I.S. gave out an alarm that a ship was nearby. Taking the ship's I.D. from the A.I.S. screen I called her name over the radio. Having made contact I asked the ship's captain if he could give a weather forecast for the area. In broken English the captain asked me to wait a minute or two, and then he came back: "Wind from west force eleven!"

Force eleven? It must be a mistake. Perhaps he meant force seven. We were to be virtually becalmed for the next four days, and for the rest of the passage did not have any strong winds. On arrival at Sal I learnt that Tropical Storm Delta had struck the Canary Islands on 28th November, causing severe damage. At least seven people had been drowned. The storm also caused power shortages, leaving twenty thousand people without power and airports closed down. My thoughts went out to Trevor and Matt; I hoped that they came through unscathed.

During the four days of being becalmed we had drifted to within fifteen miles of the coast of Mauritania. It was whilst in this windless state that I noticed with some curiosity that a trawler was always nearby. Compared to the rust-streaked African trawlers that I had previously encountered, this one was in pristine condition. The trawler's hull was smartly painted black, and in sharp contrast the booms that protruded from each side were painted yellow. There could be no mistaking this vessel for anything but a trawler. This is where I did make one big mistake, for the 'trawler' turned out to be a decoy vessel for the Spanish navy, which was engaged in intercepting the illegal immigration traffic. The first inkling of the true nature of the 'trawler' came when a high-speed inflatable boat (R.I.B.) was lowered over its side and headed towards *Mykon*. Four men aboard the R.I.B., complete with rifles slung across their backs and wearing woollen hats, could have come out of a scene from *The Guns of Navarone*. "All personnel on deck!" one of them called through a loudhailer.

All personnel? There was only me here. As this drama was being played out, a naval vessel appeared from over the horizon and headed towards us with a bone in her teeth. I am not at all familiar with classes of naval vessels, but if my memory serves me right the marking on her bow was P317. Switching on my hand-held V.H.F. transmitter I called up the naval vessel and asked what were her intentions, as she had begun circling us at about five knots. The captain, who sounded German, answered my question by directing a series of questions at me. "Why have you been off this coast for nearly four days?" "Where are you going to?" "How many people on board?" "Which was your last port of call?" After I had answered all the questions there was a radio silence that lasted for several minutes. Obviously the details that I had supplied were being checked out.

The radio burst into life again: "You say that you are going to Sal in Cape Verde, that course is two-three-five degrees, why are you heading zero-nine-zero degrees?"

"No, no, I cannot steer the yacht, I have no wind, the yacht is only *pointing* zero-nine-zero, not going anywhere. I am waiting for the wind to come back." Hoping that the captain was not a mind-reader, I silently added: "… you stupid bastard."

Realising that it was just an innocent yacht that had been encountered, the captain's attitude changed: "I take my cap off to you and hope the wind comes back soon, good luck." The R.I.B. headed back to its mother ship, the 'trawler'. The naval vessel followed, and within half an hour they had all disappeared over the horizon. Looking at the now empty sea around me, I could have been forgiven for thinking that it had all been a dream. The hand-held V.H.F. transmitting radio lying on the cockpit side-bench reassured me that it hadn't been.

The wind, when it did come back, was from the northeast and about force three to four. At first the self-steering could not cope with this following wind until I doused the main and unfurled the foresail to the size of a Genoa. The wind was then brought onto the quarter. Tacking downwind like this does add on a few extra miles, of course, but running at five knots through the water I was happy. Just before daylight, after two weeks at sea, the light beacon on Sal appeared fine off the port bow. It was 9th December. Entering the anchorage at Baia de Palmeila I dropped the hook in six metres of water about two hundred yards from the beach. There were over twenty other yachts nearby, mostly flying the German flag. Only one other solitary yacht beside me was flying the Red Ensign. This yacht belonged to an Italian couple, Claudia and Leo. They were seasoned travellers and sailed under the Red Ensign as they found that there was less hassle when clearing the yacht at immigration.

It was as I walked along the dusty road to the immigration office that the scarcity of trees and shrubs became apparent. Cape Verde seemed an odd name for these brown volcanic rock islands, but the early settlers had named them after Cap-Vert (meaning Cape-Green), now in Senegal, the westernmost point of continental Africa. These early settlers were Portuguese and first discovered the uninhabited Cape Verde in 1456, making the islands a part of the Portuguese Empire. Due to its location about three hundred miles from the African coast, Cape Verde became an important watering station and a sugar cane plantation site. The watering station must have been on one of the other islands of the archipelago, as on Sal all the drinking water now comes from a seawater desalination plant. These islands had also played an important part in the slave trade, as a transit camp for the poor African souls that were destined to spend their lives in servitude in the fields of Brazil, the West Indies or the southern states of America. With hindsight, I suppose it was the slaves who did make it to the plantations that were the lucky ones (that's if being lucky can be associated with being a slave) for many did not survive the terrible conditions on the arduous voyage across the ocean.

In 1975 Cape Verde achieved independence from Portugal and now the majority of the population ekes a scant living, mostly from the service trade. With the need to import ninety percent of its food owing to its poor natural resource base (including the scarcity of water), Cape Verde runs a high trade deficit. The result of this economic imbalance is that most of the islanders live a very frugal lifestyle.

The attitude of the locals is quite stoic, and regardless of their plight the people I met seemed very friendly and helpful, and not from any expectation of being rewarded. For example, I would be queuing at the town's communal drinking water taps (fontana) to fill the ship's water containers, and when my turn came, invariably someone would take the bottles out of my hand and fill them for me. The drinking water cost just a few cents, paid to an elderly lady who sat on an upturned paint drum and handed out receipt tickets from a roll.

There wasn't any public transport as we know it, so in order to reach the small town (Vila de Espargos) which is about two miles away, you just started walking towards it along the dusty road. After a few minutes a pick-up truck would stop, and after giving the driver a few escudos you hopped on board and joined the other passengers. The fare was government-controlled and there was never any hassle from the driver regarding payment.

Vila de Espargos reminded me of a cowboy town that you would see in a western movie, although there are recently built banks and mini-supermarkets with modern façades; they looked out of place in the old town. Inside one of the old buildings I discovered an internet café where you could pay for an international phone call at a fraction of the state-controlled service, which in 2005 was four euros per minute. There are several bars/cafés in the centre of town where I would sit at a table on the pavement with a cold beer and watch the world go by. It was there that I met a street vendor called Gilbert, who was selling necklaces and trinkets that he and his wife had made from small white sea shells and the black, beadlike vertebrae of fish. I do not wear any ornaments, rings or jewellery at all, but on this occasion I did buy a shell necklace and bracelet for myself. The idea was that I could make myself look like a native Brazilian. Werner, who had been to Natal (the same Brazilian port that I was heading for), had warned of the slum district 'favela' that I would have to go through, where muggers were a serious threat. He had advised me to pay attention to the way that the locals dress and buy similar clothes. Looking like a foreigner (e.g. wearing dark socks with Bermudas) would make me instantly recognisable as a *gringo* and a target for thieves. The bracelet and necklace, I hoped, would go some way to helping me blend in with the locals in Natal.

Each day I would head into Vila de Espargos to phone home or post letters, and each day my dinghy was left on the beach in the care of the beach children. As I have mentioned, the behaviour of these local kids was not at all as I had been warned about. When they weren't at school they were playing football on the beach, kicking what looked like a homemade ball of rags. And their honesty did amaze me, for each day I would hand out a set number of colouring books and crayons or whatever to the forest of outstretched hands of the shrieking children. The remainder of the 'bribes' which I had carried ashore in a plastic food box were left in the dinghy. Each time I returned to row back to *Mykon*, usually in the evening, the children had gone and the contents of that plastic box had remained untouched.

Near to the beach there was a ramshackle bar where the locals met and sat yarning around wooden circular tables that resembled giant cotton reels. These six-foot diameter wooden reels had been industrial cable carriers originally, as the black stencilled lettering stated. Among the locals I met Karl, a German who had made Cape Verde his home and had lived in Sal with his wife Elizbet for over thirty years. Over the years he had noticed the subtle changes in the seasons owing to global warming. Karl pointed out that the northeasterly trades in the month of December would have at one time been constant over the islands, but were now erratic.

As if to verify Karl's observations the northeasterly wind that had been blowing at force four since my arrival died away altogether for several days. I did not mind the absence of wind at all, as I was not in any hurry to leave this peaceful anchorage. I did take the opportunity during this calm spell to don a mask and snorkel and, armed with a scrubbing brush, looked at *Mykon*'s hull for signs of any barnacles or growth. There was, surprisingly, hardly anything below the waterline to scrub off, even though the anti-fouling had been on for over seven months. I had painted on two coats of anti-fouling paint in Ramsey on the Isle of Man. This navy blue paint was International Micron Extra, and at the time I thought it was a bit pricey. 'Don't spoil the ship for a ha'p'orth of tar' did come to mind.

The 'ship' was very nearly spoiled one evening, though not through the lack of tar but when a neighbouring yacht's anchor fouled my mooring and began dragging *Mykon* out to sea. At the time I was rowing back from the shore and thought my eyes were playing tricks as I saw through the darkness the silhouette of *Mykon* moving from the anchorage. A French-registered yacht that was used as a lobster fishing boat had dropped its anchor across my mooring. On weighing the anchor, the yacht's owner had unknowingly caught my nylon anchor warp. The young Frenchman, who was about twenty-five years of age, lived permanently at Sal and ran his yacht single-handed, making a living by fishing. Amid the cries through the darkness of a mad Englishman shouting blue murder, the Frenchman, on realising the predicament he had caused, stopped heading out to sea. It took quite a while to sort out the entangled cables, and after much swearing and cursing by me, *Mykon* was safely anchored once again.

The next day the Frenchman rowed across to our new anchorage and handed me a sail bag. "This spinnaker somebody gave to me; it is too small for my yacht, you take it the size okay for your yacht." I suddenly felt sorry for all the cursing that I had directed at him the night before. This unexpected gift I looked on as a going-away present, for I was sailing at noon. Most of the other yachts had already sailed away, bound for the Caribbean. My next intended landfall was the island of Fernando de Noronha, en route to Natal. Claudia and Leo, the Italian couple, had told me how they intended to visit Fernando de Noronha, which had once served as a Portuguese penal colony. It sounded an interesting place to visit.

Chapter 24

With one last glance at the beach to make sure that the tide had reached the high water mark, I weighed anchor and headed out to the open sea. It was 15th December 2005. Although I had enjoyed my stay at Sal, I was glad as usual to be back at sea again. The feelings I had could be compared to those of the pit ponies that I had worked with below ground as a boy of fifteen years. After being kept down the coal mine for twelve months, the ponies were released into a grassy field for an annual two-week break. For several days they gambolled about like spring lambs in their new-found freedom. One of the freedoms I felt when at sea again and being single-handed was not to bother about wearing any clothes. The weather was too hot and humid to be dressed, and apart from a foreign-legion-type hat, I wore nothing else. Not a pretty sight, but the fish didn't seem to mind, for as I was trimming the sails a flying fish landed on my chest with a mighty thud. This unexpected guest accompanied a plate of instant potatoes and me for dinner that evening. It was whilst having dinner that I became aware that my already loose front tooth was becoming even more wobbly. Really I should have paid a visit to a dentist at Sal and had it pulled out. Too late now.

The northeasterly trade wind had returned, as Karl had predicted, and on a broad reach we headed southward at four knots. Fine on the port bow the twinkling lights on one of the islands in the archipelago – Boa Vista – could be seen in the distance. At the same time as the sun began to sink below the horizon, a huge full moon began to rise, its silvery reflection illuminating the powerful curvature of *Mykon*'s white sails. This was paradise.

By 03:00 the next day the lights on Boa Vista had disappeared in our wake, although we were not clear of the archipelago yet for there were two more islands to pass between: Santiago and Fogo, which lay about sixty-five nautical miles to the southwest. For some reason that I could not explain, we were in an area that at times made the magnetic compass swing wildly, affecting the known variation by as much as ten degrees. This error first came to light when I noticed that although the masthead was steady on Orion's Belt, the compass card was being pulled to the west. Checking our true course on the G.P.S. confirmed the extra compass error. Irrespective of erratic compasses I hadn't any intention of sleeping that night, for we were in the trade wind area frequented by Caribbean-bound yachts. In the friendly glow of the cabin lamp I set about making a pot of tea and tuned in to the B.B.C. overseas broadcast, hoping to listen to a play. If I was going to stay awake all night I might as well enjoy myself. It was whilst rooting under the bunk for a fresh pack of tea bags that I pulled out a long-forgotten plastic box that contained a catapult and bag of stones for ammunition. Jane, my dear friend who had lived alone in a cottage in the mountains, about a mile away from our cottage (she died two weeks after I had left on this voyage), had given this catapult to me to help ward off any pirates. It may sound amusing in this day and age to mention pirates, but off the coast of French Cayenne in particular the pilot book advises yachts to exercise extreme caution. It is not unknown for yacht crews to be murdered by marauding drug gangs who will then take over the yacht to use for smuggling purposes. I restowed the plastic box that contained the catapult and its primitive ammunition, hoping that I would never have to become involved in some sort of modern-day David and Goliath contest.

By daylight the last islands in the archipelago – Santiago and Fogo – lay fifty nautical miles ahead. Having kept a vigil for any shipping all through the night, I was ready for a few hours' sleep. Besides the lookout duties, I had been kept busy during the night dodging the main boom that was trying to knock my head off when the wind backed to the north-northeast. The wind shift meant that now we were almost running free and *Mykon* started to roll continuously, threatening to gybe the main sail. I put a stop to this threat by rigging a preventor guy to the end of the boom. The rolling used to drive me to distraction, as I always had to have one hand gripping onto something to keep my balance. If the rolling motion had been even and regular, things would not have been too bad. It was the unexpected violent roll, usually at a time when I was trying to get out of the cabin with a hot cup of tea, that made me swear at *Mykon*. Rolling or no rolling, I would not have any trouble sleeping. After checking the fishing line that I was trolling and having one last look around the horizon, I went below to lay my head down.

It was four hours later that the tinny rattling of the alarm clock made me sit up and fumble half-asleep to put a stop to the annoying din. "I am going to buy a battery alarm clock as soon as I get ashore." I have lost count of the number of times that I've uttered these words. It was 11:30 ship's time, and in keeping with my pathetic efforts to master the sextant I prepared to obtain a meridian altitude. The yacht's heavy rolling didn't help, as the reflected image of the sun kept dipping into the water! The result of my efforts put us fifteen nautical miles further south than our true latitude. Thank God for the G.P.S.

Besides driving me insane, another adverse effect of the constant rolling was that the blades of the wind generator kept falling away from the wind. I remedied this by making fast a lanyard to the generator's directional vane so the propeller was constantly facing into the following wind. Whilst I had been asleep a big fish had taken the lure that I had been trolling – it had also taken most of the line. The fishing line, a heavy-duty braided twine with a breaking strain of forty kilograms (eighty-eight pounds), had parted at the sheet winch where I had made it fast. Incidentally, the colour of the braided fishing line was red: this is the first colour in the spectrum to disappear in water. I regretted that the invisible line had fooled some poor fish that was now swimming around with a tin lid hooked into its mouth. My sympathies didn't last very long, I'm afraid to say, as I opened an oval-shaped tin of tuna for dinner that evening, keeping the lid to make another lure. It was during that evening that we passed between Santiago and Fogo, the last two islands of the Cape Verde archipelago.

During the night the wind backed to the northeast and I altered course slightly, bringing the ship's head to south-southwest. I wanted to eventually cross the Equator at about twenty-seven degrees west. The old pilotage instructions for sailing ships had recommended that for the month of December, between twenty-five and twenty-seven degrees west were the coordinates for the southbound crossing. The self-steering gear was finding it hard to cope with the following wind. It was only the preventor guy that stopped the boom from crashing across to the old weather side when she gybed. As soon as daylight appeared I set about trimming the rig in order that we could sail downwind with less demand on the Aries steering paddle.

I found that by sheeting the foresail hard in so that it lay fore and aft, it acted as a steering sail. The mainsail was then single-reefed in order to balance her and then boomed out fully with the preventor guy. With the reduced sail area I lost one knot of the speed through the water, but a straighter course compensated for this. I was happy with three and a half knots.

Later that day, after I had finished the boat drill and cutting my hair and so on (yes, it was a Saturday – 17th December) I decided to try out the spinnaker that I had been given by the French yachtsman at Sal. The spinnaker turned out to be just the right size for *Mykon* and set beautifully. I did not mind at all that a colourful picture of a motor-racing bike was festooned all the way across the balloon-like sail.

Of course it meant hand-steering under this rig. Who cared? It was such a beautifully sunny day. I could not believe my eyes when I saw the head of the sail fall away from the masthead and float gently down into the water ahead of *Mykon*. The snap shackle on the spinnaker halyard had shaken open. It was to take almost an hour to haul the sail back on board, as it had fouled on *Mykon*'s keel. The weight of the water trapped in the roach of the sail made it feel as if I was hauling a net full of fish. My main concern was that I had lost the use of the spinnaker halyard that was now two blocks at the masthead. In an emergency it could have been used as a main halyard. After the decks had been cleared and foresail and main had been reset to their former rig, I wrote in the to-do book 'retrieve halyard'.

"I think we deserve a cup of tea, *Mykon*," I called into the cockpit, and set about filling the measuring jug with a cup of water from the miniature galley pump. The forty-litre flexible plastic water tank that fed the galley had been refilled at Sal, so I was puzzled to find that only air was being drawn from the pump. On lifting the bottom boards in the cabin I found about three inches of water swilling about. The plastic tank had split. My immediate reaction was of profound shock, for it was a serious loss. In a separate book, where I kept a strict record of the drinking water being used, I found that there was still enough remaining for another thirty days. I felt better after this revelation, but decided to reduce my drinking water consumption from three and a half litres per day to two, just to be on the safe side. If I was not almost bald I could have said that I was having a 'bad hair day'. I decided to forgo the tea and have a hot whisky toddy instead. Sitting in the cockpit with my back resting on the cabin bulkhead, legs outstretched, whisky in hand, I looked at the bubbling wake. It was indeed a wonderful world.

The next few days of calm weather and a steady wind put me in a good frame of mind as we rolled merrily along towards the Equator. I found that I was coping better with the endless rolling now that my leg muscles were becoming stronger as they were being constantly braced to keep my balance. It was whilst I was balancing in the cockpit having my weekly salt water 'bath' and was covered in the soapsuds of washing-up liquid (bar soap doesn't lather in salt water) that I had a shock. The saucepan that was attached to the fishing line that I was trolling went flying off the sidebench. I'd caught a fish! I was glad that nobody was around to witness the surreal sight of a man covered in soap bubbles, naked except for a legionnaire's hat, hauling on board a four-foot barracuda. It was an evil-looking fish, too, something like a freshwater pike only bigger; its small sharp teeth had punctured the tin lid lure.

Being careful that it didn't snap my bare feet as it lay thrashing about on the cockpit sole, I ended its distress with the galley knife. Catching the barracuda came at an appropriate time, for it was Christmas Eve. Barracuda would be on the Christmas dinner menu.

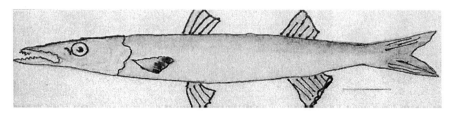

Barracuda.
Sketch: Trevor Wilson collection.

I had decorated the cabin with a miniature artificial Christmas tree that stood about nine inches high, and a plastic snowman, both held onto the pilot desk with Blue Tac. Paper decorations that I had bought in Puerta Naos were festooned about the cabin. It all looked colourful and festive. I hoped the weather would stay calm.

As events turned out, by Christmas Day the wind had disappeared altogether and the sea became smooth, with a giant, unbroken swell. Our position was six degrees north and twenty-seven degrees west. We had reached the Doldrums. My spirits were not in the Doldrums, though, for it was Christmas Day. The dinner was cooking merrily away on the stove, complete with a Christmas pudding and brandy sauce. Janet had brought the pudding and my Christmas present with her when she came out to Lanzarote. My face lit up when I opened my present, an illustrated book called *Sea Birds of the World*. This book would make my sea bird tea towel redundant.

There wasn't a bird in sight that day, although the surface of the sea was alive with numerous sailfish chasing skipjack tuna, which were leaping out of the water in a frantic effort to escape. Before darkness fell I lit the pressure paraffin oil lantern and hung it on the backstay. The vanes on the wind generator were motionless. In the cabin the brass oil lamp that hung in gimbals above the chart table lent its friendly glow to the one-man Christmas party that I was having. From the cassette player a medley of Christmas carols filled the cabin and I joined in the singing, making up any words that I'd forgotten as I went along. After several whiskies I thought that my renditions would not be out of place in a church choir. I found pulling the crackers was cheating a bit because it was always me that ended up with the paper hat, novelty and motto.

Chapter 25

At noon on Boxing Day I found that during the previous twenty-four hours we had drifted three nautical miles to the southwest. To take advantage of this calm spell I decided to 'make hay whilst the sun shines' as the saying goes.

I set about retrieving the snap shackle end of the spinnaker halyard that was mockingly sticking out of a block at the masthead. The method that I use to climb the mast single-handed is by using equipment made for rock-climbing. The kit consists of two rope clamps called ascenders, a length of webbing measuring from my waist to my heel with a foot stirrup in one end and a climber's step-in harness. The first rope clamp is shackled to the harness above waist height, the second to the non-foot-stirrup end of the webbing. Stretch tight a mast halyard, clamp the harness ascender to it and underneath it clamp the foot stirrup ascender. After taking your weight initially on the foot stirrup move your waist ascender upwards. Sit in the waist harness taking your weight off the foot stirrup. Move the foot stirrup further upwards. Repeat these actions until the desired height is reached. To come down from the mast, simply reverse the procedure. Any tools that I will require when aloft I place in a bucket left on deck to be hauled up on a lanyard when I have reached the desired height. The rate of travel is only about nine inches with each step so it's important not to forget any of the tools that you will need!

Climbing the mast single-handed.

It took about fifteen minutes to reach the masthead. Just as I was lowering the maverick end of the halyard to the deck, a constant bleeping sound came from the cabin. It was the alarm from the A.I.S. unit. Looking around the horizon from this unusually high vantage point, I spotted an oil tanker heading northwest. On returning to deck level I found that it was no longer visible. After deriving the ship's name that was displayed on the A.I.S. console I switched on the V.H.F. transmitting radio (it had been turned off to conserve the ship's battery) and sent out a general call. From the conversation that followed I learnt that the tanker was in ballast and bound for New York for orders. Most important, though, I was told that we had been spotted on the ship's radar from a range of twelve nautical miles. We chatted for about fifteen minutes, but before we signed off I was told he would report my position and that 'all was well' to the Falmouth Coastguard.

Returning to the spinnaker halyard that I had just retrieved, I cut off the self-opening snap shackle and replaced it with a Dee shackle. Before I had set out on this voyage, all the snap shackles that were destined to go aloft I had replaced with Dee shackles, except of course the one on the spinnaker halyard. Sod's Law?

In this windless area I had fully furled the foresail to stop it slatting on the rigging. The mainsail I had left fully set, hoping it would act as a warning flag to any shipping. To stop the creaking noise from the mainsail boom as it swung gently with every roll, I guyed it off with a piece of spare cordage. Rigging that piece of spare cordage was to prove a serious mistake on my part.

It was about three o'clock the next morning when my subconscious senses suddenly alerted me from my sleep. With eyes wide open and ears straining to interpret the unfamiliar noise, I lay motionless on my bunk, staring intently at the deckhead. Rain. Swinging my legs smartly out of my bunk, I readjusted the head-torch that I wore at all times during the night. Before I had time to climb onto the cabin steps – *whoosh! – Mykon* suddenly heeled over with such violence that I was thrown across the cabin.

Gripped by fear, I scrambled to reach the companionway, which was now above my head. *Mykon* was not recovering from the knockdown, and lay on her beam ends. In the cockpit I was met by a scene that resembled the chaos of a gunship battle of the nineteenth century. The wind had reached force eight and the rain that was being carried horizontally was filling the mainsail as we lay heeled to the sudden onslaught. The heavy drenching rain had filled the bunt of the almost horizontal sail and was pouring off it like a waterfall. The weatherside shrouds and stays now looked like the delicate threads of a spider's web, and were bar-tight under the sudden strain. A deafening, intense cracking noise and a nanosecond's illumination from the thunder and lightning was crashing into the sea only yards away.

"Hurry up, Trev, or you will lose the mast!" I kept repeating out aloud, as if hearing these words would help me to think straight. My heart was racing like mad. After I had freed the mainsheet to spill the wind, nothing happened. It was then I remembered that I had made the mainsail boom fast with a piece of spare cordage. By this time I was wearing my mental blinkers and ignoring all of the chaos that was going on all around us. I set about uncleating the boom. Immediately it was freed, the wind spilled from the mainsail and the lee decks started to lift clear of the water. The righting motion of the two-ton keel had begun to take effect, causing the yacht to weathercock into the howling wind. I had to act quickly to douse the mainsail, which was now threatening to shake itself to destruction.

Ignoring the deafening mêlée that was going on all around us, I made my way to the mast, half-blinded by the heavy rain. There had not been time to put my safety harness on, so on reaching the mast I jammed my bare feet under the grab rails on the cabin roof. With an urgency born of desperation I grabbed at the luff and doused the mainsail hand-over-hand. The numerous and sudden illuminations from the lightning lit up the deck with the silent speed of a camera flash. Immediately following these flashes, a sharp cracking sound of thunder reverberated through the air with such intensity that I froze in fear. With the mainsheet steadying the boom and the sail lashed down along its length, I sat in the cockpit, gasping for breath. I needed a rest to gather my wits for I was in a state of shock.

Sitting in the rain was not at all unpleasant: the opposite in fact, for the rain was warm. Although the onslaught of the bad weather was still raging, I felt safer now that we were under bare poles. Taking a deep breath, I tried to pretend that everything was normal, and set about collecting some of the torrential rainwater. Kneeling on the cabin sole I placed the tube of the water-catching device into a plastic washing-up bowl. After ten minutes the flowing water tasted salt-free and

I began to refill the water bottles that I had used. The thunder was still doing its best to frighten the wits out of me. And succeeding. Just as I was concentrating on carefully pouring the precious drinking water into the fifth plastic five-litre bottle, the cabin was filled with a tremendous bang. The yacht began to shake with such violence that I thought the hull would fracture. We had been struck by lightning. The water-collecting was immediately abandoned as I rushed on deck, half expecting to see that the aluminium mast had melted away.

Everything looked normal, but a low, humming drone filled the air. You may have walked through a field during a heavy downpour of rain and the electric pylons are giving out a humming sound. That was the very sound that was coming from *Mykon*'s rigging. Immediately following the next thunder bang, the humming stopped. To this day I cannot explain this phenomenon. The only apparent damage caused by the lightning strike was that the cylindrical radar reflector was put out of action. (Confirmed two weeks later by a passing ship that could not see us on their radar.)

In the space of only forty-five minutes the bad weather, the rain, the thunder and lightning had all passed, leaving a clear sky filled with stars. If it had not been for the twenty extra litres of rainwater that were in the newly refilled plastic bottles I might have thought it had all been a dream. We were to experience four more sudden violent thunder storms whilst we were in the Doldrums and being carried along by the North Equatorial Current. By the time New Year's Eve had arrived, I had collected forty litres of rainwater, which replaced the loss from the flexible water tank that had split. On the ninth day of being virtually becalmed I felt a gentle zephyr of wind on my face. We were actually moving through the water at one and a half knots!

It was Monday 2nd January 2006 and our position was 00.55 degrees north and 29.20 degrees west. Fine on the starboard bow and at a distance of four nautical miles a group of rocks appeared that looked like the fingers of a giant's hand sticking out of the water. They were the St Peter and St Paul Rocks, the final resting place of many becalmed sailing ships that were carried onto them by the west-flowing Equatorial Current. The closest piece of land is the island of Fernando de Noronha, 391 nautical miles to the southwest. Fernando de Noronha, as you will recall, was an intended port of call, but I would have to be content with a near-miss as we had been carried too far to the west. When the southeasterly trades were met we would be hard on the wind and heading southward, the west-going currents setting us away from the islands.

Luckily on this particular day we had steerage way – just, for I had to make a decision to sail to the north of the Rocks as the current was setting onto them at a rate of two and a quarter knots. This manoeuvre put us even further to the west and finally we crossed the Equator at 30.10 degrees west.

'Crossing the Line' was a time for celebration, and I opened the tin of Madeira cake I had bought at Porto Santo. The ration of whisky that I had intended to save for the crossing party had been drunk on New Year's Eve when I decided to have two celebrations: one for each time zone. So it was 'tea and tabnabs' as we say in the Merchant Navy.

Eating the cake, my loose front tooth was bent over, aggravating the nerve ends. I had tolerated this pesky tooth for months: enough was enough, so I decided to try to pull it out with a pair of pliers. Each time I pulled on the tooth the pain was quite intense, so I involuntarily stopped pulling. Sitting in the cockpit I racked my brains for a solution. I remembered as a boy seeing in the *Beano* that one end of a piece of string was tied to some character's tooth that required extracting and the other end to a door knob. The rapid slamming of the door pulled out the tooth. Of course the problem with that method was that on *Mykon* I did not have a door knob or door to swing it on. I did have a catapult though. Taking a short length of extra-strong fishing line, I tied a four-ounce lead weight to one end. The other end I tied to my loose tooth. The lead weight was duly placed into the leather pouch of the catapult. I pulled the elastic until it could stretch no further. With eyes firmly closed and mouth wide open, I found that my fingers were having trouble receiving the message from my brain telling them to let go. "Go on, let go!" I willed my fingers. "It will all be over in seconds." I let go. The first inkling of the extraction being a success was the salty taste of my blood-filled mouth. I didn't see my tooth disappear into the sea, as I had kept my eyes shut the whole time.

I consoled myself with the knowledge that there is a part of me attached to a lead weight and fishing line lying on the Equator.

Although I had crossed the Equator many times whilst in the Merchant Navy, this seemed different. To see the Southern Cross in the night sky, the Pole Star now out of sight below the northern horizon, all added to the sense of *Mykon* actually travelling over the Earth's curvature.

Hard on the southeasterly trades, the course that we held made us leave the island of Fernando de Noronha unreachable, sixty nautical miles away to our east. We had a visitor though, probably from the island, a frigate bird. As it swooped down to mast height I could clearly see that the bird had an angular W-shaped black wingspan which reached about six feet tip to tip, and a long, deeply forked tail. The sighting of these birds by the mariners of old must have been a welcome sight, for they usually stay within fifty miles of the land.

It was the sighting of what appeared to be a floating many-tiered wedding cake coming towards us that distracted me from my bird-watching. After making contact with the huge passenger cruise ship I discovered that although we were in visual contact by the ship's watch-keepers, we did not appear on their radar screen. I wondered if the lightning strike had put our cylindrical radar reflector out of action. The original plastic 'blipper' type radar reflector that came with the yacht, and which I had kept as a spare, was temporarily sent aloft on one of the flag halyards. Natal lay only one hundred and ninety nautical miles to our southwest, so a more permanent fixing of the radar reflector could be carried out when we reached there.

And it was two days later that we reached the mouth of the Potengi River, with the skyscrapers of Natal clearly visible along its banks. The building of a massive road bridge spanning the mouth of the river was underway. At that time (January 2006), the two constructions from either bank still had about two hundred yards to go before they would meet. The partly built bridge was a good feature marking the approach to the channel. I just had to remember to keep the port hand buoys to starboard. (The I.A.L.A. buoyage system B is used in South America.) As we sailed towards the middle of the bridge, several small sailing vessels passed by, heading out to sea. They were the local fishing fleet, consisting of about twenty *jangadas*. Although these wooden, engineless vessels looked primitive they moved gracefully and swiftly through the water with their single lateen-shaped sails filled with the prevailing trade winds. "Bom dia!" the fishermen shouted across to us as they sped by. These fishermen often sail over ten miles offshore, and although these *jangadas* were only about fifteen feet in length, they would return to shore with enormous catches of tuna, swordfish or sometimes shark.

With the engine out of gear but ticking over in standby, *Mykon* entered the river under her Genoa-sized foresail only, as there was plenty of wind and room to manoeuvre. About a half-mile up river from the bridge and close to the portside bank, I saw several yachts moored.

Spilling the wind as we approached, I found a suitable spot well clear of the other yachts and dropped the hook. It was Thursday 12th January 2006.

We had crossed the Atlantic! From Sal it had taken twenty-eight days to reach Natal. Sailing and drifting (in the Doldrums for nine days) we had covered a total of 1580 nautical miles, averaging fifty-six nautical miles per day.

Chapter 26

Rowing ashore from the anchorage, I found the landing place on the riverside on a white sandy beach. Next to the Natal Yacht Club several yacht dinghies had their painters made fast to the palm trees above the high water mark. The yacht club charged only a nominal fee to use the anchorage and for the use of all the club's facilities, which included a shower block, a small swimming pool and meals served either in the restaurant or outside under a shady veranda. Irrespective of a yacht's length the standard charge per day was sixteen reais (about four pounds sterling), and considering the yacht club was enclosed by a security-patrolled wire fence, it was a bargain. I found the staff at the club very helpful and trusting. On first landing ashore I did not have any Brazilian currency, but the staff said that I could pay later for any of the ice-cold bottled beer or food that I might want that evening.

It was whilst I was sitting on the veranda having a drink that someone called out, "Trevor!" It was Claudia and Leo, the Italian couple I had met in Sal. The couple, you may remember, that sailed their yacht under the Red Ensign. Although it had only been relatively briefly that we had met, it was like meeting old friends. They had made the crossing from Sal in twelve days compared to my twenty-eight, although they did say that they had motored through the Doldrums, using nearly six hundred litres of diesel in doing so.

I stayed at Natal for seventeen days, and in that time I met lots of interesting people. One of them was Louis, a native Brazilian who was a school teacher and supplemented his pay by being an unofficial interpreter.

I met Louis at an internet café where I was enquiring about telephoning the U.K. Louis, who was about fifty years of age, spoke fluent English and offered to guide me around the city. Payment (if any) would be left to my discretion. My potential guide seemed a genuine person, and although he was dressed in a clean tee-shirt and cotton shorts he didn't look like a school teacher. With his straw hat and plastic supermarket bag flung over his shoulder, Louis looked a bit peasant-like. This appearance was a deliberate ploy to dress down to avoid being mugged. In the cheap plastic bag Louis had expensive equipment: a digital camera, back-up hard drives and an electronic note pad, which was something to do with the journalism that he was also involved in. As I had also dressed (so I thought) to blend in with the locals I asked Louis if I would pass for a Brazilian.

"Not bad, but one thing that really gives you away are those sandals, that's the first thing a mugger looks for on a *gringo*." After I had bought a pair of rubber flip-flops and put my sandals in a plastic bag, Louis said that I would pass for a native, but on no account must I speak to anyone. "With me, you are safe from muggers, so don't worry." Among the other advice I was given was that if I was challenged by muggers, in no circumstances try to run away or resist. Stay calm and comply with their demands, and you are unlikely to be hurt. Finally I was told not to fight back, as I would be outnumbered and would probably be killed. "The police are winning though: last year there were thirty thousand murders in Brazil but only twenty-five thousand this year." Was Louis trying to cheer me up? It was whilst in the downtown centre of Natal that Louis pointed out a print shop where I had my passport copied. Apparently passports are sought after by the criminal fraternity. For the remainder of my stay in Natal I only carried this plastic laminated copy of my passport when ashore. I.D. must be produced on demand by the police.

I hope that I have not painted too bad a picture of Brazil by mentioning the consequences of being mugged if sensible precautions are not taken. In every city of the world there are good and bad people. It was the latter that stole from a nearby French yacht an expensive outboard motor and dinghy that had been left overnight with its painter made fast to the stern rail. I'm afraid by morning the French couple discovered only a severed dinghy painter trailing in the water. We had all been advised by the Natal yacht club staff to stow dinghies on deck at night. Within a short walk from the security of the yacht club was a *favela*, the slum district that Werner in the Azores had mentioned. The *favela* was a lively place where, by the roadside, fishermen could be seen hacking off lumps of shark etc. to sell to the locals.

It was not out of bravado that I made an excuse to myself to go shopping in the ramshackle and dirty supermarket in the slum district. I wanted to see for myself the Brazil not mentioned in the holiday brochures. One colourful character that I met was an old alcoholic who had a rickety wheelbarrow. For the price of a bottle of firewater he would trundle my shopping to the gates of the yacht club. In his younger days he had been a fisherman sailing a *jangada* that he had built himself.

Fish, as you may well imagine, are a principal part of the locals' diet in the *favela*, but beef is also cheap to buy. The production of beef came about because the sandy soil of Natal prevented the city from being a producer of sugar cane during colonial times. (History lesson courtesy of Louis.) For centuries, the economy of the state was based on the raising of cattle in the dry interior lands. The cattle were turned into jerked beef or used as traction. When I asked for a typical dish of Natal other than fish, I was given 'Carne de Sol' (Sun meat) which has its origin in that jerked beef.

It was at the *barracas* or huts on the beach that served food and drinks night and day that I found the most interesting meals. This particular beach was called Ponta Negra, a beautiful crescent-shaped swathe of fine silver sand. I never failed to be amazed at the surfers who, with the skill and agility of alpine skiers, would ride the large waves that rolled onto the shore. For the briefest of moments I thought that just for once, I would have a go at surfing, but the memory of falling off the marina pontoon in Praia da Vitória soon put paid to that fanciful idea. There would be plenty of time to practise balancing afloat though, for I would soon be leaving Natal and heading north. That day came on Sunday 29th January.

It was early morning when I weighed anchor, and I wasn't feeling too lively after the 'going-away party' I had the evening before with Claudia and Leo and six other sea roamers. Under full sail and on a beam reach, *Mykon* sped down river towards the open sea. We overhauled a fleet of *jangadas*; they too were racing seaward with a silent urgency to a fishing spot known only to them.

Chapter 27

The pilot book advised that when sailing from Natal to the Caribbean islands a good offing of the South American coast was essential to avoid counter inshore currents. A distance offshore of about three hundred miles would also ensure meeting the southeasterly trades. Norfolk, Virginia, was our destination of course; the final port of *Erma*'s incredible voyage from Estonia with her precious cargo of sixteen refugees. My sailing plan was to call at Scarborough in Tobago, then sail northwards, calling at Grenada and Martinique in the Windward Islands before proceeding to St Kitts in the Leeward Islands. After negotiating the strait between the Dominican Republic and Puerto Rico (the Mona Passage) I would sail northwards to the latitude of Norfolk before heading westward to the port where, in December 1945, *Erma* ended *her* voyage. April 2006 was the time that I wanted *Mykon* to arrive in Norfolk, well before the start of the hurricane season.

That was the plan anyway. An extra port of call that I added to the itinerary was Devil's Island (*Île du Diable*), the notorious French penal colony (until 1946) located off the coast of French Guiana. The horrors of this penal settlement became notorious in 1895 with the publicity surrounding the plight of the Jewish French army captain Alfred Dreyfus, who had been wrongly convicted of treason and sent there on 5th January of that year. Having read the book *Papillon* by Henri Charrière, who was an ex-Devil's Island convict himself, I became intrigued and decided to call there en route to Tobago. Incidentally, Devil's Island is the most northerly of a group of three known collectively as Salut. There would be plenty of time to daydream about the prison relics and rusting guillotines overgrown with jungle vines, as Devil's Island lay fourteen hundred nautical miles to our northwest.

Two days out from Natal we passed one of the islands of the Fernando de Noronha group: Rocas Atoll. The islands of the archipelago are about two hundred nautical miles offshore: far enough, I decided, finding that the southeasterly trade winds were constant. Altering to a course west of north, we headed for the Equator. With a free wind I decided to experiment with a different running rig. I wanted to boom out twin foresails. Only having one spinnaker pole, I doused the mainsail and after guying off the boom used this as a substitute spinnaker pole. The course held wasn't too straight, but the Aries self-steering was coping, and that was good enough for me. The twin foresail idea came to an abrupt end when after about twenty minutes or so the topping lift that held the spinnaker boom fell away from the mast. Nipping smartly up forward I found the bracket that had held the topping lift to the mast lying on deck.

I could not understand it: new vangs and plates, cleats etc. on the mast had been renewed on the pre-sailing winter over-haul. It was with profound shock that on examining the fallen bracket I discovered that the rivets had been melted. Looking up the mast I could plainly see that the original circular drill-ings that once held the rivets had been distorted under intense heat. Apart from the radar reflector being put out of action by the lightning strike, I thought that we had been fortunate to be let off so lightly. How wrong could I have been?

The loss of the topping lift didn't really cause me to be too concerned: it was the vangs that held the rigging to the mast. How many more rivets on the mast had been melted?

This was the question that worried me. After lots of pondering I convinced myself that the mast would have fallen down long before now, as we had been in several blows after being struck by the lightning. I promised myself that in Tobago I would have a thorough mast survey carried out.

It was to be three days later, whilst becalmed and almost astride of the Equator, that the rigging would be put to the test again. We were back in the Doldrums, an area that I had re-named the 'sea of storms' owing to the rapidity with which the weather could change from tranquillity to anger. I would look in wonder to the western horizon, where all the beautiful colours of the spectrum appeared with the setting of the sun. There were deep, dark greens blending into lime greens, blood reds fading to crimsons and yellow streaks in the sky outlined in black; and the clouds. There were so many different shaped clouds that a cloud expert would have thought he had died and gone to heaven. As I've mentioned, all of this tranquillity and natural beauty could soon be replaced by a sudden violent blow, as happened during the night of Friday 3rd February.

The winds had reached force nine during the blow, and I had deliberately hove to under deep-reefed main and backed storm jib. The sight of lightning flashing on the horizon filled me with dread. After counting fifteen seconds between seeing the lightning flash and hearing the thunder I estimated that it was three miles away. Hoping that the saying about lightning not striking twice was true, I went below to hook the stove strap around my waist and put the kettle on. In the snug cabin, lit up with every lamp available, the sound of the howling wind and heavy rain being driven at us in the darkness outside seemed worlds away. Usually during bad weather, especially at night, I would stay down below. During *this* blow, however, I could not stop worrying about the mast's rigging, and was constantly shining my head-torch to the masthead. If there had been anything amiss with the rigging, there was precious little I could do to put it right in those conditions, so really the inspection was futile. It was whilst directing my head-torch at the deep-reefed mainsail that for a moment I had a shock.

From the lee side of the sail the black silhouette of a bird, about the size of a pigeon, appeared. It remained almost stationary against the strong wind with the rapid movement of its outspread wings. The bird kept disappearing to the leeside of the sail, a good place to be in those weather conditions.

By three o'clock in the morning it was all over: the violent wind, rain and thunder had disappeared, and so had the bird. The rigging had held fast and this put my mind at ease, although I was still going to have the mast and rigging surveyed in Tobago.

It was more by luck than judgement that we crossed the Equator at a narrow point of the Intertropical Convergence Zone (I.T.C.Z.) and found a light northeasterly wind that I convinced myself was the beginning of the trades. I had not known until this voyage that the belt of low pressure girdling the earth at the Equator was called the I.T.C.Z. Until then it had just been the Doldrums to me.

The northeast wind increased to a constant force three to four, and from noon to noon we were averaging eighty-six nautical miles over the ground. Just before daylight each morning, the brilliance of Venus would shine a path in our wake. This was champagne sailing. Adding to these halcyon days, we had a regular nightly visitor in the form of a storm-petrel. Two or three hours after the sun had sunk below the horizon our nocturnal guest would land on the top of the spray cover and, after eyeing me up with several tilts of its head, would begin preening its feathers. Meanwhile it would occasionally spit a fluid in my face. I took this as a *thank you* for its nightly lodgings. From the excellent book that Janet had given to me for Christmas, I deduced that the bird was a Markham's Storm-petrel. The Markham's territory is usually on the western side of South America, but this one of course was on the eastern side. For anyone interested in ornithology reading these words, the bird was totally brown, with webbed feet, its body was about nine inches long, and its beak was hook-shaped.

Six days after crossing the Equator and steering northwest I altered to west by north and struck a course for Devil's Island, which lay 737 nautical miles ahead. I didn't see my visitor again. The northeasterly trades were now carrying us through the water at 4.6 knots, but we had met with the Equatorial Counter Current, running against us at 1.5 knots. The pilot book estimated that the current would be encountered much further north in February. I wished the Equatorial Counter Current had read the book. We averaged just over seventy-two nautical miles over the ground from noon to noon, and I was happy with that, for on the evening of Sunday 19th February the three islands of Salut stood fine off the starboard bow. The northernmost one was Devil's Island, or as they say in French Guiana, *l'Île du Diable*.

As we were approaching the islands, a small fishing smack headed in our direction. I wondered if they were going to come alongside. This was when I realised that apart from a hat, I wasn't wearing any clothes. Nipping smartly below, I pulled on a pair of swimming trunks, just in case we had visitors. As things turned out the fishing smack passed by with a few waving hands from the crew.

As I was not going to the anchorage at Devil's Island until daylight the next morning, I decided to have a go at catching a fish or two myself. Although the wind was only blowing at force three to four I had deep-reefed the mainsail and shortened the jib. After all, we were only biding time by gilling about off the islands until daybreak. After sailing at about one and a half knots and trolling a spinner I had hauled my supper on board. The two silver fish that I caught were about eighteen inches long and eel-like, except for the underside of the mouth, which was flat and looked a bit like the black sole of a shoe. As I was leaning over the side and concentrating on gutting the fish, making sure the blood and entrails were falling clear of the ship's side, I suddenly recoiled in horror as a shark's head broke the surface. Even in the fading light, as it thrashed about in a frenzy on the surface I could see that it was about eight feet in length. Little wonder that not many prisoners had escaped from Devil's Island, I thought to myself, as I recollected the story of *Papillon*. The fish that I had caught tasted delicious after I had boiled and mixed it with mashed potato and onions to make a kind of fish cake. I sat in the cockpit to eat my fish dinner, and through the darkness I could clearly see the black silhouettes of the three islands of Salut. One other important thing I noticed was that the stars were starting to be covered. I had already deep-reefed the main, so if we were in for a blow, we would be ready.

It was about three o'clock in the morning when the first sign of the approaching bad weather sounded on the cabin roof. Rain. The initial gentle patter quickly developed into a heavy deluge, and the rapid increase of tempo sounded like someone beating a muffled wet drum skin. The onshore wind made the islands a lee shore, and standing on a starboard tack we headed further out to sea. Continually checking our progress from my pocket G.P.S. I was relieved to see that we were indeed clawing away from the land. But the sight of the lightning flashing and the sound of distant thunder made me wish for the morning to come, when hopefully the violent wind would have blown itself out. During this bad weather I could not help thinking about those melted rivets that had fallen to the deck with the topping lift bracket. I kept reminding myself that the rigging had stood up to a similar blow only sixteen days back, and I felt reassured. The alternative of clawing off the lee shore I could not bear thinking about. 'When in doubt get the teapot out', that was what we used to say in the Merchant Navy, and that's what I decided to do.

The waist strap that I had fitted around the stove was still a novelty to me and I derived a simple sense of satisfaction from being able to fill the kettle using two hands.

It happened whilst I was concentrating on pouring the kettle of hot water into the teapot. The yacht, which had been heeling to port with the onslaught of the violent squall, suddenly rolled to starboard. Even above the noise of the howling wind and rain, the alien metallic sound of the tortured mast and rigging being carried away was unmistakable – a deafening crashing sound that reverberated through the cabin.

I rushed on deck to find that my worst dreams had been realised. The mast, sails and rigging were lying in the water. Still attached to the yacht by the leeside shrouds, the mast was being rammed into the side of the hull with every roll. In the beam of my head-torch I could see the main sheet, jib sheet and all the running gear in a tangled mess all over the deck. The mast was threatening to batter itself through the hull.

"Quick Trev – the bolt croppers!" I called out loud. As I frantically tried to position the cutting edge of the bolt croppers onto the fallen stays I kept losing my balance with the violent rolling. Several times I reached out to steady myself by trying to grab hold of the mast stays that were no longer there. Time was of the essence, but I do not know how long I had been on deck before I felt the crunching sound of the hull fracturing. The huge hissing wave that engulfed us was the prelude to *Mykon*'s demise, for we had been driven onto submerged rocks. Only the grab rails on the cabin top prevented me from being swept over the side with the bolt croppers and head-torch, which were carried away in the crashing water.

The yacht was going down by the head as I waded into the cabin, where I found the water level up to the top of the galley stove. Grabbing hold of the valise of the life raft I dragged it from under the starboard quarter berth. "Don't panic, Trev, and you will get out of this," I kept repeating.

The end of the painter that before launching must be made fast to a solid fixture on the yacht was situated under a

Velcro strip on the top of the life raft valise. I thanked God that I had made myself familiar with the life raft and its launching with my Saturday boat drills, the last drill being only the previous day. The life raft was quite heavy (designed for six persons) but a survival strength that I suddenly possessed made its weight of no consequence as I lifted the valise onto the cabin step. After attaching a four-foot length of painter to a cleat I launched the life raft, which mercifully inflated immediately.

It was some advice told to me by a friend, Dave Calvert from the Royal Welsh Yacht Club in Caernarfon, that probably saved my life. Dave had recently been on a sea survival course and had learnt that a very short length of the life raft's painter attached to the yacht was best, as it saved time in retrieving the launched raft from the end of its standard thirty-foot painter. Time was vital, as I was to find out, for just as I had boarded the raft and severed the painter with my deck knife, *Mykon* disappeared below the surface.

It had taken only ten minutes for her to go down since the initial impact with the rocks. Before we had been blown clear of the unseen rocks that were lurking just below the surface, a huge wave came crashing through the canopy opening of the life raft. I was worried at first in case the violent wind capsized the raft, so this extra weight of seawater swilling about I regarded as ballast; for a while.

Chapter 28

Once the raft had been blown clear of the rocks I set about bailing out the seawater. The torrential rain that was being driven through the opening of the canopy sometimes seemed to be filling up the raft faster than I could bail. When most of the seawater had been bailed out I set about taking stock of the situation that I was in.

The first thing I reassured myself of was that I was not in any immediate danger. Land or help was not far away. I had also thrown aboard the raft a grab bag containing – among an assortment of items – enough food in the form of sunflower seeds etc. to last ten days, a solar still to make drinking water and a fishing kit.[2] I also had a ten-litre plastic container of drinking water, which I had thrown into the raft seconds before I abandoned ship. Gallons of rainwater had collected in the folds of the raft canopy, and I scooped up a measuring jugful, in an effort to save some of it. After frustratingly looking around in vain for something in which to stow this drinking water, I drank four jugfuls of it; one after the other. The solution (although not ideal) came when I cut off the tops off several thick plastic pockets that contained distress flares and filled them with rainwater. After zipping up the canopy door flap I felt as if I was cocooned in a womb-like environment; a safe and pleasant world, far away from storms and shipwrecks.

2   A full list of the contents of the grab bag can be found in the back pages.

I suppose I was burying my head in the sand.

The thought of *Mykon* lying on the seabed kept coming back, though, and it really depressed me. To get out of that mood I told myself that I should count myself lucky that I was not down there with her. I also felt better by assuming that the low synthetic canopy of the life raft would not attract the forked lightning that lit up the sky and was a precursor to the thunder bangs that followed a few seconds later all around us. Land was close by, I kept telling myself, about seven miles to leeward, and if the wind stayed in its present direction I would be blown onshore. If the worst came to the worst there was in the grab bag an Emergency Position Indicating Radio Beacon (E.P.I.R.B.) which I could activate. In the bag there was also a small liquid-filled pocket compass with a luminous card. Having the means of knowing roughly in which direction we were heading, it soon became apparent that the wind was being deflected by the curvature of the land and blowing the raft parallel to the coast. The nearest landfall on the new heading was now six hundred miles away on Trinidad or Tobago.

This was when I decided to activate the E.P.I.R.B. After setting off the distress beacon I lashed it to the top of the raft buoyancy chamber, its aerial pointing outboard and skyward, unobstructed by the canopy. In the darkness a small orange lamp on top of the E.P.I.R.B. unit blinked on and off every few seconds, indicating that it was sending out a distress signal. Several hours later the sound of an aircraft made me hurriedly unzip the canopy and look into the night sky.

There it was! A small spotter plane flying low over the sea and coming towards us. The see-sawing of its winking red and green navigation lights made me realise that the strong winds must have been making it hard work for the pilot. Grabbing hold of the signal torch from the kit supplied with the life raft (which I had paid to have serviced by its makers before the voyage) I struggled desperately to turn it on, only to find that it didn't work. I needed to have enough light to see how to unwrap and activate the plastic-encapsulated hand- flares that were now strewn loosely over the raft floor. Their outer flare containers had been half filled with rainwater. Before I had time to dive into the grab bag where I had stowed a spare torch, the plane was heading away from us. My pathetic cries of "Come back, come back, I'm here!" were swept away into the darkness, unheard.

By daylight the rain had stopped and the wind had returned to its gentle northeasterly force of three to four. The sun was starting to evaporate the night's rainfall, forming a mist above the jungle trees that I could see on the distant coastline. So near yet so far, I told myself as I gazed at the land that we were being carried away from by the Equatorial Current. For a time I tried paddling towards the shore with the two-foot-long paddle supplied with the raft kit. After half an hour I realised that not only was it a futile effort but I kept thinking of the shark that I had seen the night before, so I gave up paddling. Although I had activated the E.P.I.R.B., I started to prepare for a prolonged time at sea, just in case the distress signal had not been received for some reason.

The drift towards Trinidad or Tobago would take about twenty-five days if the current carried the raft at one knot. Until I knew the output of the solar still I decided to ration myself to half a litre of drinking water per day. As I intended to be poking my head out of the canopy opening on the lookout for ships, I needed my head protected from the sun's rays. From the grab bag I took out a cotton sun hat. With this colourful hat, together with the swimming trunks I had been wearing when I abandoned ship, I probably could have been mistaken for a holidaymaker floating on a fancy air bed.

It was very much sooner than I expected that I knew I wasn't to be mistaken for a holidaymaker. A voice called through the opening of the raft's canopy: "Bonjour! Bonjour!"

Dropping the grab bag in shock, I turned around to see a

smiling head leaning over the gunwales of a rescue craft. The letters 'SNSM'[3] were emblazoned on the vessel's side. "Hello! Hello! Thank God to see you!"

Immediately my examination of the contents of the grab bag, and the preparations for survival that I was in the process of working out, meant nothing. I was saved! Three sets of arms were reaching out to help me aboard the rescue craft, and not realising that they were also going to haul the life raft on board, I grabbed my knapsack containing my passport, credit cards etc. Just before I left the raft the winking lamp of the E.P.I.R.B. reminded me that it was still sending out its distress call, so I disarmed it. Once I was safely on board the rescue craft, the crew hauled the life raft onto the after deck. Sitting on top of the outer chamber of the still inflated life raft, we bounced along at about fifteen knots, heading for Cayenne in French Guiana.

After about two hours we passed close to Devil's Island, where two yachts lay at anchor. *If only ...* I began to think, but quickly dismissed such thoughts as trivia when I reminded myself of the good fortune of being rescued. On reaching the buoyed channel on the approach to Cayenne, the water had turned into a muddy brown colour from the sediment of the river bed, and many fronds of palm trees that lined each bank came floating past. Signs of life on shore gradually developed and we tied up to a wooden jetty in a yacht marina where, much to my surprise, an ambulance was waiting to take me to a nearby hospital.

---

3 Société Nationale de Sauvetage en Mer

Chapter 29

After being diagnosed at the Cayenne Hospital as suffering from dehydration, I was hooked up to a saline drip. Having been drinking over three litres of water per day for the past few weeks, and only that morning having consumed several jugfuls of rainwater, I was puzzled that I should be dehydrated. But who was I to look a gift horse in the mouth? After all, the treatment was free, wasn't it?

I was placed in a single-bed ward that was spotlessly clean and had all the en-suite facilities of a modern hotel room. The saline drip to my arm was suspended from a wheeled frame that enabled me to walk about whilst still being fed the solution. This mobility proved to be very handy, for the nurse informed me that the British Consul wanted to talk to me on the telephone in the reception area. The Consul wanted to know if he could help me in any way. I asked if he could obtain some clothing, for which I would pay, of course. "Sorry, could not possibly do that." Then I asked if he could arrange some transport to get me to the airport so that I could return home, again saying I would meet the cost. "Sorry, could not possibly do that." Finally I asked if he would inform my family of the situation that I was in. No prizes for guessing his reply.

"Is there anything at all that you can do to help me?" I asked after hearing him say sorry for the third time.

"When you get to the airport, give me a ring and I will let you know." With those final words the British Consul put the phone down, probably satisfied at a job well done, and I returned to the ward slightly bewildered.

However, the next morning I did receive some very welcome and unexpected help when I had a visit from one of my rescuers. The French lifeboatman had contacted the French Red Cross (Croix-Rouge Française) and obtained a small parcel of clothes for me. The lifeboatman, who spoke in broken English, apologised for being unable to obtain any shoes for me, but I thanked him for his kindness and made it known to him that it did not matter at all about the shoes. After we had shaken hands my benefactor wished me luck and went on his way.

The nurse who had accompanied the lifeboatman to my ward told me to get dressed, as I had been declared fit to be discharged, and she would sort out some footwear for me. Returning to the ward the nurse burst into laughter: "You look like … you look like … how do you say? You look like a clown, that is it!" She handed me a pair of hospital slippers made of light blue paper. I hope that I am not in any way sounding ungrateful, but I think that the cotton trousers, with their large black and white check diamond pattern, might have been made for a giant. (I am only five feet six inches tall.) The extra-large, bright yellow tee-shirt that sported a large picture of what looked like 'Mr Happy' on the front completed my outfit. Not only did the nurse have a pair of slippers for me, she also had in her hand the bill for my night's stay in the hospital. This sent me reeling, for it was for one thousand two hundred euros. Ever thankful that I had stowed my credit card in my grab bag, I paid up and left the hospital feeling slightly worse than when I was admitted.

The torrential tropical rain was falling in drops that seemed to be the size of electric candle bulbs, and my paper slippers fell to pieces.

I walked along the pavement in search of a shoe shop, with my knapsack slung across my shoulder and one hand holding onto my trousers to stop them falling down. I only needed a walking stick and bowler hat and I probably could have passed as Charlie Chaplin.

If there is such a person as a modern-day Good Samaritan, then I met him that day in Cayenne in the guise of a patrol policeman. Not only did he take me to a shop where I bought a pair of shoes and socks and a belt, he also took me to a travel agent where I bought an airline ticket for home. It was in the taxi on the way to the Cayenne-Rochambeau Airport that I put on my new shoes and socks. These (the only ones available) went well with my odd attire, for the black socks had a gold teddy bear down the sides and the shoes were made of plastic with a crocodile skin pattern.

My flight home was via Paris and then to Manchester. After a flight of nine hours the Air France plane touched down at Orly Airport. Finally my connecting flight from Charles de Gaulle Airport landed at Manchester.

It was the 22nd of February and the snow was falling heavily. As I sat on the station bench waiting for the train that would take me home, I had time to reflect on the loss of *Mykon* and how I could finance buying another yacht to continue my voyage in the wake of *Erma* to Norfolk, Virginia. (I had only been able to obtain third party insurance for *Mykon*.) My train duly arrived and I was putting aside any thoughts of financing another voyage when I suddenly had an irrational craving for bread and cheese!

The snow was still falling heavily as I boarded the train, and I was glad to feel the warmth inside the carriage. I could not help noticing the strange furtive glances that I was being given by my fellow train passengers, who were sensibly wrapped up in winter scarves, hats and heavy coats. They could have been forgiven for thinking that I had escaped from some mental institution from the way in which I was dressed. I must have looked a little odd in my 'clown outfit' that was still wet following the downpour in Cayenne. If I had been dressed in sackcloth that day I would not have cared, for I was on my way to a little cottage in the Welsh mountains where a woman with the patience of a saint was waiting for me. It was as I was walking along the snowy lane to our cottage that the answer came to me. A book! I would try to write a book to finance buying another yacht.

This is that book. Thank you for sharing my adventure.

The End.

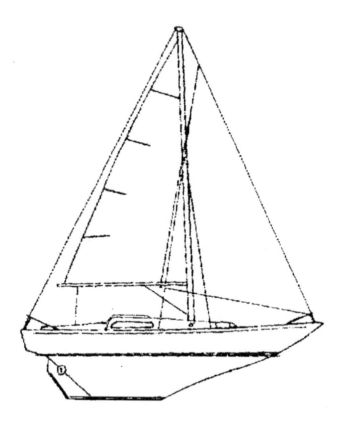

Details of *Mykon*.
Sketch: Trevor Wilson.

Class: Cutlass 27
L.O.A.: 27 ft
L.W.L.: 20 ft
Beam: 7 ft 8 in.
Draft: 4 ft 6 in.
Displacement: 6496 lbs
Sail area: 290 sq. ft

Details of Voyage:
Total time at sea: 107 days
Total distance sailed: 7503 nautical miles
Total time on voyage: 224 days
Diesel fuel used: 14 litres

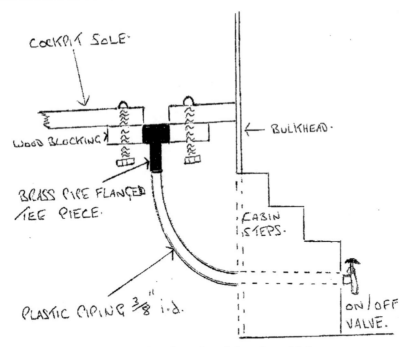

Rainwater Catcher that I fitted on *Mykon.*
Note: on/off valve when not in use was stowed under the cabin steps.
When catching rainwater the self-drainers in the cockpit were
plugged off.
Sketch: Trevor Wilson.

Glossary of Nautical Terms

A

Abaft – towards the stern.

Abeam – bearing at right angles to keel.

Adrift – afloat and unattached in any way to the shore or seabed.

Amidships – in the centre line of the ship.

Athwartships – at right angles to the centre line of the ship.

Azimuth compass – an instrument for finding the sun's magnetic azimuth. The azimuth of a bearing from the observer measured in as an angle clockwise from true north.

B

Back spring – mooring lines to prevent vessel surging fore and aft.

Beam – the beam of a ship is its width at its widest point.

Beam Ends – the sides of a ship. *On her beam ends* means the vessel is on her side and possibly about to capsize.

Bends and hitches – various knots in rope.

Binnacle – case for ship's compass.

Bitter end – the last part of a rope or cable made fast to bitts or eye-bolt used for anchoring.

Bitts – posts mounted on ship's bow to fasten mooring ropes or cable.

Bosun's chair – cradle usually made of timber with a triangular rope sling attached. Person sits in it and is hauled aloft.

Bulkhead – an upright wall within the hull of a ship.

Bulwark – the extension of the ship's side above the weather deck.

C

Carry away – of rigging, mast, anchor cable etc., to break under massive pressure from natural or man-made forces.

Cleat – a fixed point used to secure a rope on a vessel.

Clinker-built – the hull of a boat built with planks, each of which overlaps the one below.

Coaming – the raised edge of hatchway used to help keep water out.

Cockpit – a well, usually in the after part of a yacht, where the helmsman sits.

Companionway – staircase from deck to cabin.

Collision course. To determine: Extract from International Regulations for Preventing Collisions at Sea: 'If the distance of any vessel is reduced and her compass bearing does not change a risk of collision shall be deemed to exist'. A simple explanation would be to imagine two ships steaming towards each other head on; the compass bearing would be constant until for example one ship altered course to starboard (as the International Rules of the Road state). The compass bearing between each vessel would gradually alter as the ship that had turned to starboard steamed on her new course thus preventing a collision.

D

Davits – crane for ship's lifeboats.

Deckhead – ceiling.

Deep sea – away from coastal passages, to sail across oceans.

Derricks – ship's cranes; *to top the derricks* – to hoist them in readiness to lift cargo.

Dodger – canvas screens either side of the cockpit that shelter the helmsman.

Double ended – when both the bow and stern of a vessel are of a pointed shape.

Douse – to lower quickly (e.g. *douse a sail*) or to switch off (e.g. *douse an engine*).

Draft – the depth of a ship's keel below the waterline.

Dropped the hook – anchored.

Dutchman's Log – a pre-measured length of cordage attached to a log or piece of wood that is dropped over the ship's side and timed until all the cordage has run out. The ship's speed can be calculated from this datum.

E

Earrings – small lines by which the uppermost corners of the larger sails are secured to the yardarms. In a yacht, a gaff or gunter rig.

E.P.I.R.B. – Emergency Position Indicating Radio Beacon.

F

Fathom – a unit of length equal to six feet, roughly the distance between a man's outstretched hands.

Fender – an air- or foam-filled cushion hung over the yacht's side to prevent banging into dock walls or other vessels.

Fiddle – guard rail around stove or table to secure pots and pans.

Fine – nearly or just. Another ship, for example, observed just off the port bow would be described as *fine off the port bow*.

Forecastle or *fo'c'sle* – the bow section of a ship, formerly the crew's quarters.

Freeboard – the height of the ship's hull above the waterline.

Full and bye – sailing into the wind but not so close-hauled that it might be possible to be taken aback.

Furl – to roll or wrap a sail around the mast or spar to which it is attached.

G

Gantline – rope attached to bosun's chair or painting platform.

Genoa – large triangular foresail.

Ghosting winds – light zephyrs of wind.

Gig boat – ship's boat used to row crew ashore and to carry lines between ship and quayside.

Gunwale – upper edge of the hull.

Gybe – of a sail, to swing from one side of the vessel to the other, usually as a result of wind moving to a different direction when sailing downwind.

H

Halyard – line used to raise the head of any sail. Originally ropes used to haul the yardarms aloft.

Hand – to hand the sail, same as to furl the sail, to shorten sail.

Hatch coamings – raised sides of cargo hatch to prevent water going into the ship's hold.

Head valves – stop taps for the water system of the ship's toilets.

Heave to – to stop a sailing vessel by lashing helm in opposition to the sails.

Helm down – push tiller to leeward.

I

I.A.L.A. – International Association of Lighthouse Authorities. It was formed in 1979 to unify the world's buoyage system.

In the offing – something visible from the ship.

J

Jib – a triangular sail in front of the ship.

Junk – flat-bottomed, square-sailed vessel, with high forecastle and poop.

Junk-rigged – to carry a Chinese sail.

K

Keel – the central backbone of the hull.

Know the ropes – to be familiar with the great lengths of ropes and cordage involved with the running of a ship.

L

Lanyard – a rope that ties something off.

Lay – the direction of the twisted strands of a rope; *To lay a course* – to steer a course that is required.

Lazyjacks – ropes forming a 'Y' shape either side of the main boom to guide and hold the mainsail onto boom when lowering sail.

Leech – the aft or trailing edge of a fore and aft sail or vertical edge of a square sail or the leeward edge of a spinnaker.

Lee side – the side of the ship sheltered from the wind.

Lee shore – coast or land downwind of ship.

Leeward – in the direction that the wind is blowing.

Leeway – the amount that a ship is blown to the leeward by the wind.

List – of a vessel, to lean over to one side.

Lubber's line – a vertical line inside the compass binnacle or case indicating the ship's heading.

Luff – the forward edge of a sail. Also to steer a sailing vessel more towards the direction of the wind.

Lying ahull – riding out a storm or bad weather by dousing all the sails and allowing the vessel to drift.

M

Main halyard – rope used to raise and lower mainsail.

Mainmast – tallest mast on a ship.

Make fast – to secure a rope or cable to an anchor point, e.g. mooring ropes to a set of bitts.

Messroom – dining room where crew eat together.

Mole – pier or breakwater made of stone.

Monkey's fist – ball-shaped weighted knot about the size of an orange, used on the end of a heaving line to carry the line when thrown from ship to quayside or tug-boat etc.

Moor – to tie up to a mooring buoy or post or to dock a ship.

N

Navigate – to guide a vessel from one point to another.

No bottom – when the depth of water is too deep for the weighted measuring line to reach the sea-bed, the cry from the leadsman was "*No bottom!*"

O

Oilskins – bad weather gear worn by seamen.

Old Man – Captain.

Overreach – when tacking, to hold a course too long.

P

Painter – rope used to fasten a boat.

Parachute sea anchor – canvas or synthetic material drogue (i.e. a thing which is dragged), streamed usually from the bow to keep the ship's head into the wind and sea during bad weather.

Parrel – a hoop of metal, wood or rope used to fasten a yard to a mast or in a Chinese rig to fasten the luff of the sail to the mast.

Pintle – male fitting of rudder hinge.

Pitch – see-sawing effect of a vessel rotating on the beam axis causing the bow to pitch up and down.

Plimsoll Line – loading marks on ship's side. These markings by international law should be above the waterline.

Points off – the man on lookout duty, when referring to the relative position of a ship, light etc. that has been sighted, would refer to its position in *points off* the bow or stern, *a point* being one thirty-second part of a compass rose or full circle. If for instance a light was sighted approximately forty-five degrees off the port bow, that would be referred to as four points off the point bow, as one point equals eleven and one quarter degrees.

Port – left hand side of a vessel when facing towards the bow.

Preventor – a line attached to the mainsail boom and led to a cleat up forward, usually when running before the wind, to prevent the boom from accidentally gybing.

Pulpit – guard rails at the bow of a yacht.

Pushpit – guard rails on the stern of a yacht.

Q

Quay or *Quayside* – platform where ships can lie alongside, usually inside the protective harbour wall.

Quarter – side of ship that is between amidships and astern.

R

Radar reflector – a fixture, usually set aloft, that allows radar beams emitted from another ship to be echoed back to their radar screen, thus determining its presence to them electronically.

Reaching or *on a reach* – when sailing about 60 to 160 degrees off the wind.

Red Ensign – flag of the Merchant Navy. Sometimes called the *Red Duster*.

Reef – reduce the sail area, usually in strong winds.

Reefing pendants – rope ties used when shortening sail.

S

Scud – the name give by sailormen to the lowest clouds, usually seen in squally weather.

Scuttles – lidded openings in ship's side or deck.

Ship's head – direction in which the vessel is pointing, usually relative to the lubberline of the compass. Captains would enquire "How's your head?" to the helmsman when wanting to know ship's compass heading.

Shrouds – standing rigging running from the mast to the sides of the ship.

Smack – small single-masted fishing boat.

S.N.S.M. – Société Nationale de Sauvetage en Mer.

Snowball hitch – derisory term given to an unsuitable knot in a rope that comes adrift (i.e. a knot that melts when the sun comes out).

Soldier's wind – when sailing on a reach, vessel being relatively easy to steer.

Sole – floor; *cabin sole* – floor of cabin.

Sounding – measurement of depth of water under keel; *take a sounding* – make such a measurement.

Spar – pole used to support various sails and pieces of rigging.

Spinnaker – large balloon-like sail flown in front of vessel when sailing before the wind.

Spinnaker pole – used to control the spinnaker sail or other headsail.

Stand on – to hold your course, usually when you have right of way according to the International Rules of the Road.

Standing on a new tack – having brought the vessel's head through the wind and steadying on the new course.

Starboard – right hand side of vessel when facing towards the bow.

Stay – rigging running fore and aft from the mast, e.g. *forestay* and *backstay*.

Stern – rear part of the ship.